Aristokratia, Vol. I, 2013
978-0-9871581-8-5
Edited by K. Deva
©Manticore Press, 2013

ARISTOKRATIA

Contents

The Beginning

K. Deva

I would like to begin this introduction by explaining what Aristokratia is - and what it is not. Firstly, Aristokratia is a concept both new and ancient. It is old because it looks back to the traditional foundations of culture and civilisation to lay its intellectual roots. It is new because it cultivates the growth of an entirely original system. Aristokratia does not represent the idle philosophers who dwell in their ivory towers and the literary prostitutes who write whatever they are paid to; rather we look to the heretics and the visionaries who concern themselves not with the piteous state of the arts and humanities of today, but with the strong and vital culture of tomorrow.

Secondly, Aristokratia is not a vessel for plebeian politics. It does not promote any political platforms, theories or ideologies. It does however, criticise theories at the philosophical and speculative level. As for the naïve romanticism of the revolutionaries; this you will not find nor will you find the post-modernist rhetoric which populates the works of pseudo-intellectuals.

Finally, Arisokratia operates from the perspective of a belief in meritocracy. Merit is accumulated by deeds and personal worth alone. Neither birth, wealth, status, sex, ethnicity nor any other superficial factor is deemed to be a sufficient indicator of merit. In this terminology Aristokratia relies on the Ancient Greek term 'rule by the best'. This places the hierarchy on a vertical axiological plane which is transcendental rather than on the entirely different plane of horizontal and mundane governance. As such, Aristokratia deals with cultural models and the nature of civilization itself, rather than with the form of politics found on the horizontal axis.

To a extent, Arisokratia derives its intellectual heritage from authors such as Nietzsche, Plato, Aristotle, Spengler, Evola, Guénon, Ortega, Gómez Dávila and Baudelaire; individuals whose ideas revolved around a concept of aristocracy, but adhered to its original meaning not the contemporary understanding of the term, which deviates considerably from the original meaning.

As a publication, Aristokratia unequivocally and unapologetically postulates ideas which challenge popular thought. Furthermore, to encourage diversity of content we present contrasting opinions within a single volume. Arisokratia therefore does not express a unified concept, but rather an array of ideas. The only thing that they have in common is the subject matter or the theme, and whilst one author may espouse a particular idea, another author within the same issue may challenge it. The editorial purpose for this is to encourage active thought in the reader, rather than bland acceptance.

Arisokratia deals with the following topics: High Culture, Theories of Civilization, Philosophy, Aesthetics, Traditionalism, and Gnosis.

For details on future editions, please visit our website: www.aristokratia.info

Aristocratic Radicalism:
The Political Philosophy
of Friedrich Nietzsche

The expression 'Aristocratic Radicalism,' which you employ, is very good. It is, permit me to say, the cleverest thing I have yet read about myself.

— Nietzsche, Dec. 2, 1887.

Gwendolyn Taunton

Friedrich Nietzsche is perhaps the most often quoted philosopher, and yet paradoxically also the least understood. The average reader will only lightly peruse his content - pause over a few remarks – and then cease to read any further. This has led to numerous misconceptions about his work. In order to understand Nietzsche's writing it must be read in full for statements which appear contradictory are not when read in the appropriate context. Furthermore, to complicate the issue, in some parts meanings are lost in translation and still other segments have been entirely edited out for being deemed too much for the 'fragile readers' to cope with.

All of these factors contribute to creating readers who have a very superficial grasp of basic concepts such as the Übermensch, or the Apollonian/Dionysian dichotomy - they delve no deeper. While these are indeed facets of Nietzsche's work, they are only components, and if isolated from other core concepts the true nature of his philosophy cannot be interpreted – and thus Nietzsche's most well-known ideas become the most misunderstood.

To understand Nietzsche one must read all his books and piece the ideas together to reconstruct his legacy of thought. In this regard

11

the level of complexity deployed by Nietzsche is intentional, for he was not writing for the average reader – in fact to do so would have been abhorrent to Nietzsche. In *Thus Spake Zarathustra* ('Of Reading and Writing') Nietzsche refers to 'Idle Readers' and their inability to understand not the words but the essential *spirit* with which an author writes – and this is why they are doomed to misunderstand any literary work. Nietzsche's 'spirit' in particular, is obfuscated from all but the most astute readers. The intended audience for Nietzsche's writing was in fact a very small one, and it is to these few that he addressed his real ideas. To test the reader, Nietzsche deliberately obscured certain passages and made esoteric references to myth and ancient history. Even parts of the typography were encrypted. It is for this very reason that many people reject Nietzsche's writing on the grounds that it is incomprehensible – some readers do not present the adequate ability required to *translate the spirit* of his works. Nietzsche's targeting of his desired audience however, has had the unintended consequence that his ideas have been completely misunderstood by legions of others.

Misintrepretation of Nietzsche is at its most common place in the political playground, where a number of feuding parties try to claim Nietzsche's ideas in order to reinforce their own tenuous positions. This is amply illustrated by the fact that academics and amateurs alike fallaciously attribute to Nietzsche a diverse range of ideologies, including nationalism, anarchism, and democracy. So how can one reconcile all these different ideas with what Nietzsche actually wrote? The answer is simple: One doesn't. None of them are Nietzsche's creation, nor did he endorse any of them.

The majority of writers who present Nietzsche's political theories to the public do so to disseminate propaganda and plunder through his texts like barbarians, pillaging citations and raping aphorisms to support obvious political agendas. This article will present Nietzsche's true political philosophy, in his own words and from an unbiased, apolitical stance. It will not be a sugar coated placebo for 'Idle Readers', and it may be a bitter pill for the barbarians to swallow. It is however, the real and authentic opinion of Nietzsche.

ARISTOCRATIC RADICALISM

In his correspondence to another writer by the name of George Brandes, Nietzsche's political system is named as Aristocratic Radicalism. Coming from a background in Classical Philology, Nietzsche was not working within a paradigm of aristocracy as we understand it in its modern context; rather he was basing it upon the Ancient Greek definition of aristocracy.

Originally, the term aristocracy came from the Greek words ἄριστος (*aristos* - excellent), and κράτος (*kratos* - power) – *aristokratia*. It is presented in polar opposition to *demokratia* (democracy). The literal translation is 'rule by the exceptional', in contrast to democracy which is 'rule by the masses'. Thus *demokratia* and *aristokratia* presents a clear dyad which Nietzsche explains in the *Will to Power*:

> Aristocracy represents the belief in an élite humanity and higher caste. Democracy represents the disbelief in great human beings and élite society: "Everyone is equal to everyone else." "At bottom we are one and all self-seeking cattle and mob."[1]

What he is implying by this statement is that the fundamental difference betwixt the two is that aristocracy seeks to create a higher, noble type of humanity, whilst democracy seeks to reduce everyone down to the lowest element, to create a mass where people are devoid of individuality. Nietzsche does not perceive democracy as a collective of individuals (which is the way the contemporary civilian imagines it to be) but rather as a system which strips individuality from citizens, replacing them with mindless automatons. It is for this reason that Nietzsche uses the bovine imagery of 'cattle' and the 'Herd'. It would be erroneous to assume that Nietzsche is against democracy because it promotes equality; on the contrary he believes democracy promotes the greatest of all inequalities by insisting that all is equal and refusing

---

[1] Nietzsche, F., ed., Kaufmann, W., *The Will to Power*, (New York: Vintage Books, 1968), p.397.

to acknowledge that recognition of difference can be beneficial.

The paradigm of aristokratia/demokratia is the foundational political premise from which all else proceeds. Nietzsche takes us back to basics by resurrecting the old dichotomy. In more modern terminologies however the distinction is not in fact that clear cut – by way of example, Thomas Hobbes describes an aristocracy as a commonwealth in which the representative of the people is an assembly in *Leviathan*. Or, more simply expressed, a government where only an elect portion of the general public can represent the people. This is found in modern societies such as the United States which presents itself as a democracy but is in fact governed by a plutocratic élite. Considering the current political state, in which democracy is represented essentially by a two-party system of privileged entities the application of the term 'democracy' to modern Western politics in some countries may not even be applicable and a plutocracy governed by corporations is more likely the correct definition. Certainly knowledge and wisdom are no longer respected in governments as they were in Ancient Greece, for we find very few humanitarians in office.

It seems that plutocracy becomes evident in all civilizations whose power is on the wane. Whether under aristocratic or democratic rule, they both succumb to greed when in an epoch of intellectual decline. Privilege bestowed upon the members of an élite system is derivative of what the people (as a collective category) esteems as valuable at any given point in time. As the modern system is based more upon capitalism, wealth is currently the defining characteristic of assigning social merit. The problem of attributing personal status to this materialistic aspect is somewhat dubious and quite possibly symptomatic of the 'reign of quantity', an idea expressed by René Guénon.

When Nietzsche uses the term aristocracy it is in a different manner and quite apparent that he is advocating something entirely radical and not an order of rank based on wealth and/or privileged birth. Nietzsche's theory of aristocracy is purely a 'reign of quality' based on

14

individual worth. As this article progresses, we shall make it evident that in both the Ancient Greek vernacular and in Nietzsche's books aristocracy is closer to a being a meritocratic system. The common interpretation of aristocracy is of a ruling power that is passed by title, birth right, or a class that wields power over those lower in the hierarchy. But today what is left of the aristocrat, who has no real power, a meaningless title and a bloodline that long since ceased to bear nobility? There is no merit here, nothing but the empty shell of a degraded political system, perpetuating their existence as a living anachronism from an era fallen to ennui.

In essence then, Nietzsche's primary task is to create a transition point which shifts the emphasis from the old regime towards a new and eminently more useful cultural stratification. This can only be performed by redirecting the current value structure to reassign merit to a more beneficial form of aristocracy. This would not only be more in line with the original Greek definitions, but would also be akin to what was implied by Julius Evola in his use of the term 'Aristocrats of the Soul',[2] and bears some similarity to his '*Theory of the Absolute Individual*'.[3]

The best place to begin examining Aristocratic Radicalism is the correspondence between Nietzsche and another author, George Brandes. Not only did George Brandes write the book simply titled '*Friedrich Nietzsche*' in 1915, he also composed a much earlier and more obscure work '*An Essay on Aristocratic Radicalism*' in 1889, in which he names Nietzsche's political system as Aristocratic Radicalism. More importantly, Nietzsche was alive in this period, and Brandes consulted Nietzsche in private correspondence regarding assigning this name to his creation. Nietzsche responded to Brandes by saying that;

> The expression Aristocratic Radicalism, which you employ, is very good. It is, permit me to say, the cleverest thing I have yet read

---

[2] See, Evola, J., *Ride the Tiger: A Survival Manual for Aristocrats of the Soul,* Inner Traditions.

[3] This is a very early monograph by Evola which is heavily inspired by Nietzsche.

about myself. (Nietzsche to Brandes, Nice, 2nd December 1887)[4]

Another point which should be noted here is that Brandes agreed with the majority of Nietzsche's ideas, and personally selected the term Aristocratic Radicalism as the name which best described his own political beliefs, later suggesting it to Nietzsche: "I used the expression Aristocratic Radicalism because it so exactly defines my own political convictions." (Letter, Brandes to Nietzsche)[5]

> A new and original spirit breathes to me from your books. I do not yet fully understand what I have read; I cannot always see your intention. But I find much that harmonises with my own ideas and sympathies, the depreciation of the ascetic ideals and the profound disgust with democratic mediocrity, your Aristocratic Radicalism. (Brandes to Nietzsche, Copenhagen, 26th November 1887, Brandes 1889).[6]

Consequently, Brandes called his critical review of Nietzsche's oeuvre, a text published in the first half of 1889, *An Essay on Aristocratic Radicalism*.[7]

ARISTOCRATS OF THE SOUL

Firstly, as was mentioned at the start of this article, Nietzsche's use of the term aristocracy is essentially in a meritocratic sense, and this is why it becomes 'radical'. It is not a belief in maintaining the traditional aristocracy, rather it is intended to establish a new system of aristocracy and as such it is completely separate from any other system of political thought. Furthermore, in Aristocratic Radicalism, the aristocratic principle is not to be confused with, and does not

---

[4]Tobias, N. A., *The Challenge of Aristocratic Radicalism*, p.1.
[5]Ibid., p.1.
[6]Ibid., p.1.
[7]Ibid, p.2.

necessarily presuppose, an aristocratic class or a caste society.[8] If anything, the main problem with Aristocratic Radicalism occurs when one tries to define exactly who qualifies as a member of Nietzsche's new aristocracy. Whilst it is obvious that Nietzsche is advocating a hierarchical system, the exact hierarchy itself is much less easy to define, for as other writers have noted, individuals to whom Nietzsche ascribes an aristocratic status are of higher value not because of birth, class, ethnicity or any other tangible indicator. The system is based on personal qualities alone.

Nietzsche's claim is that they are of higher value because they realize higher states of the soul.[9] An unusual claim for a philosopher linked to the 'death of god' – however, Nietzsche's philosophy of religion is not strictly 'atheism'. Whilst it does denounce the Judeo-Christian Tradition, Nietzsche actually speaks with great admiration of other Traditions, such as the Hindu and the Hellenic. Nonetheless this does make defining the quantifying characteristics of Nietzsche's new aristocracy more difficult. In light of this we have to accept that Nietzsche is using the terminology of the 'soul' as an abstract concept, and indeed we do find Nietzsche describing 'greatness' of the soul as linked with other personal qualities in *The Will to Power*:

> Type: True graciousness, nobility, greatness of soul proceed from abundance; do not give in order to receive – do not try to exalt themselves by being gracious; - prodigality as the type of true graciousness, abundance of personality as its presupposition.[10]

The soul, as Nietzsche describes it is indeed an abstract expression, and Nietzsche is definitely basing his aristocratic model on a meritocratic one, centred no less on benevolence. Graciousness, nobility, giving – this is a very far cry from the cold, hierarchical models often misattributed to Nietzsche. It is evident that whatever else the term

---

[8]Hörnqvist, M., *The Few and the Many: Machiavelli, Tocqueville and Nietzsche on Authority and Equality* (Sweden: Uppsala University), p.11.
[9]Tobias, N. A., *The Challenge of Aristocratic Radicalism*, p.7.
[10]Nietzsche, F., ed., Kaufmann, W., *The Will to Power*, p.493.

may have meant for either Nietzsche or Brandes, aristocratic sentiment was not simply equated with the dominance of brute force.[11] But there are even more personal qualities Nietzsche associates with aristocracy – and this intangible aspect of their personality sets the individual apart from the group collective or 'Herd' as Nietzsche calls it. He is therefore, elevating the worth of certain individuals to a higher value than that of other individuals within the collective.

> Herd-animals - now culminating as the highest value standard of 'society'; attempt to give them a cosmic, even a metaphysical value. Against them I defend aristocracy.[12]

Aristocratic Radicalism is a system which places the 'aristocrat' as a type of individual who remains aloof and distinct from the collective Herd. Kaufmann, a well-known authority on Nietzsche argues that Nietzsche was an existentialist concerned with the creativity of the human spirit and with the strengthening of individualism.[13] What Nietzsche creates for us therefore, is a culture in which the new aristocracy is founded on personal merit, guided by powerful creative 'free spirits' that are both noble and courageous, exhibit intellectual tolerance of ideas, have the ability to accept contradictions, possess dynamic vitality and self-control, are devoid of bad conscience, have adopted the attitude of *amor fati*, and exhibit self-acceptance.[14]

Although separate from the collective, there is to be no cruelty directed towards the 'Herd' by this new aristocracy, for the personal characteristics of those selected would not be predisposed to such negative traits. Nietzsche is extremely quick to point out that personal

---

[11]Lang, B., Authors Responsibility in ed. Golomb, J., & Wistrich R.S., *Nietzsche, Godfather of Fascism? On the Uses and Abuses of Philosophy* (New Jersey: Princeton University Press, 2002), p.56.

[12]Nietzsche, F., ed., Kaufmann, W., *The Will to Power*, p.493.

[13]Robert C. Holub, The Elisabeth Legend in ed. Golomb, J., & Wistrich R.S., *Nietzsche, Godfather of Fascism? On the Uses and Abuses of Philosophy*, p.219.

[14]Golumb, J., Philosophical Anthropology, in ed. Golomb, J., & Wistrich R.S., *Nietzsche, Godfather of Fascism? On the Uses and Abuses of Philosophy*, p.35.

flaws such as these would not only automatically exclude an individual from the aristocracy, but also from the topic of philosophy itself:

> Hatred for mediocrity is unworthy of a philosopher: it is almost a question mark against his 'right to philosophy'. Precisely because he is an exception he has to take the rule under his protection, he has to keep the mediocre in good heart.[15]

Poor conduct should also automatically exclude one from the ranks of the aristocracy and from professions such as philosophy where an individual is in a trusted position of authority and must provide advice to the community or people as a whole. Nietzsche explains in the extract below;

> What I fight against: that an exceptional type should make war on the rule - instead of grasping that the continued existence of the rule is the precondition for the value of the exception.[16]

However, though essentially guiding the wider cultural group, this new aristocracy is not fully part of it, and Nietzsche advises what could be best described as a 'polite distance'.

> Without the pathos of distance such as develops from the incarnate differences of classes, from the ruling caste's constant looking out and looking down on subjects and instruments and from its equally constant exercise of obedience and command, its holding down and holding at a distance, that other, more mysterious pathos could not have developed either, that longing for an ever-increasing widening of distance within the soul itself, the formation of ever higher, rarer, more remote, tenser, more comprehensive states, in short precisely the elevation of the type 'man', the continual self-overcoming of man. (Nietzsche 1886/2008: 257)[17]

---

[15]Nietzsche, F., ed., Kaufmann, W., *The Will to Power*, p.476.
[16]Ibid., p.476.
[17]Tobias, N. A., *The Challenge of Aristocratic Radicalism*, p.7.

The *pathos of distance,* as Nietzsche calls it is not performed out of need to create a rift, but instead to facilitate understanding. One cannot effectively observe a group if one identifies as part of it – Nietzsche's aristocrat must not only be part of the group, but also separate from it in order to both shape the current of its growth and to accurately understand the needs of the collective whole. From the perspective of an anthropologist, the Aristocratic Radical is operating in a participant/observer capacity, in which despite being a part of the collective, they remain distinct from what Nietzsche defines as the 'Herd' mentality, and are able to differentiate themselves from mainstream thought in order to fulfil their function as creators/thinkers. In terms of anthropology this also relates to Arnold van Gennep's theories on the liminal. Van Gennep's structure consisted of a pre-liminal phase (separation), a liminal phase (transition), and a post-liminal phase (reincorporation). This concept was later elaborated on by Victor Turner who noted that in the transitional state between two phases, individuals were "betwixt and between" the social construct. In the early stages of development before the differentiation process had been completed, one who was naturally possessed of the required temperament would feel isolated from the 'Herd' mentality – in the later stages of progress the 'Aristocrat' will also be able to cross the liminal boundaries back into the collective. And in the final stage of development, an Aristocratic Radical who would progress from the initial role as a liminal/outsider archetype to that of the creative Artist/Philosopher who can shape the social model – which is the paradigm for Nietzsche's Übermensch.

The Übermensch is not only the basis of Aristocratic Radicalism it also one who is in essence an artist or a philosopher of the highest order. Nietzsche uses the term 'artist' here in an *unfamiliar sense*; not as a painter or a sculptor, but essentially a *creator of civilization*. The people themselves are the canvas upon which the Übermensch paints, creating a model of society that is an art form. The citation below clearly indicates that part of the requirement for Nietzsche's aristocracy is the creative principle found in both the arts and in philosophy.

The artist-philosopher. Higher concept of art. Whether a man can place himself so far distant from other men that he can form them? Preliminary exercises: (1) he who forms himself, the hermit; (2) the artist hitherto, as a perfection on a small scale, working on material.[18]

Furthermore, the ideal model for Nietzsche's new aristocracy will also possess a high intelligence, as obviously in order to fulfil the relative functions required, the higher cognitive faculties must be utilised. In this new status quo, Aristocratic Radicalism is in fact an 'aristocracy of intellect'.[19] We see this expressed in an academic study of Aristocratic Radicalism;

[...] contrary to the concept of 'aristocracy' that is orthodox and familiar, the benefit of inclusion among the aristocracy is not that one thereby wields political power (cf. Fossen 2009; Franklin 1999), but rather that one thereby counts axiologically. In radical contrast to the status quo, 'aristocratic radicalism' is an aristocracy of moral value. On the other hand, the conjunction is 'radical', because AR2 [aristocratic radicalism] asserts that, contrary to the concept of 'aristocracy' that is orthodox and familiar, one merits inclusion among the aristocracy not in virtue of the family into which one was born, but rather in virtue of the intellect with which one 'do[es] much'.[20]

Nietzsche's new aristocracy is not one based on birth, wealth, or even social class. It is a meritocracy of the mind, based on intelligence and personal qualities, and is the natural hierarchy in society itself. What renders it radical is not only the fact that it redefines the meaning of aristocracy, but that it advocates recognition of the fact that not all people are equal in capability, and that only those who are truly exceptional should be entitled to occupy a position of power. Nietzsche asserts that 'an aristocratic society [is] a society which believes in a

---

[18]Nietzsche, F., ed., Kaufmann, W., *The Will to Power*, p.419.
[19]Tobias, N. A., *The Challenge of Aristocratic Radicalism*, p.6.
[20]Ibid., p.6.

long scale of orders of rank and differences of worth between man and man[21] and thus is the antithesis of contemporary democracy. Aristocratic Radicalism is not a continuation of the traditional aristocracy for according to Nietzsche, "Aristocrats so far, spiritual and temporal, prove nothing against the necessity for a new aristocracy."[22]

One of the main points in Aristocratic Radicalism is to shift the impetus from aristocratic birth to that of aristocratic temperament. The result of this is that class nobility due to ancestry is removed – rather it becomes a matter of whether or not one *acts* as nobility – and nobility of character is a requirement which Nietzsche dwells upon at length. The reason which importance is attached to the attribute of nobility is because in traditional aristocracies it was a preparatory school for personal sovereignty, and it was "The noble class [is that] which inherits this training".[23] The descriptions on what Nietzsche considers to be noble are cited in *The Will to Power*.

What is noble?

Endurance of poverty and want, also of sickness.

Avoidance of petty honours and mistrust of all who praise readily; for whoever praises believes he understands what he praises; but to understand – Balzac, that typical man of ambition, has revealed it – *compreendre c'est égaler*.

The conviction that one has duties only to one's equals, towards the others one acts as one thinks best: that justice can be hoped for (unfortunately not counted on) only inter pares.
[...]
Always to experience oneself as one who bestows honours, while there are not many fit to honour one.
[...]

---

[21]Ibid., p.8.
[22]Nietzsche, F., ed., Kaufmann, W., *The Will to Power*, p.500.
[23]Ibid., p.406.

Always disguised: the higher the type, the more a man requires an incognito. If God existed, he would, merely on grounds of decency, be obliged to show himself to the world as only a man.

[…]

Pleasure in forms; taking under protection everything formal, the conviction that politeness is one of the greatest virtues; mistrust for letting oneself go in any way, including all freedom of press and thought, because under them the spirit grows comfortable and doltish and relaxes its limbs.

[…]

Pleasure in princes and priests, because they preserve the belief in differences in human values even in the valuation of the past, at least symbolically and on the whole even actually.

[…]

Disgust for the demagogic, for the "enlightenment", for "being cozy", for plebeian familiarity.[24]

What is noble? That one constantly has to play a part. That one seeks situations in which one has constant poses. That one leaves happiness to the great majority: happiness as peace of soul, virtue, comfort, Anglo-angelic shopkeeperdom à la Spencer. That one instinctively seeks heavy responsibilities. That one makes enemies everywhere, if the worst comes to the worst even of oneself. That one constantly contradicts the great majority not through words but through deeds.[25]

One of the recurrent themes in Nietzsche's descriptions of nobility is the motif of endurance; endurance which is performed in the name of a task or cause even if it may run contrary to the opinions of the majority. It is not enough merely to exist; in order to be considered part of Nietzsche's new aristocracy one's existence must serve a higher purpose, which is performed by setting oneself "as lofty and noble

---

[24]Ibid., p.496-498.
[25]Ibid., p.498.

a goal as you can."[26] Therefore nobility is analogous with the spirit of self-sacrifice, an interpretation which is very far removed from the averages persons understanding of the Übermensch. Nietzsche sees the nobility of man in his capacity for promising something, answering for himself and undertaking a responsibility — since man, with the mastery of himself which this capacity implies, necessarily acquires in addition mastery over external circumstances and over other creatures, whose will is not so lasting.[27] We see this summarised below in George Brandes' book on Nietzsche:

> But be that as it may: owing to our familiarity with the notion of making sacrifices for a whole country, a multitude of people, it appears unreasonable that a man should exist for the sake of a few other men, that it should be his duty to devote his life to them in order thereby to promote culture. But nevertheless the answer to the question of culture — how the individual human life may acquire its highest value and its greatest significance — must be: By being lived for the benefit of the rarest and most valuable examples of the human race. This will also be the way in which the individual can best impart a value to the life of the greatest number.[28]

Nietzsche's ideas have been claimed by many movements to enhance their own theories and as a result he has been linked to a contrasting assortment of ideologies in order to fabricate an intellectual continuity of thought. Unfortunately by doing this Nietzsche's true opinions are often distorted into supporting ideas to which he was often vehemently opposed. What is certain however, is that Aristocratic Radicalism was intended by Nietzsche to replace the existing status quo, for he makes direct and impassioned pleas to his readers for this new class of philosophers to create a new social construct;

We to whom the democratic movement is not merely a form

---

[26]Brandes, G., *Friedrich Nietzsche* (New York: The Macmillan Company, 1915), p.18.
[27]Ibid., p.30.
[28]Ibid., p.13.

assumed by a political organization in decay but also a form assumed by man in his decay...in the process of becoming mediocre and losing his value, whither must be direct our hopes? Towards new philosophers, we have no other choice, towards spirits strong and original enough to make a start on antithetical evaluations.[29]

Nietzsche explicitly links mediocrity to liberalism and democracy, for both are doctrines of the middle. This also relates directly to his theory on the will to power, and it is certainly no coincidence that the majority of ideas connected to Aristocratic Radicalism occur in the text which bears the same name. It is the will to power itself which is feared under democratic regimes, indeed according to Nietzsche: "The will to power is so hated in democratic ages that their entire psychology seems directed toward belittling and defaming it".[30]

The will to power is something which can manifest in many different guises. Like the Übermensch and Dionysius it is an integral part of all Nietzsche's works, and is something he considers to be both healthy and virtuous. It's absence and fear of individuals whom possess it are hallmarks of what he calls 'slave morality' and is a symptom of a culture in decline. This is why Nietzsche says of his contemporaries "... men, not noble enough to see the abysmally different order of rank, chasm of rank, between man and man – such men have so far held sway over the fate of Europe, with their 'equal before God,' until finally a smaller, almost ridiculous type, a herd animal, something eager to please, sickly, and mediocre has been bred, the European of today."[31] This epidemic of destructive mediocrity is something Nietzsche also links to the rise of the finance industry and liberalism.

The power of the middle is, further, upheld by trade, above all trade in money: the instinct of great financiers against everything

[29]Lang, B., <u>Authors Responsibility</u> in, ed. Golomb, J., & Wistrich R.S, *Nietzsche, Godfather of Fascism? On the Uses and Abuses of Philosophy*, p.55.
[30]Nietzsche, F., ed., Kaufmann, W., *The Will to Power*, p.397.
[31]Hörnqvist, M., *The Few And The Many: Machiavelli, Tocqueville And Nietzsche On Authority And Equality*(Sweden: Uppsala University), p.9.

extreme. [...] They need occasionally to arouse fear of other extreme tendencies - by demonstrating how much power they have in their hands, but their instinct itself is unswervingly conservative – and "mediocre" – wherever there is power, they know how to be powerful; but the employment of their power is always in one direction. The honourable term for mediocre is, of course, the word "liberal".[32]

The supreme manifestation of the will to power is the ability to impose upon becoming the character of being and is also connected to Nietzsche's notion of self-overcoming. This he refers to as *Selbstüberwindung* which is a concept originating in recognition of the role of sublimation. Sublimation, as the mental mechanism that orders and subdues instinctual drives, is responsible for the attainment of "self-mastery".[33] These concepts will be realized in the ideal Übermensch. However, if the will to power is not sufficient in an individual they shall not succeed in the process of differentiation and will seek to re-join the Herd. Individuals with a sound psychic make-up and personal authenticity are endowed with a will to power of higher quality and greater vitality. Their will expresses the master morality, in contrast to the slave morality typical of those possessing lesser power or *macht*, although the later may be endowed with greater physical force or *kraft* and this distinction between kraft and macht is crucial to any understanding of Nietzsche's mature doctrine of power: it represents the philosophical emphasis on the transition from physical force to mental and spiritual power.[34] Through this process of self-sublimation the actualised macht essentially becomes a work of art; another reason why the Übermensch is compared to an artist. The authentic selfhood of the Übermensch, like that of "the exceptional Greeks", is achieved by one's ability to bring about a "transfiguration of nature," a purification of the primitive, coarse element of force into

---

[32]Nietzsche, F., ed., Kaufmann, W., *The Will to Power*, p.462.
[33]Golumb, J., Philosophical Anthropology in ed. Golomb, J., & Wistrich R.S., *Nietzsche, Godfather of Fascism? On the Uses and Abuses of Philosophy*, p.20.
[34]Ibid., p.20.

refined, creative power.[35] In Heidegger's analysis of what Nietzsche calls values there are also conditions that make the will to power possible. They do not exist independently, but only as conditions that are useful for the preservation and enhancement of the constructs of domination into which the will to power forms itself: "Values are the conditions with which power as such must reckon ....Values are in the first place the conditions of enhancement that the will to power has in view".[36]

The way in which Nietzsche speaks of power as an abstraction is reminiscent of the Hindu concept of Shakti. Nietzsche constantly speaks of power being in itself the 'enhancement of power'; the powering of power is empowering to 'more' power".[37] Will and power therefore "are self-same in the metaphysical sense that they cohere in the one original essence of the will to power"; in thinking the "essence" of either will or of power, we do not think them alone, but, rather, think will to power. Hence, the will to power means empowering to the point of excelling. This too is linked to the virtues that Nietzsche lists as being aristocratic, as is expressed here;

> The will to power appears [...] among the strongest, richest, most independent, most courageous, as "love of mankind," of "the people," of the gospel, of truth, God; as sympathy; "self-sacrifice," etc.; as overpowering, bearing away with oneself, taking into one's service, as instinctive self-involvement with a great quantum of power to which one is able to give direction: the hero, the prophet, the Caesar, the saviour, the shepherd.[38]

The manifestation of the will to power itself is also linked to the process of differentiation. Like Aristocratic Radicalism itself, it is fundamentally individualistic: it is the power of the individual in will

---

[35]Ibid., p.21.
[36]Blitz, M., Heidegger's Nietzsche in *The Political Science Reviewer*, p.64.
[37]Ibid., p.62.
[38]Nietzsche, F., ed., Kaufmann, W., *The Will to Power*, p.407.

and ability that marks the basis of the principle.[39] In regards to how the will to power correlates to the process of individuation it is not that one opposes society as an individual, but rather it represents all individuals who posit themselves against the collective. The individual instinctively considers himself as equal or above all other individuals; what he gains in this struggle he gains for himself not as a person but as a representative of individuals against the totality.[40] In this regard, individualism should be regarded as a subconscious manifestation of the will to power, in contrast to contemporary society in which one is taught to conform to the law of the average and 'slave morality'. It is from these differentiated individuals that influence is exerted upon society in the wider perspective – Aristocratic Radicalism is intended to form the loci and focal points of the causal power structure. Individualism is followed by the formation of groups and organs; related tendencies join together and become active as a power; between these centres of power friction, recognition of one another's forces, reciprocation, approaches, regulation and an exchange of services.[41] Thus, every Aristocratic Radical maintains the central position within their respective collective as the creative principle until eventually society is presided over by a new aristocracy of creators. Because of the obvious difficulty in qualifying as part of Nietzsche's aristocracy the manifestation of the will to power in these individuals is explicitly identified as a virtue and linked to endurance. Adversity strengthens the will to power and intensifies it in the correct type and, it is for this reason that Nietzsche relates this to his 'disciples';

> Type of my disciples – To those beings who are of any concern to me I wish suffering, desolation, sickness, ill-treatment, indignities – I wish that they should not remain unfamiliar with profound self-contempt, the torture of self-mistrust, the wretchedness of the vanquished: I have no pity for them, because I wish them the only thing can prove today whether one is worth or not – that one

---

[39]Lang, B., Authors Responsibility in ed. Golomb, J., & Wistrich R.S., *Nietzsche, Godfather of Fascism? On the Uses and Abuses of Philosophy*, p.59.
[40]Nietzsche, F., ed., Kaufmann, W., *The Will to Power*, p.411.
[41]Ibid., p.412.

endures.[42]

Returning to the political elements of Nietzsche's hypothesis, Nietzsche believes the will to power is scorned and denigrated in the modern era because of democratic values. The doctrine of equality reduces everyone to exactly the same, faceless substance, and those who express any form of individualisation become a potential victim of the Herd's wrath. Under such a regime the will to power when it manifests, is feared by the Herd. In these conditions, the unequal and those below average will be rewarded because it will lessen the will to power and reduce the threat of change entering into what is otherwise a closed system of thought. Nietzsche expressed this here;

> Our virtues are conditioned, are demanded by our weakness......
> Equality, a certain actual rendering similar of which the theory of
> 'equal rights' is only the expression, belongs essentially to decline:
> the chasm between man and man, class and class, the multiplicity
> of types, the will to be oneself, to be standing out – that which I
> call *pathos of distance* – characterises every strong age. The tension,
> the range between the extremes is today growing less and less
> – the extremes are themselves finally obliterated to the point of
> similarity.[43]

Thus excessive doctrines of equality act as a vessel for the vilest and most insidious form of inequality; by punishing that which dares to think differently and by doing so inherently restricting intelligence and creativity, as well as removing individuation out of fear of the will to power.

> The Herd feels the exception, whether it be below it or above it,
> as something opposed and harmful to it. [...] Fear ceases in the
> middle: here one is never alone; here there is little room for
> misunderstanding; here there is equality; here one's own form of

---

[42]Nietzsche, F., ed., Kaufmann, W., *The Will to Power*, p.481.
[43]Jenkins, M., *Aristocratic Radicalism or Anarchy? An Examination of Nietzsche's Doctrine of Will to Power*, p.20-21.

being is not felt as reproach but as the right form of being; here contentment rules. Mistrust is felt toward the exceptions; to be an exception is experienced as guilt.[44]

Nietzsche also points out that what he refers to as the 'Herd' is diametrically opposed to what he defines as an aristocratic society and lessens the will to power by conveying the supposition within the Herd that one should seek the safety of the meridian – to be a "zero."

The Herd instinct, then – a power that has now become sovereign – is something totally different from the instinct in an aristocratic society; and the value of the units determines the significance of the sum. Our entire sociology simply does not know any other instinct than that of the Herd, i.e., that of the sum of zeros – where every zero has "equal rights", where it is virtuous to be zero.[45]

RELIGION, CULTURE AND ANTIPOLITICAL STRATAGEM

Enough, the time is coming when we will relearn politics.
– Nietzsche

Despite Nietzsche's harsh criticism of the religion to which he was contemporaneous, Aristocratic Radicalism also has a spiritual dimension. We shall elaborate further on the Hindu influences underlying Aristocratic Radicalism later; but in the following citation it will be clear that there is a strong Hellenic influence upon his thought, which is also evident in his numerous references to Dionysus. Here Nietzsche advocates asceticism as a practice which leads to creating the new aristocracy. For he says that, "The teaching *mēden agan* applies to men of overflowing strength – not to the mediocre. The *enkrateia* and *askēsis* is only a stage toward the heights; the "golden nature" is higher."[46]

---

[44]Nietzsche, F., ed., Kaufmann, W., *The Will to Power*, p.159.
[45]Ibid., p.33.
[46]Ibid., p.495.

Despite Nietzsche's common association with atheism, his attitude towards religion stems from a dislike of the Judeo-Christian environment of his day, and contains strands of religious philosophy. To the casual reader, the material found in *The Antichrist* and *Twilight of the Idols* could be a simple product of atheism, but it is actually another carefully constructed dyad in his works; that of Rome and Judea. This is not crude anti-semitism however, which is something that Nietzsche disapproved of, rather it is based on the religious values inherited from the Abrahamic Traditions passed into modern democratic society from ancient times. Nietzsche's philosophy of religion is inherently different to atheism and is tied to another concept, the 'Ladder of Cruelty' in which humans create the scenario for the 'Death of God' as a final act of cruelty towards themselves. This is also expressed in 'The Parable of the Madman'. Following the 'Death of God', what is left now that the highest ideal has been murdered? What Nietzsche provides to fill the void left by the 'Death of God', is undoubtedly a world presided over by Übermensch, and a world where all people are evolved enough to qualify as his new aristocracy. It is quite obvious from the 'Parable of the Madman' that he does not expect this to happen. So rather than remove Christianity, Nietzsche instead attempts to replace it - substituting Christianity for another Tradition. It is for this reason that he places his words in the mouth of the prophet Zarathustra, praises Dionysus, and draws upon eastern sources such as the *Book of Manu* and Buddha. When Nietzsche breaks into the first person, he identifies with his new prophet Zarathustra, who he refers to elsewhere as 'Europe's Buddha'.[47] The writer Mistry also notes: 'It is essentially in opposition to Christianity that Nietzsche appreciates Buddhism, though paradoxically, and for the most part, he polemicizes [sic] against both religions conjunctly'.[48] Likewise, Dionysus is a clear substitute for Jesus, as seen in such statements as 'Dionysus vs. The Crucified'. Nietzsche's identification with (and also as) Zarathustra and Dionysus is a complex one, but not an issue that

---

[47]Bilimoria, P., <u>Nietzsche as 'Europe's Buddha' and 'Asia's Superman'</u> (26 September 2008, *Springer Science & Business Media*), p.370.
[48]Ibid., p.370.

we shall dwell at length upon here. Suffice to say that both Zarathustra and Dionysus are intended as substitutes for Christianity, in a format which is compatible with Nietzsche's paradigm of a religio-cultural system.

During the period of interaction with Richard Wagner, both of them corresponded heavily on mythography, reworking Hellenic and Nordic myths to promote their own ideals. The eventual fall-out with Wagner was due to his increasing incorporation of Christianity – something which Nietzsche considered absurd – even more so since Wagner was also anti-Semitic. In Nietzsche's philosophy it is impossible to divorce Christianity from its older parent Tradition of Judaism. The theory which deals with this topic is known as the 'slave revolt' hypothesis. In Nietzsche's telling of events, the Christians are the low-caste branch of Judaism, who came to power by destroying the Roman Empire via an act of ressentiment. To destroy Rome, Judea weakened it by introducing Christianity and this was disseminated to the most impoverished elements of society by cultivating ressentiment, a strategy used to create a 'slave revolt' against Rome. This is also why Nietzsche speaks more favourably of Judaism than Christianity – because in his theory the Christians are the unwitting servant caste of Judea. Thus, Nietzsche promotes the 'Death of God' not to attack religion, but specifically to attack religions which weaken the will to power. In the Rome/Judea dyad, Judea won by spreading Christianity to weaken the Romans. As such, he views the creation of Christianity as a 'Holy Lie' deployed as an act of political sabotage to weaken the will to power of the Romans and aristocratic values. This is the basic premise of Nietzsche's 'slave revolt', and many of his ideas are a direct reversal of this, essentially calling for a 'master reversal' to be enacted by the intellectual élite.

Nietzsche also links Christian values to the decline of the political climate in the modern West, because to Nietzsche's thinking, Christianity offers the "poor and lowly" a "gateway to happiness" and "to this extent the rise of Christianity is nothing more than the typical socialist doctrine."[49] Indeed, he also believes socialists use Christian ideas for their own purposes: "The socialists appeal to the Christian instincts; that is their most subtle piece of shrewdness".[50] In *The Antichrist*, Nietzsche calls the "equality of souls before God" the "pretext for the rancour of all base-minded, this explosion of a concept which eventually became revolution, modern idea, and the principle of decline of the whole order of society".[51]

There is no doubt Nietzsche considers Christianity to be "the counter-principle," or *Gegenlehre* to his Aristocratic Radicalism. He also believed the socialist ideal represented the "residue of Christianity and Rousseau in the de-Christianized world",[52] stating that it is "nothing but a clumsy misunderstanding of [the] Christian moral ideal".[53] It is at this point that Nietzsche's more complicated and obscure political ideas begin to emerge, such as the *Geisterkrieg*. The term Geisterkrieg appears only once in Nietzsche's writings, however it appears to be a hidden theme underlying much of his writing. Hugo Halferty Drachon explains in an article from the *Journal of Nietzsche Studies* the meaning of the Geisterkrieg;

> To get a better sense of what is meant by this term, I think it is fruitful to contrast it with two related concepts: *geistlicher Kampf* (Christian "spiritual Warfare") and *Kulturkampf* (Bismarck's infamous onslaught on the Catholic Church). If 'spiritual Warfare' provides the broader intellectual context to Nietzsche's 'Geisterkrieg,' 'Kulturkampf,' as I shall argue, gives it a more immediate political aspect. That Nietzsche never uses and indeed specifically avoids these terms, with which he was familiar, is quite telling. Geisterkrieg is Nietzsche's own version of a war both Paul and Bismarck fought in, a war he directly engages with and wishes to reorient, or reverse,

---

[49]Buccola, N., The Tyranny of the Least and the Dumbest: Nietzsche's Critique of Socialism, in *Quarterly Journal of Ideology* (Volume 31: 2009, 3 &4), p.7.
[50]Ibid., p.7.
[51]Ibid., p.8.
[52]Ibid., p.6.
[53]Ibid., p.7.

by staking his own claim in it, most ostensibly by renaming it.[54]

Geisterkrieg is implicitly a form of warfare in both a spiritual and political context, directed at enemies of his own philosophy. Nietzsche's aim with his Geisterkrieg is therefore to re-ignite the battle, to reaffirm the noble valuation of "good and bad" against the ressentiment values of "good and evil" and planning his own "Revaluation of all Values" to reverse the revolt in slave morality.[55] Geistlicher Kampf and Kulturkampf are thus past versions of the on-going war between Rome and Judea, which Nietzsche now wishes to launch on his own account, and he renames the war Geisterkrieg to mark his own position within it.

While the more common 'war of spirits' is grammatically superior as a translation for the Geisterkrieg, 'spirit' not only appears rather indeterminate but again seems to bring us back to the Christian conception Nietzsche was trying to get away from.[56] The best interpretation of the Geisterkrieg is as a 'Mind-war'. This might be the best rendition insofar as Nietzsche writes in his aphorism titled "Preparatory human beings" in *The Gay Science*: "[W]age wars for the sake of thoughts and their consequences": the war in question is about the idea of what type of mankind shall be bred.[57] The term Geisterkrieg also appears in a letter addressed to Emperor William II (December 1888), where he repeats his claims of "Why I am a Destiny," concluding: "[T]he concept of politics has entirely merged into a Geisterkrieg, all the images of power have exploded—there will be wars such as have never been seen".[58] The Geisterkrieg is therefore far more encompassing than purely being an expression of anti-Christian sentiment. In sum, almost everything Nietzsche wrote

---

[54]Halferty Drochon, H., The Time is Coming When We Will Relearn Politics in *Journal Of Nietzsche Studies*, Issue 39 (Pennsylvania: The Pennsylvania State University, 2010), p.66.

[55]Ibid, p.68.

[56]Ibid., p.69.

[57]Ibid., p.70.

[58]Ibid., p.69.

is part of the wider Geisterkrieg against the religio-political regime, and moreover the Geisterkrieg has extended long past his death to influence others. The Geisterkrieg is a fully fledged war of ideologies in which an aristocratic premise strategically counter-manoeuvres against Nietzsche's two avowed enemies, Judeo-Christianity and Socialism/Democracy, which he believes stem from the subliminal impulse of 'slave morality' - the antithesis to his own concept of the will to power, and Aristocratic Radicalism.

Through analysing Nietzsche's concepts of Geisterkrieg (Mind-War) and *grosse Politik* (Great Politics), Drochon argues that Nietzsche did move towards a view that started to offer a coherent political structure.[59] What Nietzsche begins with the Geisterkrieg, he continues with grosse Politik by stating that "the levelling of the European is the great process which cannot be impeded; it should be speeded up even further".[60] In this regard the statement Nietzsche writes is a key strategy which entails not fighting against the current; rather the astute strategist would encourage it because in the 'great levelling of individuals' to the meridian there will eventually be a total collapse due to entropy and stagnation of thought - in other words the total decline of the west. Thus Nietzsche's goal is not to attack his enemies - rather he perceives their fall to be inevitable - but by accelerating the 'levelling', the demise can be expedited. In the meantime, he perpetuates intellectual conflict with the Geisterkrieg. This is advocated in order to attain this "higher form of aristocratism [which] is that of the future" and Nietzsche states that what is imperative is "the necessity of cleaving gulfs, of distance, of the order of rank"; thus Nietzsche's "Mind-war" and his "Great politics" are designed to "cleave gulfs" and create an "order of rank" to achieve his ideal society.[61]

To gather insight into exactly what Nietzsche was creating as a model for this ideal society, information can be found in his correspondence with George Brandes. In his letters to Brandes, Nietzsche describes

---

[59]Ibid., p.66.
[60]Ibid., p.77.
[61]Ibid., p.77.

himself as the forerunner to a socio-political system yet to come in which his name will be linked to a crisis of such magnitude that the earth has never seen before, leading to his "Revaluation of all Values" - which is presumably a reference to the success of the Geisterkrieg. This is also found in *Ecce Homo*, where he writes that this "terrible truth" will come into "conflict with the lies of the millennia," "[t]he concept of politics will have then merged entirely into a Geisterkrieg, all power structures from the old society will have exploded—they are all based on lies: there will be wars such as the earth has never seen. Starting with me, the earth will know grosse Politik".[62]

In his correspondence to Brandes, Nietzsche describes the Geisterkrieg as not being a war between nations, races or classes, but instead between individuals who incarnate as either *ascending* or *descending* life. These individuals do join together as groups, as Nietzsche explains in the following note: "Individualism is followed by a development in groups and organs: correlative tendencies joining together and becoming active as a power, between these centres of power, friction, war, awareness of the forces on either side, reciprocity, reapproachment, the regulation of mutual services. Finally: an order of rank."[63] Thus, it is a conflict between individuals, who by acting as thinkers, generate groups around them in turn. Nietzsche's Aristocratic Radical is embodied in one who is ascending life, in contrast to those who would weaken it by denouncing the will to power.

The Party of Life is another term for Nietzsche's élite, however the Party of Life not only indulges in grosse Politik, but also seems to exert influence at the platform specific level of 'petty politics'. In light of these theories, one can now begin to understand Nietzsche's infamous phrase "enough, the time is coming when we will relearn politics".[64]

Grosse Politik is another concept of Nietzsche's which has all but disappeared, and is intimately entwined with that of the Geisterkrieg.

[62]Ibid., p.65.
[63]Ibid., p.73-74.
[64]Ibid., p.79.

Grosse Politik addresses politics from a level above that of petty political parties. It is for this reason that Nietzsche declines to participate in politics at a party specific level. This is why Nietzsche refers to himself as *antipolitische*, which is different from *unpolitisch* – referring to someone who is utterly indifferent to politics.[65] Grosse Politik influences politics by shaping culture and the thoughts of the collective – for Nietzsche, politics becomes 'grand' when it sustains and assists in cultivating human greatness and cultural grandeur.[66] The first indication of the arrival of grosse Politik is found in *Beyond Good and Evil* where he proposes that Europe shall;

> acquire a single will - by means of a new caste dominating all Europe, a protracted terrible will of its own which could set its objectives thousands of years ahead - so that the long-drawn-out comedy of its petty states and the divided will of its dynasties and democracies should finally come to an end. The time for petty politics is past: the next century will bring with it the struggle for mastery over the whole earth - the compulsion to Great politics.[67]

This is an obvious reference to Aristocratic Radicalism and it is for this reason that Nietzsche places great emphasis on the personal qualities and temperament found in the new élite; politically, they may be interpreted in terms of the qualities needed by national leaders.[68] It is also abundantly clear that Aristocratic Radicalism is intended to deliver both Nietzsche's Giesterkrieg and grosse Politik. As to grosse Politik itself, Nietzsche already has a framework drawn up:

First Principle: Great politics wants physiology as the queen of all

---

[65]Golomb, J., <u>Nietzsche & Zionism</u>, in eds, Allison, D.B., B. Babich, & B., Bergoffen, D. B., *New Nietzsche Studies, The Journal of the Nietzsche Society,* (Vol 7: 3 & 4, Fall 2007 & Winter 2008), p.59.

[66]Ibid., p.60.

[67]Halferty Drochon, H., <u>The Time is Coming When We Will Relearn Politics</u> in *Journal of Nietzsche Studies,* Issue 39, p.71.

[68]Sznajder, M., <u>Nietzsche and Mussolini</u> in ed. Golomb, J., Wistrich R.S., *Nietzsche, Godfather of Fascism? On the Uses and Abuses of Philosophy*, p.239.

other questions: it wants to create a power strong enough to breed Humanity as a superior whole, with greatest severity, against all that is degenerate and parasitical to life....

Second Principle: War to the death against vice: in vice all types of anti-nature. The Christian priest is the most vicious type of man: because he teaches anti-nature. [...] create a Party of Life, strong enough for Great politics .... It wants to breed Humanity as a whole, it measures the order of race, peoples, individuals, according to their future. [...] Third Principle: The rest follows.[69]

Grosse Politik is clearly intended to be a 'master theory' designed to be disseminated from the top down, for in *Ecce Homo*, Nietzsche contrasts grosse Politik with politics delivered at the smaller, party level: "this perpetuation of European particularism (*Kleinstaaterei*), of small politics [has] deprived Europe of its meaning, of its reason - (has) driven it into a dead-end street."[70] Not only this, but the notion of the 'state' itself is a concept which Nietzsche challenges, saying that "State I call it where all drink poison, the good and the wicked; state, where all lose themselves, the good and the wicked; state, where the slow suicide of all is called 'life.'"[71] Both the state and Nietzsche's grosse Politik, are wedded to yet a third idea – that of the cultural philistines.

From the State the exceptional individual cannot expect much. He is seldom benefited by being taken into its service; the only certain advantage it can give him is complete independence. Only real culture will prevent him being too early tired out or used up, and will spare him the exhausting struggle against culture-philistinism.[72]

---

[69]Halferty Drochon, H., The Time is Coming When We Will Relearn Politics in *Journal of Nietzsche Studies*, p.34.
[70]Sil, N. P., *Vivekananda and Nietzsche as Critics of Western Bourgeois Civilization*, p.9.
[71]Ibid., p.9.
[72]Brandes, G., *Friedrich Nietzsche*, p.13.

The exceptions then, who are Nietzsche's new aristocracy, are defendants not of the state, but of culture. The cultural-philistines live for the moment, are oblivious to any sense of past and are devoid of interest in anything 'higher' in society. The term itself errects a contrast between artificial 'culture' in the form of laws and rules arbitrated by the state, and the deeper ties which are found in concepts such as the '*Volksgeist*' and the '*Zeitgeist*'. The cultural philistine is oblivious to art, history, music, literature or any form of bond with his own community, and mistakes the artificially conveyed systems of the state to be 'culture'. Whatever presents itself to the eye, is 'culture' for the cultural philistine. The cultural-philistine regards his own impersonal education as the real culture; if he has been told that culture presupposes a homogeneous stamp of mind, he is confirmed in his good opinion of himself, since everywhere he meets with educated people of his own sort, and since schools, universities and academies are adapted to his requirements and fashioned on the model corresponding to his cultivation.[73] Today, we might correlate the cultural philistine with the qualities of the new consumerist mind-set, where text language is the norm, Apple products are status symbols, and MacDonald's is traditional food. If anything, what Nietzsche described as the cultural philistine is far more prolific in the modern era that it was in his own day. Given the spread of the 'cultural philistine' who believes culture to stem from the state and corporations, how is it possible resurrect an interest in real culture? Nietzsche answers thus;

> When the men of a community are steadily working for the production of single great men. From this highest aim all the others follow. And what state is farthest removed from a state of culture? That in which men energetically and with united forces resist the appearance of great men, partly by preventing the cultivation of the soil required for the growth of genius, partly by obstinately opposing everything in the shape of genius that appears amongst them. Such a state is more remote from culture than that of sheer

---

[73]Ibid., p.7.

barbarism.[74]

Culture therefore, will return when the people work together to place value upon producing single individuals who are capable of creating and shaping the current to produce great works. Moreover, the state which is more likely to generate the 'cultural philistine' is one which abnegates the will to power, which as we have already seen, finds its apex in Christian and democratic values.

GRAND POLITICS

What Nietzsche is defining as politics is so far removed from the contemporary system as to be a truly revolutionary concept. Essentially all political systems in modern European countries fall under the rubric of a two party 'democracy', based on an underlying plutocracy which prevents anyone without disposable wealth from gaining entry into parliament. All media, public relations and advertising are controlled to the extent that any smaller parties cannot afford to compete with the two party system. Therefore, 'democracy' as we understand it is no longer representational of the will of the people anyway, because candidates in an election are deprived of equality in media coverage during the course of a campaign – ensuring that power remains held in the grasp of the two party system and the corporate élite who fund their campaigns. Only the two main parties can compete in terms of finances, restricting the true choice of the vote to the centre right and the centre left. This effectively ensures the impotence of all other parties, even under systems where MMP is in place. What is currently defined as a democracy is in fact a plutocracy where the factor that decides the victor in an electoral campaign is in fact the propaganda/media team and the financial institutions. In relation to politics and media, Nietzsche says "I am opposed to [...] Parliamentary government and the press, because these are the means

---

[74]Ibid., p.12.

by which the Herd animal becomes the master."[75] What he means with this statement is that the media appeals to the stupidity of the masses, and not the intellectuals – thus the great majority vote not for the best candidate but the one with the most expensive campaign.

Nietzsche does not regard European democracy as a strong or vital system, referring to it as "a release of laziness, of weariness, of weakness."[76] This is also why Nietzsche connects democracy with mediocrity; because the vote is controlled by those lest qualified to make a decision; which is also why, when speaking of the government he says, "They know: *mediocritas* is also *aurea*.[77] Mediocrity is gold. "We have a different faith: to us the democratic movement [of which socialism is a part] is not only a form of the decay of political organization but a form of the decay, namely the diminution, of man, making him mediocre and lowering his value".[78] Furthermore, in regards to how Nietzsche views the party system, he believes them all to be fundamentally untrustworthy. "How treacherous all parties are! They bring to light something about their leaders which the latter have perhaps always taken great care to hide under a bushel."[79]

Closely related to Nietzsche's critique of democracy are his even more scathing remarks on socialism. Indeed, in *The Antichrist*, Nietzsche writes: "Whom do I hate most among the rabble today? The socialist rabble..."[80] The term 'socialist rabble' does not mean the voters or people – this comment is directed at the 'rabble rousers' (political agitators) who cultivate ressentiment in the collective. The socialist, then, seems to be saying: "I am wretched because 'the system' has made

[75]Nietzsche, F., ed., Kaufmann, W., *The Will to Power*, p.397.

[76]Nietzsche, F., ed., Kaufmann, W., *The Will to Power* (New York: Vintage Books, 1968), p.399.

[77]Ibid., p.461.

[78]Buccola, N., The Tyranny of the Least and the Dumbest: Nietzsche's Critique of Socialism, in *Quarterly Journal of Ideology*, p.22-23.

[79]Nietzsche, F., ed., Kaufmann, W., *The Will to Power*, p.398.

[80]Buccola, N., The Tyranny of the Least and the Dumbest: Nietzsche's Critique of Socialism, in *Quarterly Journal of Ideology*, p.2.

me so! If we overturn 'the system' and punish those who supported it, I will cease to be wretched."[81] In other words, socialism, like other forms of ressentiment, is a manifestation of the will to power in the "least and dumbest" members of society.[82] Effectively the socialist cultivates ressentiment in the same manner as the Christians toppled Rome; socialism creates a 'slave revolt' which then proceeds to the cultivation of mediocrity that empowers democracy. Socialism is therefore a means of agitation employed by individualism: it grasps that, to attain anything, one must organize oneself to a collective action, to a 'power'.[83] As Nietzsche says, the preaching of altruistic morality in the service of individual egoism is one of the most common lies of the nineteenth century.[84] The target demographic of reseentiment can thus be any group which is envied by others within the same cultural grouping; "evil…precisely the 'good man' of the other morality, precisely the noble, powerful man, the ruler, but dyed in another colour, interpreted in another fashion, seen in another way by the venomous eye of ressentiment".[85] Thus, in Nietzsche's 'slave revolt' theory, the group that identifies as oppressed will always be the one that is raised by the agitators to carry out vengeance – thus the successful political agitators will always seek to cultivate ressentiment in the lowest members of society and promise them 'equality'.

[The underprivileged] need an appearance of justice, i.e., a theory through which they can shift responsibility for their existence, for being thus and thus, on to some sort of scapegoat. This scapegoat can be God – in Russia there is no lack of atheists from ressentiment – or the social order, or education and training, or the Jews, or the nobility, or those who have turned out well in any way.[86]

Secondly, Nietzsche believed that the ruling class in industrial culture

---

[81] Ibid., p.19.
[82] Ibid., p.15.
[83] Ibid., p.25.
[84] Ibid., p.25.
[85] Ibid., p.20.
[86] Ibid., p.20.

– capitalists – "lacked noble manners" and, as such, did not command sufficient respect from the working class. In Nietzsche's mind, these two factors played off one another and created the conditions necessary for revolutionary thought and action.[87] In *The Gay Science*, Nietzsche explains the importance of "noble manners":

> Oddly, submission to powerful, frightening, even terrible persons, like tyrants and generals, is not experienced as nearly so painful as is [the] submission to unknown and uninteresting persons, which is what all the luminaries of industry are. What the workers see in the employer is usually only a cunning, bloodsucking dog of a man who speculates on all misery; and the employer's name, shape, manner and reputation are a matter of complete indifference to them. The manufacturers and entrepreneurs of business probably have been too deficient so far in all those forms and signs of a higher race that alone make a person interesting. If the nobility of birth showed in their eyes and gestures, there might not be any socialism of the masses.[88]

Though fascism was not around in Nietzsche's lifetime, the debate as to whether or not Nietzsche inspired some of the theories behind fascism appears often. As explained earlier, his political theory is correctly titled Aristocratic Radicalism, and it should be abundantly clear by now that it advocated an entirely different system to fascism. Nietzsche's influence actually predates fascist Italy and entered it via the works of Gabriele D'Annunzio. D'Annunzio generated a much wider audience for Nietzsche "to prepare for himself the superhuman reading of Nietzsche, and its use in an aristocratic key."[89] The rebellion against modernization, the need for an aristocracy of intellectuals (which D'Annunzio saw himself as leading) as well as sensuality and eroticism as marks of "real" life, the depiction of popular masses as a rabble, the cult of strength, and strong antidemocratic biases were all

---

[87]Ibid., p.10.
[88]Ibid., p.12-13.
[89]Sznajder, M., <u>Nietzsche and Mussolini</u> in ed. Golomb, J., & Wistrich R.S., *Nietzsche, Godfather of Fascism: On the Uses and Abuses of Philosophy*, p.239.

featured in his writings.[90] Like Nietzsche, D'Annunzio saw politics as a vehicle for beautiful and noble ideals.[91] Nietzsche's main influence was therefore not over German fascism, but Italian, for not only was D'Annunzio well connected with the platform in Italy - Mussolini himself had a high understanding of Nietzsche's work and ever wrote essays on Nietzsche. D'Annunzio was only briefly involved with fascism however, and later denounced it - but only after promoting Nietzsche's philosophy in politial circles through out Italy.

There are vast differences between fascism and Aristocratic Radicalism however. For one, Nietzsche adamantly opposed nationalist beliefs in a "folk soul" and thought it was a "basic error" to think of "collective" wills.[92] Therefore, rather than creating a nationalist super-power, Nietzsche instead called for the unification of Europe and for a "new caste" to dominate it, the "Good European".[93] There is no evidence of any racial agenda in any of Nietzsche's works, and he was openly opposed to Anti-Semitism.

The Vedic Tradition

Finally, to fully understand Aristocratic Radicalism, it needs to be examined in relation to Hinduism due to the profound influence of *Manusmṛti* or the *Laws of Manu* on Nietzsche. The text presents itself as a discourse given by the sage Manu, to a congregation of seers after the great floods in India c.10,000 years ago, teaching them how to face such calamities in future by organising themselves with guidelines for the social classes. Nietzsche's interest in this text dwells within its religious use: Firstly he notes the value of Hinduism as equal in power to the Judeo-Christian Tradition and looks to the Vedic past to

---

[90]Ibid., p.241.
[91]Ibid., p.242.
[92]Buccola, N., The Tyranny of the Least and the Dumbest: Nietzsche's Critique of Socialism, in *Quarterly Journal of Ideology*, p.27.
[93]Halferty Drochon, H., The Time is Coming When We Will Relearn Politics in *Journal Of Nietzsche Studies*, Issue 39, p.71.

create a counter-Tradition. In *The Book of Manu* he finds a legislative book similar to the Bible – but opposite in its underlying perspective, because *The Book of Manu* is a spiritual text for those who would *ascend life*. Nietzsche says that *Manu* is "an incomparably spiritual and superior work; it would be a sin against spirit even to mention its name in the same breath as that of the Bible".[94] From the perspective of life, *The Book of Manu* is *preservative* whereas Christian morality is *destructive*.[95] Nietzsche believes that the Christian construct of the 'Holy Lie' as he calls it is a philosophy which weakens man and the social unit by breeding admiration of the lesser and abnegation of the 'higher type'. According to Nietzsche Christianity erects its Holy Lie in the name of a "beyond" and thus commits itself to the destruction of this world and the imposition of a 'slave morality'.[96]

The Book of Manu, on the contrary, neither lowers the higher types nor raises the lower types - one stays at exactly the status they themselves have attained. Thus, to Nietzsche it has not erected a 'Holy Lie' to disempower man, instead it uses Tradition to raise man to a level which is in accord with Nietzsche's own theories. "The order of castes," Nietzsche writes, "the highest, the most dominant *Gesetz*, is only the sanction of a natural-order, natural-legal-positing of the first rank, over which no wilfulness, no 'modern idea' has power."[97] Through these and other rules, the *Manu* wages war not on the few and the powerful, but against the many, die *"grossen Zahl."*[98] This is what Nietzsche refers to when he speaks of breaking tablets and the re-evaluation of all values – it is the moment when the 'Holy Lie' of the Judeo-Christian empire topples, and a new set of 'values' is inscribed.

Like Plato, Nietzsche was in favour of adopting a class system with

---

[94]Luisetti, F., *Nietzsche's Orientalist Biopolitics* (USA: University of North Carolina), p. 6.
[95]Berkowitz, R., Friedrich Nietzsche, The Code of Manu, and the Art of Legislation, in *New Nietzsche Studies* (Volume 6-7: 2005-2006), p.7.
[96]Ibid., p.7.
[97]Ibid., p. 8.
[98]Ibid., p. 7-8.

loose correlations to the Hindu *varna* system. However, as pointed out earlier Nietzsche's qualifications for acceptance into his definition of the highest class/caste are meritocratic and are not fixed by birth, rank or privilege. Citing Nietzsche's views on this system, Roger Berkowitz from the *New Nietzsche Studies Journal* writes that;

> The order of castes rests upon the observation that there are at times either three or four kinds of men in nature. First comes the "highest caste," of whom Nietzsche says: "I name them the fewest." They are the *"geistigsten Menschen."* Only these "most spiritual men" have the privilege (*Vorrecht*, literally, a prior right) to establish beauty and the good upon the Earth. It is from their ranks that the artists and legislators emerge. The second kind of man is the muscular man - the members of the warrior class. Following Plato, Nietzsche calls these men "the guardians of *Recht*." They are exemplified, above all, by the king, as both warrior and judge - the executive of the most *Geistig*. The third kind of man includes the mediocrities, encompassing not only the businessmen, handworkers, and farmers, but also the scientists, academics, and the largest part of artists, those who busy themselves with a career.[99]

In regard to this there is no doubt that not only is class/caste self-assigned to an extent, it is also part of Nietzsche's theory on the construction of a new aristocracy. The fact that it is to be self-designated by an individual's attitude and behaviour is evident in this example - the rights a man arrogates to himself are related to the duties he imposes upon himself, to the tasks to which he feels equal.[100] Furthermore, these new creators are the ones who are to inscribe Nietzsche's values in the future – their creative acts are the essence of the 'will to power'. "To prepare a book of law in the style of *Manu* means to give a people the right to become master one day, to become perfect, to aspire to the highest art of life".[101]

---

[99]Ibid., p. 8-9.
[100]Nietzsche, F., ed., Kaufmann, W., *The Will to Power*, p.467.
[101]Luisetti, F., *Nietzsche's Orientalist Biopolitics*, p.6.

[T]hus it shall be! They first determine the whither and for what of man. With a creative hand they reach for the future, and all that is and has been becomes a means for them, an instrument, a hammer. Their "knowing" is creating, their creating is a legislation, their will to truth is - will to power.[102]

Conclusion

One thing is necessary above all..., something that has been unlearned most thoroughly nowadays – and therefore it will be some time before my writings are 'readable' – something for which one has almost to be a cow and in any case not a 'modern man': rumination.[103]

The reason readers have difficulty in interpreting Nietzsche's political system correctly is that it does not conform to any contemporary model in the West, which leads to both erroneous interpretations and deliberate falsifications. The inevitable recourse of this process is that both academics and amateurs alike have politicised an author, who, true to his own words, really was not interested in politics at the 'petty' level. It should be painfully obvious that Nietzsche was against socialism, democracy, nationalism, anarchism and indeed almost everything which revolved around the politics of the masses or ressentiment. Essentially what he was promoting was instead a hierarchical society based on intelligence, personal qualities and individual merit – close to Plato's *Republic*, though Nietzsche in no way indicates that his new aristocracy was to be composed primarily of philosophers. They are defined as 'spiritual', artists, creators and legislators. In any regard, it is obvious that in his paradigm the creators at the top of the hierarchy are overtly humanitarian in outlook and that emphasis is placed on their individual merit to society.

---

[102]Berkowitz, R., Friedrich Nietzsche, The Code of Manu, and the Art of Legislation, in *New Nietzsche Studies*, p.16.
[103]Müller-Lauter, W., Experiences with Nietzsche in ed. Golomb, J., & Wistrich R.S., *Nietzsche, Godfather of Fascism? On the Uses and Abuses of Philosophy*, p.66.

One may think that it is perhaps far-fetched to imagine this being enacted, however if it were constructed as an organisation which operated outside of the government between a network of people, this could in fact be established with great ease, with people voluntarily ascribing themselves to their chosen roles. Ironically, because it is so far removed from the contemporary political model, it is also the easiest one to enact because it could – hypothetically – be constructed to overlay the existing power structure and *thus has no need to challenge it*. By completely side-stepping the political structure, Nietzsche's Geisterkrieg has no need of garnishing votes, no need of propaganda or money – all it needs to be enacted is to win the hearts and the mind of the people – which is why it is a 'war of the spirit' against the 'cultural philistine'. Nietzsche's political system is actually *antipolitical* because it rejects the entire corpus of western politics in favour of a *natural hierarchy*. Nietzsche's Geisterkrieg does not require politics, politicians or political parties; all it requires are thinkers, artists, creators, and spiritual leaders. These people are to be Nietzsche's new aristocracy and it is they who will fight the 'mind-war'. This in turn will open the route for 'grand politics' which is essentially not a normative system either.

Grand Politics distances itself from what Nietzsche rejects as small-minded party based systems in favour of doctrines that are capable of spreading and disseminating over the entire earth. In line with his rejection of nationalism, Nietzsche favours a form of thinking which is not geographically fixed to any one time or place. Grand Politics once it was fully transcribed (bearing in mind that Nietzsche became ill with brain cancer before completing his political treatise) was to be a universal system that could be applied anywhere – not so much as a 'one world government', but a 'one world class', in which the new hierarchy would eventually disperse and displace the democratic values of Christianity in the moment which Nietzsche terms the 're-evaluation of all values'. This is the point where Europe realises it is in great decline, and unable to cease the process, looks not for others to blame for the impending collapse, but to history to see what started it – and in the process denounces the values behind the decline – which according to Nietzsche are democracy, socialism and Christianity. As they are fundamental principles, they can only be replaced and not eliminated. To this end, Nietzsche replaces democracy with aristocracy, and Christianity with *The Book of Manu*. In a similar fashion, he substitutes Zarathustra and Dionysus for Jesus. All of Nietzsche's works do not advocate the destruction of ideas, but the creation of substitutes – which of course is why Aristocratic Radicalism is a meritocracy of creators – they are the intellectual vanguard for the ideas that will change the world.

Amrtam Ayur Hiranyam
Julius Evola's Notion of Eschatology

[Only] he who knows and practices ritual action
rises again in life and obtains immortal life:
the others who neither know nor practise ritual action
will continue to be born anew, as nourishment for death

Śatapatha Brâhmana 10.4.3,10

Marek Rostkowski

The issue of life after death, the hereafter, the beyond, the land of the dead, destiny, that what is on the other side, has been known to humanity since its very origins. We can find various representations of this notion among several civilizations or religious systems. Although the fundamental dilemma concerns what exists beyond, this does not change the fact that every kind of the hereafter affects what takes place here and now. Even unbelief that there is something after death, that there exists some kind of an alternative reality and a deep conviction that with physical death comes an absolute end, conditions a particular attitude towards being.

We, however, will not concentrate ourselves on the latter but will be dealing with an idea of life after death such as is presented by an Italian aristocrat, revolutionary conservatist and Traditionalist, an eminent authority in the field of esotericism, an explorer of civilizations and spirituality, a philosopher, a painter, an alpinist and well-known expositor of Integral Traditionalism – Baron Julius Evola (1898-1974).

First and foremost, however, one needs to note that he is not an creator of the theories of one sort or another regarding the hereafter but he rather serves as a commentator or hermeneutist of numerous sources revealing to us the hidden meaning of the allegories drawn from the treasury of Tradition. This is what one always need to remember when dealing with Evola's worldview.

The 'Democratization' of Immortality

One of the ideological pillars supporting the edifice of the modern world which – in the Traditional outlook – is a manifestation of the last stage of the *Manvantara*, i.e. of the *Kali Yuga*, the Wolf Age or the Iron Age of which the vanguard in the contemporary West, is the notion of equality. Although the beginnings of this process can be observed much earlier, it is especially the last two centuries that witnessed the denial of every hierarchy, the highest authorities depreciation, and a transformation of the established order which all drowned in the sea of blood. Each of these things was carried out by people who called themselves the defenders of human rights, humanitarians in the name of equal rights for every man and fought against alleged injustices. A peculiar paradox tinged with irony is a situation where the apostles of humanitarianism by trying to put a human being on the pedestal, in fact degraded a man as much by striping and depriving him of a spiritual perspective.[1] Being supported by other theories – worked out by spiritually extirpated reason which for a modern man is a god[2] – like for example evolutionism according to which we are descended from some kind of uncomplicated element which later developed into the advanced organisms and therefore, in other words, what is higher comes from what is lower; or social contract theory which tells us that at one time people concluded a contract with one another on the strength of which they transferred the power over themselves to a superior institution, i.e. a sovereign, the idea of egalitarianism became a dogma. Its supremacy seems to be unquestionable and the range of its influence still gains new areas.

---

[1]Cf. Lings, M, *Ancient Beliefs and Modern Superstitions* (Cambridge, 2001). p.25.
[2]Herlihy, J., *Modern Man At The Crossroads. The Search for the Knowledge of First Origins and Final Ends* (Lahore, 2005), p.31.

The notion of equality penetrated also into the eschatological sphere – no matter how odd that sounds. Nevertheless, this invasion is by no means recent as its hallmarks can be seen as early as in the time of Sixth Dynasty of the ancient Egyptian empire[3] which an eminent Romanian specialist in religious studies, Mircea Eliade, mentions when he refers to one of the myths. Eliade wrote:

> Osiris was actually Orly the copping stone of the resolution that already before him had modified the Egyptian eschatologic notion [...]Osiris yet increased 'democratic' nature of far-reaching transformation of the notion of immortality: everyone can achieve immortality provided that one emerges victorious of a trial [...] although the osirian theology instead the trials of the heroic, initiatic nature (fight with bull) introduces the trials of the etic and religious character (good deeds etc.). The archaic notion gives way to the human and humanistic notion.[4]

We deal with a similar process within Christianity, which we will discuss later on. For now we restrict ourselves to claiming that for Evola the notion according to which every soul is immortal seemed at least bizarre or rather was "an ideological aberration",[5] inconceivable for a Traditional civilization.

Coming from an old Roman aristocracy Baron Evola was at the very Antipodes of the egalitarian theories. For such an orthodox proponent of hierarchy, authority, elites or, in a word, of everything coming "from Above", it was unthinkable to believe that an equal status can be attributed to, for example, an imperial *pontifex* on the one hand and on the other to a humble stallholder.[6] Such a view

---

[3]Evola, J., *Revolt Against the Modern World* (Rochester: VT, 1995), p.237.
[4]Eliade, M.,*Traktat o historii religii* (Warszawa, 1966), p.143-144.
[5]Ea [J. Evola], The Problem of Immortality, w: *Introduction to Magic. Rituals and Practical Techniques for the Magus* (Rochester: VT, 2001), p.150.
[6]It would not be without interest to mention, however, that at the same time the Italian traditionalist glorified an idea of fidelity to one's own nature as opposed to striving for becoming someone who one in reality is not, what, according to

was contrary to, described by him, the Primordial Tradition (*La Tradizione Primordiale*), i.e. the metaphysical principle of the world.[7] The principle of equality was in his eyes something simply impossible, it was "sheer nonsense" that represents "a logical absurdity".[8] Every attempt to realize it leads to reversing all right relations and established order of things. Especially from the esoteric perspective a concept of making equal the initiate with the profane – rootless and devoid of both interesting and point of reference to the higher world, to "the metaphysical reality", but also with a man remaining on the exoteric level of religion seemed to him greatly incomprehensible as well as sinister. He did not agree on any aspect of reducing all people to the common denominator but was led to everyman's existence of depreciation instead. The Italian claimed even that "Ordinary man should never say, I love," but, "Love loves through me." As the fire manifests itself in individual flames when the necessary conditions

the traditional doctrine was impossible and harmful. "Better own duty" – writes Evola – "even imperfectly done than someone else's done perfectly". Evola, J., *Etyka aryjska* (Chorzów, 1993), p.24. Therefore, a man of lower status fulfilling his own obligations was more noble than someone being higher in the hierarchy but denying his vocation. As the Author of *Rivolta contro il mondo modern* claims: "A craftsman who does his duties in a perfect way is undoubtedly more dignified than a king badly performing his function". *Idem, Orientacje* (Chorzów, 1993), p.16.

[7] Evola depicted the image of the World of Tradition in his *opus magnum* under the title of *Rivolta contro il mondo moderno* (1934). About Evola's understanding of the idea of the Primordial Tradition see Mikołejko, Z., *Mity tradycjonalizmu integralnego. Julius Evola i kultura religijno-filozoficzna prawicy* (Warszawa, 1998), p.129-156; Rostkowski, M., *Julius Evola: (Kontr)rewolucja w imię Tradycji*, Myśl.pl no. 8, p.61-64.

[8] Evola, J., *Men Among the Ruins. Postwar Reflections of a Radical Traditionalist*, (Rochester: VT, 2002), p.133 and 134. René Guénon adds that the theory of egalitarianism is "contrary to all established facts and belied even by simple observation, since equality is really nowhere to be found". Guénon, R., *Spiritual Authority and Temporal Power* (Hillsdale: NY, 2001), p. 8. In another book the French traditionalist states that since equality, which he calls hallucination, is impossible, there appear false hierarchies instead and that "the democratic slogan of equality being merely the consequence and the manifestation, in the social order, of intellectual anarchy". *Idem, East and West* (Hillsdale: NY, 2001), p.106. Cf. also Rostkowski, M., *Upiorne oblicze Zachodu. Refutacja egalitaryzmu w pismach René Guénona*, Pro Fide, Rege et Lege 2011, no 2, p.181-192.

are present, likewise love (or better said, the *being* of love) manifests itself in individual beings who love with a love that transcends and transports them, in relation to which they are more or less passive. The same applies to hatred, fear, piety, etc".[9] Those two faces of humanity – if not antinomic – are separated by *an abyssos* which makes them completely different modes of existence. In relation to this one could also mention here Evola's distinction between *person* and *individual*[10] as totally different forms of human being.

Since the conception of making all people equal in this world was for the Italian aristocrat unacceptable whatsoever, all the more so must have been as far as the hereafter is concerned. It is not here, of course, about undermining a belief that after death everyone goes to the same place. It would be difficult, as a matter of fact, to find such notions on a religious-mythological map of the world. It is rather about questioning an assumption according to which every human being, regardless of the particular destination in the afterlife, was to have an immortal soul. Before we clarify, however, the heart of the matter, we have to deal with yet another aspect of the problem. We will say a few words about a notion – seemingly contradictory to the above mentioned – of the pre-existence of the souls.

PREEXISTENCE AND REINCARNATION

The author of *Rivolta contro il mondo modern* claimed that neither death was an absolute end in itself after which there is only emptiness

---

[9]Ea [J. Evola], The Doctrine of Immortal Body, in *Introduction to Magic...*, *op. cit.*, p.197. A few chapters earlier Abraxas addresses the Reader with the following words: "you must be strong enough for this truth: *you are not the life in you*. You do not exist. There is nothing you can call "mine." You do not own Life: it is Life that owns you". Abraxas, *Knowledge of the Waters*, in: *ibidem*, p.17. Cf also: Evola, J., *The Path of Enlightenment in the Mithraic Mysteries* (Sequim: WA, 2005), p.14; *idem*, *The Yoga of Power. Tantra, Shakti, and the Secret Way* (Rochester: VT, 1992), p.63.
[10]See *idem*, *Ride the Tiger. A Survival Manual for the Aristocrats of the Soul* (Rochester: VT, 2003), p.106-111.

nor birth was a beginning. They both are merely the successive stages outlined on the map of fate. In the metaphysical perspective "birth is a change of state and so is death; the human condition of earthly existence is only a restricted section in a continuum, in a current that traverses many other states"[11] – states Evola. Human life, such as it is perceived currently, is not one, absolute and does not even have to be the most important stage. What is both before and after this life can be of much greater importance than just fleeting and often ephemeral earthly existence. Moreover, what preceded it has not only an unspecified impact but is of fundamental significance. The Self, as Julius Evola claims, preexists and, at the same time, determines the human nature[12] and it is mind as *nous* – not the soul – that survives death.[13]

This idea is related to the sphere of sexes as well. From the point of view of a Traditional men, writes the Traditionalist, "before physical embodiment, the sexes existed as superindividual forces and transcendental principles; before appearing in 'nature', they existed in the realm of the sacred, the cosmic, and the spiritual".[14] The very

---

[11]*Ibidem*, p.220.

[12]Ea [J. Evola], Freedom, Precognition, and the Relativity of Time, w: *Introduction to Magic...*, *op. cit.*, p.311. On another occasion Evola refers to the particular examples taken from Hindu civilization, Persian-Aryan civilization and Hellenic civilization. He finds even traces of all this in the philosophy of Kant and Schopenhauer. See Evola, J., *Revolt Against...*, *op. cit.*, p.91.

[13]Ea [J. Evola], *The Problem of Immortality*, *op. cit.*, p.150. Cf also G. Stucco, *Translator's introduction*, [in:] *Yoga of Power...*, *op. cit.*, p.XII. If we were to speak about survival of soul, it is possible only in case of achieving a certain degree of enlightenment. Evola, J., *Karma and Reincarnation*, http://www.gornahoor.net/library/KarmaAndReincarnation.pdf.

[14]Evola, J., *Eros and the Mysteries of Love. The Metaphysics of Sex* (Rochester: VT, 1991), p.115. Otto Weininger refuses the women the right to own the Self referring the Chinese, Mahomet, Aristotle, Tertulian or Orygenes. See Weininger, O., *Płeć i charakter*, Kraków 1911, p.229-230, 383. Thus, perhaps, his conviction that only men feel the need of immortality. *Ibidem*, p.159. Evola, in turn, quotes a couple authors from various periods undermining also some spiritual elements of women. He does not agree with this notion, though, and writes that if a woman does not have soul, one should mean by this the Spirit, i.e. *nous* and not *psyche*. And if the term

essence of human being – independent of its sensual incarnation, not belonging to merely terrestrial sphere – is something much deeper and multidimensional, going beyond the human, falling outside any definition.

A conviction or a belief about pre-existence of the Self is in accordance with a general order of the world of Tradition. We know that the characteristic direction of Tradition is vertical, i.e. leading from top to bottom. As above, in Heaven, so below, on Earth. What is superior defines what is inferior and not the other way round. Everything of this world, everything what is visible was to be a reflection, projection and so a result of the causes having their sources in higher reality. On this basis Julius Evola was interpreting, for example, very restrictive caste law in India. According to it, birth in a particular caste was by no means a matter of coincidence, a twist of fate, but had its own inevitability determined by a higher law. This birth was a manifestation of its predispositions, of its nature which existed before and independently of an earthly appearance. As a matter of fact, the words which were used for designating caste in India signify "individual nature".[15] It is, therefore, that "birth does not determine nature, but that nature determines birth; [...] a person is endowed with a certain spirit by virtue of being born in a given caste, but at the same time, one is born in a specific caste because one possesses, transcendentally, a given spirit. Hence, the differences between the castes, far from being artificial, unfair, and arbitrary, were just the

---

'soul' is taken in the latter meaning, then, in fact, "woman not only has a soul but is eminently 'soul'". Evola, J., *Eros and the Mysteries...*, *op. cit.*, p.151. About wrong consideration soul and spirit, and as a consequence, psychic and spiritual sphere equivalent, what Kant was to contributed to, see Guénon, R., *The Reign of Quantity and the Signs of the Times* (Hillsdale: NY, 2001), p.235. Later on, in the same book, Guénon makes an interesting observation: "According to the Islamic doctrine it is through the *nafs* (soul) that *Shaytan* can obtain a hold on man, whereas the *ruh* (spirit), of which the essence is pure light, is beyond the reach of his endeavors". *Ibidem*, s. 242.

[15]Guénon, R., *Spiritual Authority...*, *op. cit.*, p.8. The French traditionalist thought the institution of caste to be the most complete expression of the metaphysical doctrine in the human order. *Ibidem*, p.31.

reflection and the confirmation of a pre-existing, deeper, and more intimate inequality".[16] It is an absolute antithesis of a modern view of man.

The above presented idea can make one think of the theory of reincarnation, i.e. of transmigration of souls and their many appearances in various forms. The author of *Rivolta contro il mondo moderno* cautions against considering those notions equivalent.[17] While the theory of reincarnation – which he regards as "folkbased", "superstitious" and "lacking solid, traditional foundations"[18] – is characterized by some degenerative influences and its very appearance is according to him a symptom of a spiritual disease,[19] the doctrine of pre-existence of souls, known both in the East as in the West, has an initiatic character.[20] Moreover, Evola points out an absence of the notion of reincarnation in the Vedic era.[21] On the other hand,

---

[16]Evola, J., *Revolt Against…*, *op. cit.*, p.92. Some misunderstanding and evident errors concerning the matter rectifies René Guénon. See R. Guénon, R., *Introduction to the Study of the Hindu Doctrines* (Hillsdale: NY, 2001), p.151-156. In another book he presents a possibility of existence outside the castes. It can take place in two ways, i.e. one can be either above them (*ativarna*) or beneath them (*avarna*); moreover those two cases are extremely opposite to each other. To provide its better depiction he gives an example of the contemporary people perceiving themselves as being outside of every religion, not participating in any of them, as an antithesis of those who "having penetrated to the principial unity of all the traditions, are no longer tied to any particular traditional form". *Idem, The Reign of Quantity…*, *op. cit.*, p.62-63.

[17]Ea [J. Evola], *Freedom, Precognition…*, *op. cit.*, p.311

[18]Evola, J., *The Yoga of Power…*, *op. cit.*, p.143.

[19]*Idem, Revolt Against…*, *op. cit.*, p.259.

[20]Ea [J. Evola], *Freedom, Precognition…*, *op. cit.*, p.311.

[21]He refers here among others to the symbolic Vedic rite of "wiping out the tracks" which was performed in order to prevent the dead returning among the living. See Evola, J., *The Doctrine of Awakening. The Attainment of Self-Mastery According to the Earliest Buddhist Texts* (Rochester: VT, 1996), p.23. One needs to mention that when Evola speaks about the Vedic era he does not mean the whole ancient sacred literature of India but distinguishes the two phases of the Indo-Aryan traditions: the Vedic and the *Brāhmana Upanisad*. *Ibidem*, p.21. The origins of infiltration by the notions of reincarnation locates Evola in the period of *Upanisad* speculations. *Ibidem*, p.26. Mircea Eliade indicates a fact that the Hindu philosophy is called

considering this theory from the esoteric point of view, he writes about its impossibility. What undergoes the subsequent incarnations is not what is produced (a particular individual) but what produces (the subpersonal power incarnated in it).[22] *Il barone* indicates also the differences between the notion of "soul" in Buddhism and in *Vedanta* which cannot be simply transferred to deliberations on reincarnation nowadays. "If today – as he writes – one still wishes to speak of reincarnation, one can no longer speak of it through the soul as personality, but through other principles included in the human entity and always in a sense that excludes, furthermore, a true continuity of personal consciousness. He can tell himself that which is in the present condition is eternal and what is transmitted from being to being is no longer the 'immortal atman' (the subpersonality), but it is 'life' as 'desire', in the Buddhist sense of the term,[23] since "only what belongs to the earth comes back to the earth".[24] Marco Pallis, in turn, adds that there is the often ignored obvious fact of the existence of many other, different from the human, states, in comparison with which the chances of another incarnation in human form are extremely rare.[25] Therefore, Julius Evola recommends a considerable dose of suspicion of every doctrine giving preeminence to the idea of reincarnation.[26]

Apart of all the above mentioned, the Italian aristocrat formulates another charge concerning this theory. He considered it as not harmonizing with praised by him the olympian and heroic worldview and at the same time as a characteristic for non-Aryans[27] which

existentialist what was to be the result of dealing by India from the era of *Upanisad* only with the structure of the human condition. Eliade, M., *Joga. Nieśmiertelność i wolność* (Warszawa, 1984) p.12.

[22]Ea [J. Evola], *The Problem of Immortality...*, *op. cit.*, p.147.

[23]Evola, J., *Karma and...*, *op. cit.*

[24]*Ibidem.*

[25]Pallis, M., *The Way and the Mountain. Tibet, Buddhism, and Tradition*, (Bloomington: IN, 2008), p.181.

[26]Ea [J. Evola], *The Problem of Immortality...*, *op. cit.*, p.147. Cf. also *Various Commentaries*, [in:] *Introduction to Magic...*, *op. cit.*, p.181.

[27]One should not confuse here what Evola calls 'Aryan" or "non-Aryan' with the nazi notions. The Italian traditionalist uses those terms in the primordial and spiritual

represent the telluric and matriarchal worldview. In fact, it is "conceivable only by one who feels himself to be a 'son of the earth' *who has* no knowledge of a reality transcending the naturalistic order."[28] Where, then, in all this is a place for immortality, one could ask? Before we reach the final explanation, one needs to clarify one more – very important for our considerations – question.

IMMORTALITY AND SURVIVAL

It is widely assumed in the West that everyone who lives after death becomes immortal. No matter how ridiculous it might sound, especially for our contemporaries, it is not a pure banality. Western civilization, of which Christianity is the foundation, sees the hereafter either as a reward (the Heavens) or a punishment (the Hell) for the worldly existence. Therefore, regardless whether one is in the Father's House or burns in the hellfire, he is immortal just on the strength of his not dissolving into the emptiness having breathed his last due to having a soul that was granted by God to every human being. Meanwhile it is a far reaching simplification of this complicated matter. A conscious surviving death is by no means tantamount to immortality. Let us emphasize those two notions which Evola uses in regard to the afterlife: survival and immortality. In a sense the latter one could consider as a higher 'level' of the former. In Evola's eyes they are not, obviously, the synonyms, but neither are they an absolute axis which every destiny comes down to. There are, as a matter of fact, not only two but many more possibilities of the forms of the afterlife, since a man is far from a dichotomy soul-body.[29] The Italian aristocrat refers here to an analogy

---

sense. See Evola, J., *The Doctrine of Awakening...*, *op. cit.*, p.13-20.

[28] *Ibidem*, p.26.

[29] *Idem, Revolt Against...*, *op. cit.*, p.47. It is especially expressed by the initiatic teachings which, unlike the religions speaking about this matter in the abstract terms, deal with it from different perspectives that take into consideration various possibilities and conditions. See Ea [J. Evola], *The Problem of Immortality...*, *op. cit.*, p.145. Frithjof Schuon writes that "Every diagram of spiritual realization starts in principle from the distinction between the body and the soul, then distinguishes

to the corporeal sphere of a human. He maintains that, as in the case of a physical organism that does not disappear immediately after death but goes through a variety of phases which are subjected to the chemical-physical laws, the same happens in case of the "psychical" part of a human. Therefore, after death the "psychic" corpse or a kind of a copy of the dead's personality lasts yet for some time and in some instances it can originate in different manifestations.[30] Moreover, in one of his books, Julius Evola emphasizes a distinct borderline, which is to be the hallmark of almost every ancient religion, between survival and immortality on the one hand, and life after death of the most people on the other.[31]

Let us repeat once again that according to the Italian revolutionary conservatist not everyone who survives death, by the very fact becomes immortal. Furthermore, even avoiding Hell, Hades or their equivalents, one has no guarantee of immortality. The latter was the privilege of only those few who belonged especially among the heroes, as an Aryan notion states.[32] Those who remain on the level of survival are the Titans.[33] Even if this survival means the continuation of an individual existence in the "celestial" or "angelic" states, they still are conditioned. Although their lasting can be infinite, they are not – according to the Aryo-Oriental notion – truly eternal, 'deathless' in

---

within the soul between the sensorial soul (the psyche and the thinking mind) and the immortal soul (the true ego), and finally, within the immortal soul, between the individual soul and the Spirit (the Intellect), or in other words between the 'brain' and the 'heart'". Schuon, F., *Prayer Fashions Man* (Bloomington, in 2005), p.140.

[30]Evola, J., *Revolt Against...*, *op. cit.*, p.145.

[31]*Ibidem*, p.150.

[32]*Idem, Metaphysics of War. Battle, Victory & Death in the World of Tradition* (Aarhus, 2008), p. 102. We can find its traces in the Islamic idea of *shahida*, i.e. a martyr whose path of life and rank he thus attains is praiseworthy in the eyes of God. *Koran* says: "Those who believe, and have left their homes and striven with their wealth and their lives in Allah's way are of much greater worth in Allah's sight. These are they who are triumphant" [IX,20]. Cf. Ashraf, S. A., *The Inner Meaning of the Islamic Rites: Prayer, Pilgrimage, Fasting, Jihad*, [in:] *Encyclopedia of Islamic Spirituality*, Nasr, S. H., (ed.), vol. 1 (Lahore, 2000), p.129.

[33]Evola, J., *Revolt Against...*, *op. cit.*, p.225.

the absolute sense.[34]

The Genuine Immortality

1. The Path of the Gods and the Path of the Ancestors

We have already said that immortality is not the equivalent of survival. Considering them as being equivalent Julius Evola regards as misuse and alien to the Olympian worldview. Immortality is something different and is not only a higher or even the highest degree of the survival but is the achievement of the inaccessible heights of Being for the masses. It is the rising to the region of the gods or even higher – to the land of the heroes who became gods. It was not without a reason that the Italian aristocrat, as well as other traditionalists, spoke about the path of gods as different from the path of ancestors. The latter means "passing on from one samsaric World to another".[35] The latter follow "those who do not survive in a real way, and who slowly yet inexorably dissolve back into their original stock, into the 'totems' that unlike single individuals, never die".[36] It goes without saying that the former is within reach for only few whereas the majority follow the latter. The idea of true immortality is conceivable "for those few who, as men, have been able to conceive of themselves as more than men and who have taken part, in full awareness – even if only through some flash of insight – in states that are free of the condition of the individual".[37] "The path of the ancestors" corresponds to Hades, Nifelheim, the chthonic deities, the larval state which awaits most people after death.[38]

It is worth mentioning that the Author of *Rivolta contro il mondo*

---

[34]*Idem, The Doctrine of Awakening…, op. cit.*, p.208.
[35]Lings, M., *Ancient Beliefs…, op. cit.*, p.56.
[36]Evola, J., *Revolt Against…, op. cit.*, p.50-51.
[37]*Idem, The Doctrine of Awakening…, op. cit.*, p.199.
[38]*Idem, Revolt Against…, op. cit.*, p.51.

modern points out the absence of the notions of dark man's destiny in *the Vedas*.[39] He claims that the vision of the infernal world full of fear and misery, representing the idea of punishment, is fairly recent and alien to the pure forms of Tradition altogether which knew only the differentiation between "the aristocratic, heroic, solar, and Olympian survival for some, and the dissolution, loss of personal consciousness, larval life, or return into the cycle of generation for the others"[40] that is by no means the same as infernal destiny, such as Christianity presents it. The Italian traditionalist writes that in ancient Egypt or Mexico the later fate was not considered whatsoever.[41] On the other hand there have survived some symbolic images concerning resurrection or immortality as for example the ideogram of a cosmic human with raised arms (Y) which to be hidden in the rune of life Y from the scandinavian-teutonic tradition.[42]

The path of the gods, in turn, offers "the possibility of escape from the vicissitudes of the *samsara* and of passing as it were from the circumference along a radius to the Divine Centre".[43] Martin Lings compares it to getting out of the Plato's cave.[44] It is also known as "the solar path" or "Zeus's path" and it leads to the bright seat of the immortals being depicted as the land on heights, in heaven or as an island. In the Nordic tradition it was represented by Valhalla or Asgard and in Aztec-Inca tradition by "House of the Sun" reserved only for kings, heroes and nobles".[45]

In the similar way this notion is expressed by the Hindu tradition where we find such terms as *deva-yana* ("the path of the gods") and

---

[39]"Images of obscure hells are almost entirely absent from the most ancient parts of the Vedas" Idem, *The Doctrine of Awakening...*, *op. cit.*, p.23.
[40]*Idem, Revolt Against...*, *op. cit.*, p.51.
[41]*Ibidem.*
[42]*Idem, The Hermetic Tradition. Symbols and Teachings of the Royal Art* (Rochester VT 1995), p. 11; idem, *Revolt Against...*, *op. cit.*, p.123, 293.
[43]Lings, M., *Ancient Beliefs...*, *op. cit.*, p.56
[44]*Ibidem*, p.59.
[45]Evola, J., *Revolt Against...*, *op. cit.*, p.50.

pitr-yana ("the path of the ancestors"). The latter, which in one of the *Upanisad* books is called "the path of the mother", is related to what is dark, to night, to the six months of the sun's descent and "leads to the moon, which is the symbol of the principle of change and becoming and which is manifested here as the principle regulating the cycle of finite beings who continuously come and go in many ephemeral incarnations of the ancestral forces".[46] *Deva-yana*, in contrast, leads to *Brahman*, i.e. the unconditioned state and "is analogically associated with fire, light, the day, and the six months of the solar ascent during the year; it leads to the region of the thunderbolts, located beyond the "door of the sun".[47]

The immortals dwelled also in the mountain regions[48] where, according to the most ancient Hellenic beliefs, they were transferred once they had been stolen from death. In China the very term "immortality" consists of two words: "a mountain" and "a man", thus, the immortal is "a man in the mountains".[49] In other words, it is here about inaccessibility, about a barrier for ordinariness since the true immortality can only be achieved by a handful of the chosen ones.

2. HOLY WAR

The highest dwelling of immortality, as has already been stated, was reserved for the beings of superhuman nature, for the beings containing in themselves the principle that goes far beyond the mere human condition. Access to that place was open for the kings, the nobles or the heroes. The latter ones were transforming war into an

---

[46]*Ibidem*, p.51.

[47]*Ibidem*. Cf. *idem, Heathen Imperialism* (bmw. 2007), p.78.

[48]Thus, among others, Evolian valorization of the mountains and mountain-climbing as a form of asceticism leading to self-initiation. More about this see: *Idem, Meditations on the peaks. Mountains Climbing as Metaphor for the Spiritual Quest*, (Rochester :VT, 1998). Cf also Rostkowski, M., *Julius Evola und die Metaphysik des Bergsteigens*, "Kshatriya" 2008, no. 19, p.3-5.

[49]Darga, M., *Taoizm*, Warszawa, p.86.

ascetic experience and thus it was becoming the holy war, the Islamic Way of Allah (*jihad*), through which it was possible to experience the risk, the struggle, the agonal tension causing the absolute existential crisis. Giving one's own life, its sacrificing on the battlefield was, in fact, an effective overcoming death what is expressed in the Roman notion of *mors triumphalis*.[50] According to the purest metaphysical concept of the holy war, for those participating in it, what did really matter was not an enemy or other earthly reasons, but "the simple capacity to turn war into an ascetic preparation for the attainment of immortality".[51] One can find some elements of the Aryan notion of the holy war and heroism[52] conceived as "ascetism, catharsis..."[53] among the Aztecs, the people of northern Europe, Arabs[54] and even in Southern America,[55] which proves its universality. We find echoes of this idea even in twentieth-century Japan where *kamikaze* ("the Divine Wind"), i.e. the suicidal pilots had on their plane's fuselages the inscription: "You are gods who are free from all human yearnings".[56]

There was also a possibility of survival from a battle containing similar experience to war, as we have already mentioned, i.e. that of

---

[50] Evola, J., *Metaphysics of War...*, *op. cit.*, p.70 i 80-81. Therefore, those who seemingly died, did not succumb to death and are still alive, although in a different form. *Koran* says: "Think not of those, who are slain in the way of Allah, as dead. Nay, they are living. With their Lord they have provision" [III,169].

[51] Evola, J., *The Mystery of the Grail. Initiation and Magic in the Quest for the Spirit*, (Rochester: VT, 1997), p.131-132.

[52] More about this see *Idem, Aryjska doktryna walki i zwycięstwa*, Szczerbiec, 1996, no 8-9, p.20-24.

[53] *Idem, Metaphysics of War...*, *op. cit.*, p.89.

[54] In Islam the greater Holy war, i.e. the interior holy war (*al-jihad al-akbar*), can take place independently and beyond the lesser holy war (*al-jihad al-akbar*). The latter is war on the physical plane, while the former belongs to the spiritual plane. According to a hadith Muhammad was to say to his companions returning from one of the battles, that they were going from the lesser to the greater holy war. Having not understood the last term, they asked Him for clarification. Muhammad then answered that it was "war with one's own lesser soul (*nafs*)". Ashraf, S. A., *The Inner Meaning of the Islamic Rites...*, *op. cit.*, p.128.

[55] Evola, J., *Revolt Against...*, *op. cit.*, p.233.

[56] *Ibidem*, s. 136.

64

the existential crisis. Then, on the strength of it the extreme intensity of life is transformed into something *more than life* [*mehr als Leben*]. The value of victory was equivalent to holiness and initiation. A warrior, through "the asceticism of action and battle", experiences non-physical death and wins the interior victory, i.e. realizes superior concept of life, crosses the gates of heaven, enters paradise, goes to the heavenly regions which are not to be understood literally as they are allegories of the particular states, which were attained by the chosen ones, and "symbolic representations – concocted for the people – of transcendent states of consciousness on a higher plane than life and death".[57] Moreover, he achieves that, as it were, on his own, relying on his own power,[58] whilst experiencing the specific form of the experience. We can refer here to Mircea Eliade's attempt of interpretation of the Babylonian *The Epic of Gilgamesh*. The Romanian specialist in Religious Studies claims that according to this epic "some beings are able, even without god's help, to attain immortality, provided that they succeed in going through a series of the initiatory trials".[59] Rudolf Otto, in turn, refers to the considerations of another thinker concerning piety without belief in God, as differentiation between *sacrum* and *profanum* is more important:

> There can exist the genuine piety without formed belief in God and developed cult. There is no, however, piety worth this name without idea of what is sacred. If for religion belief in God together with His worship matters, nevertheless, as I often underlined, there

---

[57] *Idem, Metaphysics of War..., op. cit.*, p.97 i 143. In *Koran*, soul which is at the state of victory in holy war is called *radiyat an-mardiyyat an* (satisfied and satisfying) defining the state of acting of God's and man's will in unison. Ashraf, S. A., *The Inner Meaning of the Islamic Rites..., op. cit.*, p.128.

[58] One should not understand this "self-sufficiency" literally. Having said that a man could liberate himself on his own we meant that he did not need any mediators. It does not mean, however, that he is independent of anything, since human being, relying only on his own capabilities, with the use of his purely human qualities cannot go beyond human condition, escape from humanity towards the higher regions. He is in need of certain circumstances like the existential crisis we have spoken about before.

[59] Eliade, M., *Traktat o historii religii..., op. cit.*, p.54.

is yet more important criterion for the essence of religion, that is to say, the difference between the sacred and the profane.[60]

Therefore, on the strength of an internal triumph in the particular circumstances there occurs in a man the transformation on the metaphysical plane and, at the same time, physical death is not intrinsic here.

3. The Reintegration of the Primordial State

We are getting, thus, to the possibility of attaining immortality whilst being still alive. Seemingly paradoxically it is connected to the symbolic of death, except that not in the terms of the physical but rather the spiritual death. Therefore, "who really wants to live, must first die;[61] if one wants to be born for the other world, one has to die for this world, "die before you die" as the Prophet Muhammad once said.[62] This concerns the initiation understood as "active death". It refers in many respects – sometimes slightly different in meaning, but still depicting the principle – for example to "the twice-born" within the Hindu castes or even to a degree to the succession of the Vicar of Christ in Rome who assuming the Holy See die as the former individual, losing his personality, and is born in the different form, i.e. without nationality, under other name, to the new role. In order to portray the difference between the initiate and a simple man, Evola compares this relation to the one that exists between the latter and an

[60]Söderblom, N., *Das Werden des Gottesglaubens*. Quote from: Otto, R., *Świętość. Elementy irracjonalne w pojęciu bóstwa i ich stosunek do elementów racjonalnych*, (Warszawa 1999), p.213.
[61]Ea [J. Evola], *The Doctrine of Immortal Body...*, op. cit., p.198. In the *Atharva Veda*, on the other hand, the crisis of death is considered as "the effect of a hostile and demonic force that, with suitable rites, can be repulsed". Evola, J., *The Doctrine of Awakening...*, op. cit., p.23. It suggests, in a sense, a kind of artificiality of death as a brutal and unexpected interference in the course of events which can be eliminated.
[62]Ashraf, S. A., *The Inner Meaning of the Islamic Rites...*, op. cit., p.129. Schuon, F., relates to a mystical German saying: "He who dies before He dies does not die when He dies". Schuon, F., *The Transfiguration of Man* (Bloomington, 1995), p.88.

animal.[63]

Initiation, on the one hand, is a man's transfer onto the higher level of existence, i.e. *de facto* denial or overcoming his human nature;[64] on the other hand, he is fully humanized by it, if one may say so. Eliade states that "through initiation one overcomes the natural modality, the child modality and gains the cultural modality, i.e. one is lead into the realm of the spiritual principles [...] the initiation grants people their human status; before initiation one does not fully participate in humanity".[65] Having not attained the initiation, one remains on the lower level of existence with no hope of improving his fate after death. According to the Greek tradition: "those who have not been initiated, that is to say, the majority of people, are condemned in Hades to do the Danaïdes work; carrying water in amphorae filled with holes and pouring it into bottomless barrels, thus never being able to fill them up; this illustrates the insignificance of their ephemeral lives, which keep recurring over and over again, pointlessly".[66]

The most important aim, however, of every authentic initiation is the regeneration in a human his primordial condition.[67] The Vedic hereafter, as a matter of fact, was related – as the Italian traditionalist claims – to this reintegration,[68] to bringing back his state from before the Fall.

Glorification of the initial condition of humanity which existed *in illo tempore*, before civilization as such appeared, was a common element of the Taoist schools. "The Taoist wise men, like the hermits and adepts

---

[63]*Inicjacja w nowoczesnym świecie*, Społeczeństwo Otwarte, 1996, no. 11. p.IX.

[64]We find an analogy in the philosophy of Friedrich Nietzsche who wrote: "*I teach you the overman. Human being is something that must be overcome*". Nietzsche, F., *Thus Spoke Zarathustra*, (New York, 2006), p.5.

[65]Eliade, M., *Inicjacja, obrzędy, stowarzyszenia tajemne. Narodziny mistyczne*, (Kraków, 1997), p.18.

[66]Evola, J., *Revolt Against...*, op. cit., p.51.

[67]*Idem, The Hermetic Tradition...*, op. cit., p.10.

[68]*Idem, The Doctrine of Awakening...*, op. cit., p.23.

striving for attaining longevity and immortality, were trying to recover the paradisal condition, that is to say, the primordial perfection, primordial spontaneity"[69] – as we find out from the Romanian scholar. The above mentioned glorification comes from the belief – that stands in total opposition towards the whole modern science and that, at the same time, agrees with the traditional views – about progressing degradation and the world's and man's involution. Therefore, the further from the origins, the greater the decline and simultaneously the further back, the better state of affairs. Human being's height existed then *ab origine*, when – according to the numerous beliefs – he was on the same level as gods were. In accordance with Sumerian notions for example, "the primordial man participated in a way in the divine substance: through breathing life into him by Enki or thanks to the god's blood".[70]

Attaining the initiatic rite, one is transferred, in a sense, to the origins, and, at the same time, obtains characteristic of them the modality of being. The symbolic of gold is here of major importance. The traditional teachings call the first, i.e. the initial epoch gold which was followed by the silver era, then bronze era and finally the iron age. After the latter, the whole cycle began again which illustrates one of the Eddic myths concerning the rise of a new race and new sun following the twilight of the gods (*ragna-rokkr*); then, the Aesir are to gather again and reveal the mysterious golden tablets which they used to have in the origins.[71] It is the Golden Age which was the perfect era; it was divine paradise from before the original sin. In the terms of Hindu tradition it was *Satya Yuga* (*sat* – being hence *satya* – the truth), i.e. the age of *being, truth*. It is, then, among others, due to the particular conditions of the current era, that initiation is needed in order to be able to return to the origins. On the other hand, the initiation was useless or even inconceivable for people who lived *in illo tempore*, since "spiritual

[69]Eliade, M., *Historia wierzeń i idei religijnych. Od Gautamy Buddy do początków chrześcijaństwa* vol. II (Warszawa, 1994), p.18.

[70]*Idem, Historia wierzeń i idei religijnych. Od epoki kamiennej do misteriów eleuzyńskich* vol. I, (Warszawa, 1997), p.41.

[71]Evola, J., *Revolt Against...*, *op. cit.*, p.186.

development in all its degrees was accomplished among them in an altogether natural and spontaneous way by reason of their proximity to the Principle".[72]

Gold had also an integral relation to the very immortality as is expressed by the sentence: *amrtam ayur hiranyam* which means "gold is immortality".[73] "In the Hellenic tradition – as Evola writes – gold had a relationship with related the radiant splendor of light and with everything that is sacred and great; thus, anything that was bright, radiant, and beautiful was designated as "golden".[74] In China it was connected to the "yellow waters", i.e. to the future life and making gold was related to the gaining "drink of immortality" and to "summoning the immortals".[75] Frithjof Schuon claimed that gold is the colour of the heart,[76] and the latter is "the organ of Revelation",[77] the organ of gnosis,[78] the equivalent of the Spirit creating transcendental center of ego", "the organ of uncreated Intellect",[79] the place where peace is sent to by God;[80] compared with other elements it is like sun in the planetary system;[81] it is also "the third eye", "the Eye of Certainty" (*ayn al-yaqin*) perceiving the fire-flames symbolizing the Divine Truth[82] in

[72]Guénon, R., *Initiation and Spiritual Realization*, (Hillsdale: NY, 2001), p. 27.

[73]Eliade, M., *Joga. Nieśmiertelność...*, *op. cit.*, p. 292.

[74]Evola, J., *Revolt Against...*, *op. cit.*, p.185-186.

[75]Eliade, M., *Joga. Nieśmiertelność...*, *op. cit.*, p.298.

[76]This information was to come from one of Schuon's unpublished texts. Aymard, J. B., Laude, P., *Frithjof Schuon. Life and Teachings* (Albany: NY, 2004), p.182. Cf also Schuon, F., *Esoterism as Principle and as Way* (Bedfont, 1990), p.229-234.

[77]Schuon, F., *The Transcendent Unity of Religions*, (Wheaton, II, 1993), p.106.

[78]Burckhardt, T., *Introduction...*, *op. cit.*, p. 22.

[79]Schuon, F., *Prayer Fashions Man...*, *op. cit.*, s. 140. Burckhardt, Por. T., *Introduction to Sufi Doctrine* (Bloomington, 2008), p.28; Guénon, R., *The King of the World*, (Hillsdale: NY, 2004), p.15.

[80]Guénon, R., *The Symbolism of the Cross*, (Hillsdale: N, 2004), p.43. Cf *idem*, *The King...*, *op. cit.*, p.14.

[81]Burckhardt, T., *Introduction...*, *op. cit.*, p.86. Cf. Guénon, R., *The Esoterism of Dante* (Hillsdale: NY, 2001), p.47.

[82]Lings, M., *What is Sufism*, (Cambridge, 2006), p.61-62. Cf. Abu Bakr Siraj ad-Din [*idem*], *The Book of Certainty. The Sufi Doctrine of Faith, Vision and Gnosis*, (Cambridge, 1996), p.17-19.

the Islamic esoterism. "The purity of the heart" is a quality that was to characterize every caste in the Golden Age.[83] Oswald Spengler, in turn, tells us about yet another of gold's aspects. According to him it is altogether unique in comparison with other colours, as it was outside all the natural colours. He writes that "Gold is not even a colour. The colours are natural and this hardly to be seen in nature metallic sheen is supernatural".[84] Thus its intentional application or imitation in various civilizations. And for example "the Arabic art expressed the magical sense of light through golden background of its mosaics and images on board". He notices, similar in style, the symbolic meaning within the Egyptian art in reference to shined surface of the stones".[85]

The very initiation, however, understood as return to the Golden Age is not all. It is its fundamental but not the only goal, one could name it as the preliminary one after which the next will be achieved through the initiations following one another. We need to underline that we do not deal here with different types of initiation but its one type of various stages or degrees[86] on the path to the final, superior end. In many doctrines, especially those having their origins in the East, the very process of approaching to the final, the highest stage of existence is divided into phases. In Taoism, for instance, one needs to achieve the integrity of the human state. If one succeeds in that, one becomes *chen jen*, i.e. "the true man". Then, if he ascends to the higher states, he becomes *shen jen*, that is to say "the divine man",[87] *Wang*, i.e. "the King", of which the equivalent is *al-Insan al-Kamil* – "the universal man", "the perfect man"[88] or "the primordial man" *al Insan al quadim*[89] from Islamic esoterism or *Adam Kadmon* from Hebraic *Kabala*.[90] In

[83]Evola, J., *Revolt Against...*, *op. cit.*, p.184.
[84]Spengler, O., *Zmierzch Zachodu. Zarys morfologii historii uniwersalnej* (Warszawa 2001), p.158.
[85]*Ibidem.*
[86]Guénon, R., *Perspectives on Initiation*, (Hillsdale: NY, 2001), p.245.
[87]See Guénon, R., *The Great Triad*, Hillsdale, NY 2004, p.113-117.
[88]Guénon, R., *The Symbolism...*, *op. cit*, p.12.
[89]See Burckhardt, T., *Introduction...*, *op. cit.*, p.65-66.
[90]*Idem, Man & His Becoming According to the Vedanta* (Hillsdale: NY, 2004), p.40.

this sense, as René Guénon claims,[91] one should interpret the following verse: "So the last shall be first, and the first last: for many be called, but few chosen". [Matt 20,16]

Gaining the higher states, a man dies to the former and regenerates in the next ones. It is not said, however, that once he has achieved the first, he will achieve another. Everyone reaches that state which his abilities allow him to. Regarding a danger of this process, Evola states, that "there is a radical point of view, according to which he enters the beast".[92]

A certain reference, moving for a while from the sphere of initiation to that of the mysticism, can be found in Eckhart's teaching about the renouncing of oneself. It is also, in a sense, about one's own death which is to be used as a means to rebirth in God. The German mystic expresses this in the terms of exchange of what belongs to the human nature for what belongs to the nature of God. The basis of his ontic ethic (*Seinsethik*) is demanded in the internal life an exchange of what is human for what is divine. It is about renouncing oneself, about coming out of oneself in order to make thus room for God: "wherever a man renounces himself, there enters God and thus the man becomes 'divine'".[93] Thomas à Kempis, in his *De imitation Christi* writes: "And the more completely a man dies to self, the more he begins to live to God" [II,12][94] and a little later – putting words into God's mouth – "Son, to what a degree you manage to come out of yourself, you will be able to come to me".[95]

In this context one should interpret poverty's blessing in the Gospel: "Blessed are the poor in spirit: for theirs is the kingdom of heaven"

---

[91]Guénon, R., *Insights into Islamic Esoterism and Taoism*, (Hillsdale: NY, 2003), p.23.
[92]*Inicjacja w nowoczesnym świecie...*, *op. cit.*, p.IX.
[93]W. Szymona OP, *Wstęp*, [in:] Eckhart, M., *Pouczenia duchowe*, [in:] *idem*, *Traktaty*, p. 12 and 13. Cf. also J. Piórczyński, *Mistrz Eckhart. Mistyka jako filozofia* (Wrocław, 1997), p.173.
[94]*Ibidem*, p.280.
[95]à Kempis, T., *Naśladowanie Chrystusa*, (Kraków, 2009), p.123.

[Matt 5,3]. A man, by renouncing oneself for God, becomes poor in what is human and thus filling oneself with what is divine. Guénon gives an interesting interpretation pointing out that the equivalents of evangelical poverty are modesty and smallness and which also show a correlation. He writes: "According to Islamic esoterism, this 'poverty' (in Arabic, al-faqru[96]) leads to al-fana', that is, to the 'extinction' of the 'ego' [moi]; and by this 'extinction' one attains the 'divine station' (al-maqamul-ilahi), which is the central point where all distinctions inherent in outward points of view are surpassed, where all oppositions have disappeared and are resolved in a perfect equilibrium".[97]

Returning yet for a while to Meister Eckhart; he characterizes the nature of the above mentioned exchange by the following words: "In what measure you come out of all things, to what degree you dispose in them everything what is yours, in the same measure, neither less nor more, enters God with everything what is His".[98] It is an unconditional, necessary, even obligatory relationship for God Himself.

Wherever a man comes out of his "self" by obedience and renounces what is his, there must enter God. When one does not want anything for oneself, then God must want for him exactly what He wants from Himself. If I renounced my own will by the fact that I put it into superior's hands and I want nothing for myself any more, then God must want from me and if He loses anything for me, He loses at the same time for Himself. This is with everything: if I want nothing for

---

[96]Titus Burckhardt points out that this term is universally used to describe spirituality as a whole. What is poverty and emptiness on the side of man (creature) is plenitude and fullness on the side of God (Creator). Cf. Burckhardt, T., *Introduction...*, *op. cit.*, p.78.

[97]Guénon, R., *Insights into Islamic Esoterism...*, *op. cit.*, p.20. He also points out the analogy between this extinction and *nirvana*. *Ibidem*. Cf. *idem*, *The Symbolism...*, *op. cit.*, p. 41; *Letters of a Sufi Master. The Shaykh Al-'Arabi ad-Darqawi*, (Louisville, KY 1998), p. 39. Nevertheless, Martin Lings, discussing the essence of sufism, writes that "between the degree of human perfection and that of extinction in the Divine Perfection there are said to be innumerable spiritual degrees". Abu Bakr Siraj ad-Din [M. Lings], *The Book of Certainity...*, *op. cit.*, p.12.

[98]Mistrz Eckhart, *Traktaty ...*, *op. cit.*, p.15.

myself, then He wants for me.[99]

It is the determinism or the law of action and reaction which determines sequence of the processes regardless of anyone's will, including that of God.[100]

This teaching of Meister Eckhart one could equally well describe by paradox of co-existence of man-God, that is to say, a human being that exists on the divine level. His realization was also the goal of the Hindu spirituality. In India this state was understood as a situation where the liberated person "lives in time and at the same time participates in immortality; it meets the height of Being and simultaneously constitutes its part; and is a being, in whom "coexists divinity and humanity as Being and non-Being, eternity and death, the whole and a part".[101] Moreover, the fulfilment of this state was identical with its realization to oneself as it had been previously present, although in potential dimension.[102] Martin Lings, illustrating this coexistence, refers to the image from the teaching of Sufi Abd al-Karim al Jili who used the terms of water and ice.[103] It is then about acquiring of particular knowledge – *gnosis* – that opens our eyes to what was not previously visible, that enlightens us. As we read in *the Upanisads*: "Who knows the one and the other, both nothingness and becoming,

[99]*Ibidem*, p.17-18. In order to yet more clear illustrate relation between God and man from Eckhart's point of view let us refer to an author of one of the books dealing with the German mystic's thought who claims that according to the latter "A Man is not a God's servant and God is not his Master. (…) God and Man – each of them is a master and a servant AT the same time" and even that "a Man decides in what way God exists". Piórczyński, J., *Mistrz Eckhart...*, *op. cit.*, p.180 i 186. See the whole part about this: *ibidem*, p.170-187.

[100]Some people are led to such conclusions by the effort to understand the necessity of allowing by God to the Crucifixion of His Son as a means of cleansing people's sins instead of a simple act of His Power. See *Various Commentaries...*, *op. cit.*, p.183.

[101]Eliade, M., *Joga. Nieśmiertelność...*, *op. cit.*, p.110.

[102]Cf. Evola, J., *The Hermetic Tradition...*, *op. cit.*, p.58; G. Stucco, *Translator's introduction...*, *op. cit.*, p.XII.

[103]Lings, M., *What is Sufism...*, *op. cit.*, p.70.

he will overcome death by perdition, through Being he will achieve immortality".[104]

4. LIBERATION

The question of liberation appears here. We can refer to another polarization[105] that one finds in Evola's books. It is about differentiation between salvation and liberation, enlightenment or awakening. This division, as a matter of fact, is not always treated as a polarization but rather as different terms that – depending on specific circumstances – express very similar, if not the same, meanings. This concerns above all those situations where an idea characteristic of a particular civilization appears somewhere else independently and thus it must be expressed differently, i.e. in its own language. And so we can just refer to the Hindu civilization where one can find metaphysical notion of liberation, while in the Western religions there are theological notions of salvation.[106] One can also refer to a characteristic of Japanese Buddhism that is more or less equivalent to those just mentioned, It is of course the notion of *satori*.

Nevertheless, it is worth of mentioning that René Guénon treated this polarization a little more 'restrictively'. He discerned the essential differences between the notions of Orient and Occident, among which the differentiation between Western immortality/salvation and Eastern liberation is like an insurmountable gulf. For him salvation is

---

[104]*Upaniszady*, trans. S. Michalski (Kraków, 1991), p.113.

[105]One can, however, quote many more. We will restrict ourselves to pointing out just a few of them. The same applies then to the dychotomies such like: faith-knowledge (gnosis), religion-initiation, prayer-incantation and so on. About the first one see: Schuon, F., *Understanding Islam*, Bloomington, IN 1998, p.179; about the two last see: Guénon, R., *Perspectives on Initiation...*, op. cit., p.68-69 and 163.

[106]See Guénon, R., *Introduction to the Study...*, op. cit., p.83. Julius Evola, in turn, in his *Lo Yoga della potenza*, briefly states that to the Hindu notion of liberation corresponds the notion of salvation in the West Evola, J., *The Yoga of Power...*, op. cit., p.206.

of exoteric nature and one is not able here to attain the transcendent states that, in turn, are to be achieved through pure metaphysical knowledge.[107] It is also obvious depreciation of action as the path of realization and at the same time valorization of contemplation. The former, according to the French metaphysician, as belonging to the human, therefore worldly sphere, can achieve some goals only within this sphere. Julius Evola, however, considered this sort of opposition to be wrong and derived from Western philosophy rather than from the Orient. In his eyes, both through the path of action and through the path of contemplation, one can attain liberation.[108] Even here, however, this differentiation was not that rigid, since in the East one can also find the examples of the path of action present in the pages of the ancient Aryan epic – the *Bhagavadgita*, and in Tantric Yoga or actions carried out by the Japanese samurai. Action and contemplation, East and West – in their traditional sense – are the two paths leading towards one goal, i.e. towards liberation.

Indo-Aryan tradition distinguished two ways of gaining liberation. That being achieved while still alive is called *jivan-mukti*, and the other being achieved after death is known as *videha-mukti*.[109] In the first case the liberated one, although formally still having physical body and present among living people, in fact is dead to this world and reborn for the other. "One 'freed in this life' [...] 'dies no more' (*na punar miryate*)",[110] as Ananda Coomaraswamy writes. Existing

[107]Rooth, G., *Prophet for a Dark Age. A Companion to the Works of René Guénon* (Eastbourne, 2008), p.142. Cf. Guénon, R., *The Spiritist Fallacy* (Hillsdale: NY 2004), p.124-125.

[108]Evola, J., *Action, Contemplation, and the Western Tradition*, http://thompkins_cariou.tripod.com/id18.html

[109]*Idem, The Doctrine of Awakening...*, *op. cit.*, p.195. See also: *idem, My correspondence with Guénon*, [in:] *idem*, Evola, J., *René Guénon. A Teacher for Modern Times* (Sequim: WA, 2004), p.31; *idem, The Yoga of Power...*, *op. cit.*, p.4, 137. As Evola points out, original Buddhism considered, as it were, also the third possibility: *sotāpanna*, that is to say, those who achieve extinction neither while still alive nor after death. At the same time, however, they have higher knowledge and find themselves beyond the current of "becoming". *Idem, The Doctrine of Awakening...*, *op. cit.*, p.196-197.

[110]Evola, J., *Metaphysics of War...*, *op. cit.*, p.60.

in different, higher ontological states, one becomes like god for the rest of the mortals, although he is superior to gods themselves. Seneca considered the true man to be higher than god, as "while the latter is protected against misfortune by nature, a man is able to encounter it, face it and turn out to be better".[111] The *Corpus Hermeticum*, in turn, states: "Let us not to be afraid of truth. The true man is above them (heavenly gods) or at least equal to them. [...] Let us have the courage to say, that a man is the mortal god, and celestial god is the immortal man".[112] Enlightening or awakening that can be treated as synonymous with liberation,[113] concern knowledge and participating in reality to which even gods have no access. They are excluded from the possibility of attaining it, since they are "numb" by celestial pleasures.[114]

5. THE STATE OF THE UNCONDITIONED

Videha-mukti, according to Guénon, is, as it were, the higher, full form of liberation that is the absolute realization of "the Supreme Identity".[115] It is not here about ethic category,[116] but about something superior which transcends dualisms like good and evil. A man therefore, liberating himself from his body, liberates himself from

---

[111]Coomaraswamy, A. K., *The Hindu Tradition: Theology and Autology*, [in:] *The Essential Ananda K. Coomaraswamy* (Bloomington: IN, 2004), p.281.

[112]Quote from: *Idem, The Hermetic Tradition...*, op. cit., p.11.

[113]It is expressed to a great extent through the figure of Prince Siddhartha who became the Buddha, i.e. precisely "the Enlightened One". To his doctrine – called "the Doctrine of Awakening" – Evola dedicates one of his books. See *Idem, The Doctrine of Awakening...*, op. cit.

[114]*Idem, The Yoga of Power...*, op. cit., p.58

[115]Guénon, R., *Perspectives on Initiation...*, op. cit., p.210, 242. Cf. *idem, Man & His Becoming...*, op. cit., p.160.

[116]Gustav Meyrink expresses this in the following words: "They *believe* that a day is coming when good people will enter Paradise and evil people will be swallowed into the pit of Hell. We, on the contrary, *know* that a time will come when many will reawaken and be separated from those who sleep, as lords from slaves, because the sleepers cannot understand the awakened." The Path of Awakening According to Gustav Meyrink, [in:] *Introduction to Magic...*, op. cit., p.37.

the last element related to the material dimension and *de facto* is not human any more.[117] At the same time he eventually renounces this world and frees himself from its bonds. This liberation is to free one from all chains and dependences characteristic of corporeal order what equals death since, as Schuon claims, by distinguishing *Nirvana* and *Parinirvana*, "the living beings, regardless of the degree of their spirituality, of necessity remain related to the Being that belongs to the realm of Nirvana, as it represents a perfect transcendence in relation to all manifestation and to the whole cosmic enmeshment, but which, being still of the realm of Maya whereof it is the summit or quintessence, is not yet the Self".[118]

The Italian Traditionalist, in turn, admitted the possibility of attaining this modality before actual physical death. As an example he refers to Prince Siddhartha, know as Buddha, i.e. "The Enlightened One", who having discovered "The Four Noble Truths" and "The Eight Stage Path" realizes the full awakening. There is a legend, according to which Siddhartha could freely establish the moment of his death, that is to say, in order to die, he must have wanted it,[119] which means that leaving his body behind did not matter for his ontological status whatsoever.

It is about the state of the unconditioned – *Atma* in the terms of Hindu *Vedanta*.[120] This state is placed above all others, free of all dualisms, contradictions or antagonisms. To be in the state of the unconditioned means to be beyond Being and non-Being, Becoming, Truth and False, Good and Evil, beyond every element connecting one with any world. At the same time, it is altogether different than other states, including the intermediate ones between beginning of the path and the state in question itself, since "no matter what high they may be, they are still conditioned".[121] Here we can again refer to Eckhart's

---

[117]Guénon, R., *The Great Triad...*, *op. cit.*, p.113.
[118]Schuon, F., *In the Tracks of Buddhism*, London 1989, p.136-137.
[119]Evola, J., *The Doctrine of Awakening...*, *op. cit.*, p.194.
[120]See Guénon, R., *Man & His Becoming...*, *op. cit.*, p.102-107.
[121]*Ibidem*, p.153.

teaching. He claimed the divinity to be the aim of salvation.[122] We need to explain straight away that the divinity in Eckhart's point of view is not synonymous with God Himself. Moreover, it is superior to Him as God participates in conditioned reality, "becomes and elapses",[123] as Eckhart writes. Divinity, in turn, is the synonym of the nameless God:[124] "High above God and personal Lord rests '*divinity*' that is in almost the same relation to God as *Brahman* to Iśwara".[125] A similar view is presented by Frithjof Schuon who considered Personal God to be a reflection of the Absolute in the organic mirror of *Maya*[126] and, at the same time, "first determination, from which come all secondary determinations forming the cosmic existence".[127] It is, then, the opposition between *deitas* and *deus*.

We are not going to consider the nature of this divinity or reality because it would go too far beyond our main topic.[128] We can just mention that Julius Evola noticed here some kind of contradiction

---

[122]Otto, R., *Mistyka Wschodu i Zachodu. Analogie i różnice wyjaśniające jej istotę* (Warszawa, 2000), p. 41. This belief, as many others, in the possibility of gaining salvation through knowledge, links Meister Eckhart with Śankara. *Ibidem.* Rudolf Otto in his book takes on the comparison both mystics. As far as Śankara – but also Hindu thought in general - is concerned, an interesting reference, which, at the same, is not without connections with our main topic, is the idea of unity and identity of *Atman* with *Brahman*. See Eliade, M., *Traktat o historii religii...*, *op. cit.*, p. 37-38, 151, 158-160. As for union with Divinity, one can also refer to the notion of salvation or rather liberation (*moksha, mukti*) from *Vedanta*, where we find "the paradoxical image of a refusal of Paradise and choice of Supreme Union". Schuon, F., *Islam And The Perennial Philosophy*, 1976, p. 198. In this perspective paradise appears as still conditioned to a degree and so being on the lower level that the unconditioned; in other words it is not identical with the latter. We see similar ideas among the Sufis who consider paradise to be "the prison of the gnostic" or even a place „inhabited by fools". Schuon, F., <u>Some Observations on a Problem of the Afterlife</u>, [in:] *The Essential Frithjof Schuon* (Bloomington: Indiana, 2005), p.457-458.

[123]Otto, R., *Mistyka Wschodu i Zachodu...*, *op. cit.*, p.17.

[124]*Ibidem*, p.29.

[125]*Ibidem*, p.25.

[126]Schuon, F., *Esoterism as Principle...*, *op. cit.*, p.21.

[127]Schuon, F., *The Transcendent Unity...*, *op. cit.*, p.38.

[128]More about this see: *ibidem*, p.25-63.

referring to the version presented by mystical rather than esoteric schools of thought, which is different to the magical tradition. The former characterizes passive, if not quietistic, tendency expressing itself in the terms of one's melting in the impersonal reality like the grain of salt in an ocean no matter whether this is the undiversified infinity (in Vedanta called *nirguna-brahman*) or transcendent order of thing or harmony. The idea of battle, spiritual subordination are alien and useless for it. "Magic tradition does not see the spiritual world as idyllic... at the same time".[129] It is, therefore, the stated that characterizes dynamic, battle rather than passivity.

Returning to the liberation from the conditioned, in India – as Eliade states – "'to liberate' oneself is to go onto a different level of existence, to move closer to a different way of existence, transcendent in relation to the human condition". For a Hindu the metaphysical awareness is expressed not only in the terms breaking and death (breaking with the human condition, one *dies* to everything human) but inevitably carries with it the results of mystical nature: rebirth to the unconditioned state of existence. This is liberation, the absolute freedom.[130] "What metaphysics understands by immortality" – writes Ananda Coomaraswamy – "and by eternity implies and demands of every man a total and uncompromising denial of himself"[131] in order to make possible an adaptation of what in the ontological hierarchy is on the higher level. In India, as a matter of fact, but naturally not only there, the spiritual or absolute freedom was expressed in the terms of the supreme power.[132] This is the true immortality.

The only possible and true immortality according to Julius Evola is Olympian immortality. The very term "Olympic" the Italian aristocrat interprets as "inborn superiority or nature that in reality

---

[129]Evola, J., *The Path of Enlightenment...*, op. cit., p.15.

[130]Eliade, M., *Joga. Nieśmiertelność...*, op. cit., p.20.

[131]Coomaraswamy, A. K., <u>On the Pertinence of Philosophy</u>, [in:] *The Essential Ananda K. Coomaraswamy...*, op. cit., p.81.

[132]Eliade, M., *Joga. Nieśmiertelność...*, op. cit., p.235.

is supernature".[133] Olympian immortality "implies the abrogation of the naturalistic and earthly-motherly bond, the departure from the everlasting circle of generation, and ascent toward the region of immutability and pure being".[134] It is then, so to speak, about disposing of one's humanity, about overcoming human modality of existence as a condition of participation in the superior reality. F. Schuon writes: "The noble man is one who dominates himself; the holy man is one who transcends himself".[135] Gaining this aim is made by overpowering the interior lust, destroying *an-nafs*, i. e. The lust soul,[136] through the absolute control over oneself and one's desires. "The struggle for immortality is a battle for the control over sounds and ghosts that dwell in us",[137] as succinctly states Gustav Meyrink. Surrendering to the senses leads to weakness of spirit and their overcoming to its strengthening.[138] The path to the pure liberation consists in "becoming free from all real and possible determinations [...] until the garment falls away through an absolute integration into 'selfhood'. Then the formula 'ego sum' (I am) is overcome, as the '*sum*' (am) becomes resolved into '*est*' (is). This is the point of the "Supreme Identity", the Buddhist nirvana, and Plotinus's 'One'. In Hatha Yoga it is said: "Empty as a vase in the air – full as a vase in the ocean".[139] Following the victory and defeating one's own demons, physical death is of no more importance, as then it means merely disposing of the

---

[133]Evola, J., *The Mystery of the Grail...*, op. cit., p.17.

[134]*Idem, Eros and the Mysteries...*, op. cit., p.50.

[135]Schuon, F., *Esoterism as Principle...*, op. cit., p.149.

[136]*Letters of a Sufi Master...*, op. cit., p.18 i 20. One of the representations of this act – according to Seyyed Hossein Nasr – is the image of St Michael the Archangel slaying the Dragon. Nasr, S. H., Religion and the Environmental Crisis, [in:] *The Essential Seyyed Hossein Nasr*, Bloomington, IN 2007, p.32-33.

[137]*The Path of Awakening According to Gustav Meyrink...*, op. cit., p.37. The same concerns also the occult energies present in the human body, as the doctrine of tantric yoga expresses, according to which Since we live in the Age of the Wolf connected to the corporeality where the sphere of the spiritual was degraded, it is the body to be used for one's awakening. See Evola, J., *The Yoga of Power...*, op. cit., p.3.

[138]*Letters of a Sufi Master...*, op. cit., p.17.

[139]Ea [J. Evola], *The Doctrine of Immortal Body...*, op. cit., p.197.

material remains of a being who had been dead to this world already.[140] Moreover, material, physical existence becomes less important at the same time. For the unconditioned one, and strictly speaking, for its very unconditioning, physical body is altogether unimportant. Thus consent to suicidal act.[141]

Finally Evola summarizes:

> The only Immortal, in an absolute sense, is the Unconditioned, the principle beyond all manifestation. Immortality thus exists only as "Olympian" immortality in a higher sense, proceeding from a state of union with the Unconditioned. [...] In order to achieve immortality, it is necessary to *burn* every tendency that would urge one to assume this or that superhuman 'seat' ('angelic', one might say, or 'heavenly') since all this, from an initiatic point of view, still belongs to the manifested, conditioned state, and not to the unconditioned, and has no 'eternal' character.[142]

---

[140]Evola, J., *The Doctrine of Awakening...*, op. cit., p.194.

[141]*Idem, The Yoga of Power...*, op. cit., p.179, 188. Cf. also: *idem, The Doctrine of Awakening...*, op. cit., p.194; *idem, Ride the Tiger... op. cit.*, p.221-226.

[142]Ea [J. Evola], *The Problem of Immortality...*, op. cit., s. 149-150. Hence also not infrequently In the writings of the traditionalists, especially among the muslims, one questions the divinity of Jesus Christ as His corporeal nature was to relativize the Absulte. See Schuon, F., *Understanding Islam...*, op. cit., p.12-13. Cf. *The Path of Awakening According to Gustav Meyrink...*, op. cit., p.40.

FAUSTIANISM & FUTURISM:
ANALOGOUS PRIMARY ELEMENTS IN TWO DOCTRINES ON EUROPEAN DESTINY

DR K R BOLTON

ABSTRACT

This paper examines the similarities between Italian Futurism and the Faustian imperative of The West described by Oswald Spengler. Both had an analogous outlook in particular on the role of technics in the new epoch after the Great War. While Futurism saw the potentialities of the machine age with eternal optimism, Spengler saw the new epoch as necessary but inexorably tragic. Both ideas reflect above all a Nietzschean will-to-power, and while there is no evidence of a direct association between Spengler and Marinetti, the convergence of their ideas is partially explainable by the influence of Nietzsche. Hence, it can be said, according to this paper, that Futurism was Faustian and Faustianism was Futurist. Both doctrines hold lessons for the present and upcoming centuries, in positive and negative ways.

*****

German philosopher-historian Oswald Spengler (1880-1936)[1] is, when not placed down the Memory Hole by modern academia, primarily known as a seminal Thinker of the 'Conservative Revolution' movement of Weimer era Germany. Spengler's most well-known and once influential work is *The Decline of The West*[2] published as two separate volumes in the aftermath of World War I. Here Spengler established a 'morphology of history', of High Cultures

---

[1] For a detailed biography on Spengler see: K R Bolton, 'Spengler: A Philosopher for all Seasons', pp.4-59, in: *Spengler: Thoughts & Perspectives Vol. X*, Southgate, T., editor (London: Black Front Press, 2012).

[2] Spengler, O., *The Decline of The West* (London: George Allen & Unwin, 1971).

proceeding in their own life's course of organic cycles like other organisms: birth (Culture), youthful vigour (High Culture), middle aged maturity (Civilisation), senility and decay (Late Civilisation) and death. These 'cultural epochs', as he called them, were described in seasonal terms of Spring, Summer, Autumn, and Winter.[3] When the race that founded the Civilisation has become spent, what remains for succeeding generations is the fellaheen, now a-historical, who return to subsistent level, as in the present day masses of prior Civilisations such as the Egyptian Indian, Muslim, et al, existing among ruins of past glories.[4]

Therefore, history is neither universal nor applicable to a nebulous concept called 'mankind', nor a darwinistic, evolutionary lineal progression of 'mankind' from 'primitive to modern'. Each Civilisation is self-contained with a definite life-cycle. Spengler most cogently expressed his morphology of history in a passage from *Decline* that repudiates '*one* linear history' as 'an empty figment', but postulates instead 'the drama of a number of mighty cultures', each having its own life; its own death', 'waxing and waning', never to return.'[5]

Each Civilisation, while being self-contained in having its own world-outlook and 'spirit', or *zeitgeist*, nonetheless follows analogous organic cycles, although impressed with the unique spirit of the founding race. Spengler called the spiritual impetus of the Western Civilisation 'Faustian', after Goethe's play based on the Medieval morality tale of Doctor Faustus,[6] who made a pact with the Devil in his unquenchable thirst for knowledge. Hence, the Faustian soul of the West reaches to the infinity of space; its 'prime-symbol is pure and limitless space.'[7] The Faustian soul impels The West to uncover the secrets of the universe

---

[3]Ibid., 'Table I: Contemporary Spiritual Epochs'.
[4]Ibid., Vol. II, p.105.
[5]Ibid., Vol. I pp.21-22.
[6]von Goethe, J., W., (1828-29), *Faust: A Tragedy*, English translation, Bayard Taylor (London: Frederick Warne, 1871). An online edition can be read at: http://www2. hn.psu.edu/faculty/jmanis/goethe/Goethe-Faust.pdf
[7]Spengler, O., *The Decline of The West*, op. cit., Vol. I, p.183:

no matter where that might lead. This quest towards the infinite is expressed in all aspects of a High Culture and Civilisation, including its art, architecture, music, mathematics, etc. The Faustian quest has been most dramatically expressed in the impulse for exploration, and today we might say that this, as far as we can presently comprehend, finds its ultimate expression in exploring the infinity of space. Hence, we might now say, using Spengler's paradigm, that the space rockets of the 'Autumn' and the 'Winter' Late epoch of Western Civilisation are analogous to the Gothic spires of the great Cathedrals[8] in the Spring epoch; both expressing that which 'impels the ... Faustian soul towards infinity-distant Future'.[9]

FUTURISM

There seems at first sight to be little in common between Spengler and Futurism. Few if any writers have addressed the possibility, and there does not seem to have been any direct influence of Spengler's philosophy and morphology of history on the Futurist movement. Spengler is regarded as a conservative reactionary,[10] while the Futurists were revolutionaries, who vociferously and audaciously demanded a total break from the past.

Yet Spengler, as a realist who accepted the unfolding of history as he believed it must be played out, recognised that the 'Faustian soul' inexorably leads Western Civilisation literally 'full-steam ahead' to its last hurrah on the world stage, achieving its Faustian dominance over the Earth before, like Rome and Alexander's Greece before it,

---

[8]Ibid., Vol. I, p.396.

[9]Ibid.

[10]Cf. Dr Fritz Stern, in describing the German 'conservative revolution' as 'the ideological attack on modernity, on the complex of ideas and institutions that characterize our liberal secular, and industrial civilization'. *The Politics of Despair: A Study in the Rise of the Germanic Ideology* (New York: Anchor Books, 1965), p.7. The definition hardly accounts for the ideas of Spengler, Jünger, the National Bolsheviks, and the industrialists such as Reusch, who supported the movement.

succumbing to internal forces of decay and death, to be superseded by another High Culture of a race-people-state of youthful vigour, thereby setting in motion the forces of history over again.

While Conservatives talked of a 'return' to traditions, Spengler stated that no such resurrection of the old is possible, although a 'Second Religiousness' concomitant with a return to Authoritarianism ('Cæsarism') will take on new forms in the final epoch of the West.[11] Like all revivals of a Late Civilisation this would lack 'the creative young strength of the Early Culture. But both have their greatness nevertheless'.[12] However, this would not be some type of grand role playing of yesteryear, but the new religion and the new absolutism would harness the technical achievements of the Faustian, or else would succumb to the 'coloured world revolution', then under the leadership of Bolshevik Russia, which was already harnessing the West's technical achievements for its own destructive mission; a threat on which Spengler focused in his final work, *The Hour of Decision*.[13]

Given Spengler's recognition of the epochal importance of the Machine and Western technics in the last cycle of the West's life, there is a major element of Spengler's philosophy and historical morphology that can be described as 'Futurist', and as having a commonality even with the ultra-radicals of the Futurist movement. Although it is not known that there was any communication between Spengler and the Futurists, despite Spengler's frequent holidays in Italy,[14] and there is no extant correspondence on the matter, it is in Italy where a natural coalescing of Spenglerian ideas with those of Futurism converged within the Fascist movement, and in Fascist Italy.[15] With the significant input of Marinetti's Futurists into the Fascist party from its inception, Italian

---

[11]Spengler, O., *The Decline of The West*, op. cit., Vol. II, p.310.
[12]Ibid.
[13]Spengler, O., *The Hour of Decision* (New York: Alfred A Knopf, 1963), pp.204-230.
[14]Spengler, O., *Spengler Letters 1913-1936* (London: George Allen & Unwin, 1966), inter alia. See also: K R Bolton, 'Spengler: A Philosopher for all Seasons' in Southgate, T., (ed.) Spengler: *Thoughts & Perspectives Vol. X* (London: Black front Press, 2012).
[15]Spengler, O., *The Hour of Decision*, op. cit., p.230.

Fascism was indeed a unique experiment in trying to synthesise two antithetical viewpoints: the Traditionalist and the Futurist, and Marinetti remained loyal to the last to Fascist Italy.[16] Such a synthesis, despite Spengler's caution as to the outcome of Fascism, would seem to be the best that could have been achieved in terms of the Spenglerian epoch of Caesarism, although he saw more historical significance in Mussolini the individual than in the party.[17]

Most significantly, the Futurists, like Spengler, regarded Western Civilisation as decadent and in need of 'heroic surgery', as one might say. Like Spengler, also, they saw the epoch emerging from the aftermath of World War I to be that of the Machine and technics. Like Spengler, they demanded that Western technics must be harnessed for the great deeds to be undertaken by the West, or at least by Italy, and not in the service of democratic and humanistic doctrines in the service of a nebulous 'mankind'. It is therefore instructive to look at the ideas of the Futurists, before considering Spengler's thinking on technics and the epoch of the Machine.

FUTURISM IN ITALY

Ultimately, one can readily find the common source of inspiration for both Spengler and Futurism in Friedrich Nietzsche, whose aim was 'a revaluation of all values'.[18] For the poet Filippi Marinetti (1876-1944), the most prominent of the Italian Futurists, Nietzsche was a seminal influence.[19] Spengler accounted Nietzsche along with Goethe to have been the most significant influences on his thinking. In the preface to *The Decline of The West* Spengler acknowledges in 1922 the debt he owes to them: 'and now, finally, I feel urged to name once more those to whom I owe practically everything: Goethe and Nietzsche. Goethe

---

[16]Berghaus, G., *Futurism and Politics: Between Anarchist Rebellion and Fascist Reaction 1909-1944* (Oxford: Berghahn Books, 1996), pp.218-276.
[17]Spengler, O., *The Hour of Decision*, op. cit., p.187-188.
[18]Nietzsche, F., *Twilight of the Idols* (Middlesex: Penguin Books, 1968), p.21.
[19]Günter Berghaus, op. cit., inter alia.

gave me method, Nietzsche the questioning faculty…'[20]

Marinetti's ideas had begun for form even prior to the Great War, with the publication of the 'First Futurist Manifesto' in 1909. The manifesto was published in the Parisian paper *Le Figaro*. The 'Futurist Political Programme' was published in 1913, and the Futurist Political Party founded in 1918, followed in 1919 with their adhere to Mussolini's *Fasci*.[21]

THE DECADENCE OF PACIFISM

The rejection of pacifism as an ideal, and the reality of conflict, was a marked feature of the philosophy of both the Italian Futurists and of Spengler. Indeed, Spengler's final essay, shortly before his death, was a repudiation of pacifism, which he saw as a symptom of decadence. This essay was written in answer to a question on world peace put to well-known individuals such as Eleanor Roosevelt and Mahatma Gandhi, et al by the Hearst magazine, *International-Cosmopolitan*, published in January 1936.[22] Spengler began by stating that someone who knows history and the enduring characteristics of humanity can only answer the question. 'There is a vast difference, which most people will never comprehend, between viewing future history as it will be and viewing it as one might like it to be… Peace is a desire, war a fact; and history had never paid heed to human desires and ideals'.[23]

For Spengler history was a Nietzschean will-to-power among all healthy life forms, which might take economic, social, political and military shape between individuals, classes, peoples, races and nations. Violence is always the ultimate recourse, pacifism a symptom

---

[20]Spengler, O., *The Decline of The West*, op. cit., Vol. I, xiv.
[21]Lyttelton, A., (ed.), 'Italian Fascisms', *Roots of the Right* (London: Jonathan Cape, 1975), p.207.
[22]Spengler, 'Is World Peace Possible?', *Cosmopolitan*, January 1936; *Spengler: Selected Essays* (Paraparaumu, New Zealand: Renaissance Press, 2005), p.43.
[23]Ibid.

of decadence that is only heard from the Late West. 'Talk of world peace today is heard only among the white peoples, and not among the much more numerous coloured races. This is a perilous state of affairs'. When individuals talk of peace, their pleas are meaningless, but when entire peoples become pacifistic 'it is a symptom of senility'.[24]

> Strong and unspent races are not pacifistic. To adopt such a position is to abandon the future, for the pacifist ideal is a static, terminal condition that is contrary to the basic facts of existence. Should the white peoples ever succumb to pacifism they will inevitably fall to the coloured world, just as Rome succumbed to the Teutons.[25]

While appeals to nationalistic militarism are commonplace on the Right – although appeals to militarism are no less common from the Left, albeit usually taking on a 'class' façade – what differentiates both Spengler's Faustianism and Marinetti's Futurism in their warlike appeals goes above and beyond mere jingoism. Spengler saw war as the hard reality for survival and a Nietzschean will-to-power vis-à-vis the arming and mechanisation of the 'coloured world' behind the leadership of Bolshevism.[26]

Marinetti and the Futurists also saw pacifism as a symptom of decadence, of a bourgeois civilisation that yearned above all for comfort and safety. The 1909 Futurist manifesto had exclaimed with drama typical of the movement: 'Sing the love of danger, the habit of energy and boldness'.[27] The Futurist manifesto declared:

> 7. Beauty exists only in struggle. There is no masterpiece that has not an aggressive character. Poetry must be a violent assault on the forces of the unknown, to force them to bow before man.

---

[24]Ibid.
[25]Ibid.
[26]Spengler, O., *The Hour of Decision*, op. cit., 'The Colored World-Revolution', pp.204-240.
[27]Berghaus, G., op.cit., p9.

9. We want to glorify war – the only cure for the world – militarism, patriotism, the destructive gesture of the anarchists, the beautiful ideas which kill, and contempt for women.[28]

Although Spengler did not *glorify* war as the Futurists did as intrinsic to their aesthetics, for Spengler war was simply a fact, and pacifisms a symptom of decadence.[29] Such considerations as 'war and peace' therefore were not a matter of either glorification or opposition but of hard reality; the product of the inexorable forces of history.

Here we see on the question of pacifism accord between the Futurists and Spengler's Faustian ethos: pacifism as a 'symptom of senility', stated Spengler, while Marinetti et al declared struggle as the generator of the new aesthetics, and war as 'the cure of the world'. Hence, the Futurist declaration implies that there is something to 'cure' in the first place, something organic that is diseased. We might see here that both Spengler and the Futurists were attempting to deal in similar manner with the same issue: the etiolation of Western Civilisation. The aesthetic of the new Western epoch of will-to-power is ushered for both Spengler and the Futurists by struggle. The Futurists described the new – Futurist – arts in militaristic terms, as did Spengler. 'Art, yes: but in concrete and steel' said Spengler;[30] while the Futurists declaimed: 'Beauty exists only in struggle'. Hence, the aesthetics of the coming epoch were identical for both Spengler and the Futurists.

The Futurists, with Italy's entry in the Great War, Marinetti having been a leading interventionist campaigner, enthused that the world conflagration was a great Futurist event that would herald a new epoch. In a passage analogous to that of Spengler's contention that the art of the new epoch demands an art reflecting struggle, the Futurist

---

[28]'The First Futurist Manifesto', 1909; Lyttelton, A., (ed.), *Italian Fascisms*, op. cit., p.212.

[29]Spengler, O., 'Is World Peace Possible?', op. cit.

[30]Spengler, 'Pessimism?', *Preussische Jahrbücher*, CLXXXIV, 1921, in *Oswald Spengler: Selected Essays* (Paraparaumu, New Zealand: Renaissance Press, 2005), p.17.

war manifesto in 1915 had demanded of Italian artists:

> Futurist poets, painters, sculptors, and musicians of Italy! As long as the war lasts let us set aside our verse, our brushes, scapulas, and orchestras! The red holidays of genius have begun! There is nothing for us to admire today but the dreadful symphonies of the shrapnel and the mad sculptures that our inspired artillery molds among the masses of the enemy.[31]

It was this militarist aesthetic that was to later be placed at the service of Fascist Italy, and while Traditionalism and Futurism both flourished in uneasy co-existence rather than in synthesis, the Futurist aesthetic was manifested through Fascist Italy in the great architecture and monuments of the era as well as the graphic propaganda,[32] while Hitlerian Germany relegated anything of a modernist character to the realm of decadence.[33]

FUTURISM AND FAUSTIANISM

More than the common rejection of pacifism by Spengler and the Italian Futurists however, was the full-hearted embracing of the epoch of the machine and technics, which for the Futurists became a cult and a means of individual transcendence, and for Spengler an historical necessity.

Futurism and Faustianism are terms that imply the same outlook and origins. Both strive – again, Nietzschean like – for the beyond.

Spengler would have been unlikely to have seen in the Futurist arts anything other than another decadent product of the epoch, that should no longer even be attempting to either mimic the great art of

---

[31]Marinetti, 'War, The World's Only Hygiene', 1915.
[32]Berghuas, G., op. cit., 'Accommodation with the Fascist Regime', pp.218-276.
[33]Spotts, F., *Hitler and the Power of Aesthetics* (London: Hutchinson, 2002), 'The Modernist Enemy', pp.152-168.

previous Western epochs (e.g. the Old Masters) or to create a new art for the Late epoch of The West. Western Man was historically obliged to focus on matters other than the aesthetic, although the Futurists regarded their new aesthetic, like the Dadaists, as part of their revolt against bourgeois culture. Their art was 'Faustian', insofar as they attempted to depict speed, steel, and the technical dynamism of the epoch, as the Surrealists attempted to depict the new insights of psychology. What Spengler thought of such artistic rebellions however is stated by him in general:

> Expressionism, yesterday's vogue, produced not a single personality or artistic work of any note. As soon as I began to question the sincerity of that movement I was shouted down by a thousand voices. Painters, musicians, and poets tried to prove me wrong, but with words, not with deeds. I shall stand corrected when they come forth with the equivalent of Tristan, the Hammerklavier sonata, king Lear, or the paintings of Marées.[34]

He would hardly have been impressed with the noise 'music' which the Futurists pioneered, or paintings that include the depiction of the moustache by gluing to canvass toothbrush bristles. Spengler sharply condemned the new movements as being counter to the new epoch of Western Faustian technics, and considered them to be 'flaccid' and 'superfluous'. The epoch of the great arts of The West had gone, and at best the old masters could be copied; at worst, the 'artsy-craftsy approach' that had arisen in architecture, painting, poetry, religion, politics, even philosophy' are treated as 'handicrafts' that can be taught as techniques within a studio. These movements, Spengler stated, reek to high heaven, and not only want to be tolerated but to hold full sway, purporting to be 'German', and to claim the 'future'.[35] The one area of the arts that had yet to be fulfilled was that of the novel, until then epitomised by Goethe. 'The art of the novel requires outstanding personalities, superior in vigour and breadth of vision,

---

[34]Spengler, O., 'Pessimism?', op. cit., p.16.
[35]Ibid.

reared in cultural excellence, high-minded but tactful in their views'.[36] However, again Spengler returns to the harsh realities facing The West in the Late epoch, that can only be fulfilled not by art movements but by industrialists and army officers: 'Nowadays however, practical men such as industrialists and army officers are using better, sounder, clearer, more profound language than the tenth rate scribblers who think style is a sport'.[37]

The arts were passé in this epoch, stated Spengler, and nothing great would likely emerge 'in the proud tradition of Mozart, Johann Strauss, Bruckner, and the young Schumann'. He regarded the present musicians as 'orchestral acrobats' and 'incompetents', and 'not since Wagner had one great creator of melody appeared'.[38]

Art had lost 'validity'. That is not something to be lamented, stated Spengler, but embraced as signifying an epoch that required greatness in other directions: 'Eras without genuine art and philosophy can still be great eras; the Romans have demonstrated this for us. Yet for those who are always a step behind the times, the arts are synonymous with Life itself'.[39] The denizens of the new epoch had yet to face the harshness of the era:

> Not for us, however. People have told me that life without art is not worth living. I ask in return: For whom is it not worth living? I should not care to have lived as a sculptor, ethical philosopher, or dramatist in the days of Marius and Caesar. Nor would I care to have been a member of some Stefan George Circle, attacking Roman politics from behind the Forum with the grand pose of the litterateur. No one could have a closer affinity for the great art of our past – for there is none today – than I. I should not care to live without Goethe, Shakespeare, or the great monuments of older architecture. I am thrilled by any sublime Renaissance masterpiece,

---

[36]Ibid.
[37]Ibid.
[38]Ibid., p.17.
[39]Ibid., p.16.

precisely because I am aware of its limitations. I love Bach and Mozart more than I can say; but this cannot make me speak of all the thousands of writers, painters, and philosophers that populate our cities as true artists and thinkers. There is more painting, writing, and 'outlining' going on in Germany today than in all the other countries put together. Is this culture? Or is it a deficiency of our sense of reality? Are we so rich in creative talent, or are we lacking in practical energy? And do the results justify in any way at all the noisy self-advertisement?'[40]

The Futurists however, rebelled against the 'flaccid', the 'artsy-craftsy', and the 'superfluous', not by attempting to 'improve' upon tradition, which Spengler stated was impossible in the Late epoch of a Civilisation, but by a total *rejection* of tradition. The Futurists shared Spengler's outlook on the new epoch, but revolted against it precisely by the method of what Spengler condemned in regard to the modernists in Germany: 'noisy self-advertisement'. They took no inspiration from the prior epochs of greatness, and regarded such nostalgia as a distortion of the present epoch which had other tasks, that, as Spengler pointed out, could achieve 'greatness' of another type.

Specifically, there is something about the Italian Futurist audacity in Spengler's final paragraph in his essay on 'Pessimism' which for the most part could be transposed into an Italian Futurist manifesto, when writing of the artistic 'ideals' of the present:

These ideals should be dashed to pieces; the louder the noise, the better. Hardness, Roman hardness is taking over now. Soon there will be no room for anything else. Art, yes: but in concrete and steel. Literature, yes; but by men of iron nerves and uncompromising depth of vision. Religion, yes; but take up your hymnbook, not your classy edition of Confucius, and go to church.[41] Politics, yes;

---

[40]Ibid., p.16.
[41]An allusion to the 'Second Religiousness' that Spengler stated emerges during the Late epoch of a Civilisation, when that Civilisation embarks on an historical finale. For The West in its epoch of youthful – 'Spring' - vigour, that Religiousness was

but in the hands of statesmen and not idealists. Nothing else will be of consequence. And we must never lose sight of what lies behind and ahead of us as citizens of this century. We Germans will never again produce a Goethe, but indeed a Caesar.[42]

The Futurist movement did indeed intend to 'dash to pieces; the louder the noise, the better,' the 'flaccid' ideals, and their art was definitely one of 'concrete and steel'. They condemned with the utmost Latin drama what Spengler called the 'faint hearted romanticism of the poets and the writers, the philologians' dreamlike nostalgia for the distant past, the patriots' habit of timidly consulting previous history before arriving at any decisions, the urge to compare, symptomatic of insufficient mental independence.'[43] This is what Spengler called 'the historical disease, of 'gazing nostalgically into the remote past', leading to pretentious plans for improving the world', with the only practical result being the 'exhausting of] crucial energies through senseless quarrelling, spoiling our chances to discover real opportunities...' [44]

What was required, drawing from history, stated Spengler, was not 'knowledge, which is 'relatively unimportant', but 'experience' placed into perspective. What might be too easily misunderstood from Spengler's morphology of history, with its focus on cyclic analogies between Civilisations, is that such a paradigm is not intended to provide our epoch with a 'model' with which to imitate or revive, but examples of analogous epochs of Civilisations provide 'to show us the relationships that exist between inborn character and external conditions, between Tempo and Duration'. 'We are not given patterns to imitate. Rather we can observe how something happened, and thus

represented by Gothic Christianity and the Crusades, and the Gothic Cathedral, with the spire ascending towards infinity. The 'Second Religiousness', which is yet to emerge, would be a revival of that spiritual vigour, although not of the same depth as the original.

[42]Spengler, 'Pessimism?', op. cit., p.17.
[43]Ibid., p.12.
[44]Ibid., p.13.

learn what consequences to expect form our own situation'.[45]

Hence, it might be seen from these statements that the tendency to consider Spengler as regressive or nostalgic, as wanting to return Germany, Europe or 'The West' to prior epochs; as a kind of revived pageantry of the Gothic era, is a misinterpretation. Spengler realised more than many that one cannot revive something that has been not only dead but long buried.

What Spengler called 'dreamlike nostalgia for the distant past' was repudiated with gusto by the Italian Futurists. The 'First Futurist Manifesto' vehemently broke with the past:

> We are on the extreme promontory of the centuries! What is the use of looking behind at the moment when we must open the mysterious shutters of the impossible? Time and Space died yesterday. We are already living in the absolute, since we have already created eternal, omnipresent speed.[46]

The Futurists contemptuously repudiated the nostalgia and regression of much of Italian patriotism, stating:

> Museums: cemeteries! Truly identical in their sinister juxtaposition of bodies that do not know each other. Public dormitories where you sleep side by side for ever with beings you hate or do not know. Reciprocal ferocity of the painters and sculptors who murder each other in the same museum with blows of line and colour. To make a visit once a year, as one goes to see the graves of our dead once a year, that we could allow! We can even imagine placing flowers once a year at the feet of Gioconda! But to take our sadness, our fragile courage and our anxiety to the museum every day, that we cannot admit! Do you want to poison yourselves? Do you want to rot?

---

[45]Ibid.
[46]Marinetti, F., 'The Futurist Manifesto', Point 8 (1909), Lyttelton, *Roots of the Right*, op.cit., pp.211-215.

What can you find in an old picture except the painful contortions of the artist trying to break uncrossable barriers which obstruct the full expression of his dream?

To admire an old picture is to pour our sensibility into a funeral urn instead of casting it forward with violent spurts of action and creation. Do you want to waste the best part of your strength in a useless admiration of the past, from which you emerge exhausted, diminished, trampled on?

Indeed, daily visits to museums, libraries, and academies (those cemeteries of wasted effort, calvaries of crucified dreams, registers of false starts!) is for artists what prolonged supervision by the parents is for intelligent young men, drunk with their own talent and ambition.

For the dying, for invalids and for prisoners it may be all right. It is, perhaps, some sort of balm for their wounds, the admirable past, at a moment when the future is denied them. But we will have none of it, we, the young, strong and living Futurists!

Let the good incendiaries with charred fingers come! Here they are! Heap up the fire to the shelves of the libraries! Divert the canals to flood the cellars of the museums! Let the glorious canvases swim ashore! Take the picks and hammers! Undermine the foundation of venerable towns![47]

The Futurists ridiculed the Right's preoccupation with what they termed 'the boring memory of the Roman grandeur', which would be replaced 'with an Italian grandeur a hundred times bigger.'[48]

While Spengler's was anything but such contempt for the past,[49] as

---

[47]Ibid.

[48]'Second Political Manifesto of Futurism' (11 October 1911), Point 3; Berghaus, G., op. cit., p.69.

[49]Spengler's home overlooking the River Isar was adorned with fine paintings and

stated above, he regarded 'nostalgia' and preoccupation with revivals of artistic forms that were unique to the past epochs of The West, as deviations from the historical path, which leads to a new epoch; one of force and steel, which is what the Futurists sought to usher. Any such imitations would necessarily be inferior to the original artistic impetus that organically grew within previous epochs and could never regain the same vigour.

While Spengler abjured the new art movements as puerile, much of the art of the Italian Futurists was intended as an affront to Italian cultural stasis, and what Spengler called 'flaccidity'. The Futurists were doing in Italy what Spengler counselled: dashing to pieces; 'the louder the noise, the better'. The Futurists intended to provoke and there performances would often end in rioting. They were consciously the storm troopers of *squadisti* of the arts. Marinetti stated that he would introduce 'the fist into the artistic battle', 'enabling the brutal entrance of life into art'. He called the theatre a form of 'cultural combat', which would lead artists out of their ivory towers, 'to participate, like the workers or soldiers, in the battle for world progress'.[50] This was Spengler's dashing to pieces of artistic flaccidity in action, while forcing artists to come to terms with the demands of a new epoch. As for the aesthetic works of Futurism, other than the banal theatrics that were intended to provoke, the Futurist arts under the Fascist regime evoked the graphic depictions of steel, guns and machines that seem to be a logical development of the arts towards the new Faustian epoch that Spengler saw as possibly being ushered – provisionally - by Fascism. Such Futurists graphics and architecture depicted what Spengler described in prose as the coming age of 'Caesarism': 'Roman hardness'; art 'in concrete and steel'. The very contours of Futurist graphics, such as the poster art, convey hardness and an austere discipline in contrast to early Futurist provocations.

Chinese and Greek-style vases, fine rugs, and a vast library. K R Bolton, 'Spengler', op. cit.
[50]Berghaus, G., op. cit., p.73.

The Machine

The Italian Futurists gloried in the prospect of the coming Machine Age, and the epoch of technology, speed, dynamism. There was much optimism in regard to the machine and the way it might impact upon Man in a type of techno-human dichotomy that would lead to a higher human synthesis. Ernst Jünger,[51] the celebrated German war veteran and novelist and a collaborator with the 'National-Bolshevik' movement in Germany, was among those who heralded the coming age in which there would be a Nietzschean transcendence of 'The Worker' as he and the Machine entered a new phase of higher being: The Worker-as-Hero. The most evident form this took was to be in Stalinist Russia[52] where work became the new realm in which heroism could be achieved, the individual transcendent, and the 'Hero of Soviet Labour' recognised as a new aristocracy. 'The total character of work'[53] said Jünger, had become 'a new and particular will to power'.[54] Spengler and Jünger had read each other's works, *The Decline of The West* and *Der Arbieter* respectively.[55] Spengler proffered his own version of 'socialism', 'Prussian Socialism', which shared nothing in common with Marxism – a product rather than the antithesis of Capitalism - but was based upon the Prussian élan of duty to the state within which all classes were part of an organic whole. Spengler however saw elements of Marxism still in Jünger's ideas.[56] National Bolshevism with its cult of the industrial worker, Spengler's conception of technics as the ultimate form of the Faustian soul in the finale of Western Civilisation and the cult of technics fostered by the Italian Futurists as the only tolerable aesthetic and form for the emerging epoch, shared a broad

---

[51]Bolton, K. R., Jünger and National Bolshevism, in *Jünger: Thoughts and Perspectives, Vol. XI,* (ed) Southgate, T., (London: Black Front Press, 2012).

[52]Overy, R., *The Dictators: Hitler's Germany and Stalin's Russia* (London: Allen Lane, 2004), pp.258-259.

[53]Jünger, E., *Der Arbeiter: Herrschaft und Gestalt* (Hamburg: Hanseatische Verlagsanstalt, 1932), p.99.

[54]Ibid., p.70.

[55]Spengler to Jünger, April 11 1924, *Spengler Letters,* op. cit., p.156.

[56]Spengler to Jünger, ibid., September 5 1932, p.272.

common belief, however, in the character of the 20th and proceeding centuries. All these elements demanded that The West looks forward rather than back, despite the affiliation of those such as Spengler with Conservatism.

The 'Manifesto of Futurism' celebrated the Machine as a means of transcendence:

> 3. Literature has up to now magnified pensive immobility, ecstasy and slumber. We want to exalt movements of aggression, feverish sleeplessness, the double march, the perilous leap, the slap and the blow with the fist.

> 4. We declare that the splendour of the world has been enriched by a new beauty: the beauty of speed. A racing automobile with its bonnet adorned with great tubes like serpents with explosive breath… a roaring motor car which seems to run on machine-gun fire, is more beautiful than the Victory of Samothrace.

> 5. We want to sing the man at the wheel, the ideal axis of which crosses the earth, itself hurled along its orbit.

> 11. We will sing of great crowds agitated by work, pleasure, and revolt; the multi-colored and polyphonic surf of revolutions in the modern capitals, the nocturnal vibration of the arsenals and the workshops beneath their violent electric moons: the gluttonous railway stations devouring smoking serpents; factories suspended from the clouds by the thread of their smoke; bridges with the leap of gymnasts flung across the diabolic cutlery of sunny rivers; adventurous steamers sniffing the horizon; great-breasted locomotives, puffing on the rails like enormous steel horses with long tubes for bridles, and the gliding flight of aeroplanes whose propellers sound like the flapping of a flag and the applause of enthusiastic crowds.

It is in Italy that we are issuing this manifesto of ruinous and incendiary violence, by which we today are founding Futurism, because we want to deliver Italy from its gangrene of professors, archaeologists, tourist guides and antiquaries. Italy has been too long the great second-hand market. We want to get rid of the innumerable museums which cover it with innumerable cemeteries.[57]

The similarity with the aforementioned Jünger is apparent, as is the analogy with Spengler's Faustian vision for the Western finale. Indeed, one can perceive pure Faustianism throughout, and most cogently in the closing line of the manifesto: 'Standing on the word's summit we launch once again our insolent challenge to the stars!'[58] The 'challenge to the stars' is the very epitome of the Faustian quest towards 'infinite space'.

Spengler had an intense interest in the technical innovations of his day, and was invited as a guest by the great industrialists to see the achievements of industry and technology. In 1924 Spengler was invited to take part in a trial of an airship.[59] In 1923 he had been invited as a personal guest of Hugo Junkers to the Leipzig Fair, to fly aboard the Junkers limousine airplane from Berlin to Leipzig, with the Reich President and other notables. Of interest, Junkers had written to Spengler:

It would give me particular pleasure to use this opportunity to make you, as the author of one of our most important intellectual productions, acquainted with one of the latest products of German technique...[60]

The Junkers letter indicates both the esteem Spengler gained in important quarters, and the coconsciousness that he evoked in the

---

[57]Marinetti, 'Manifesto of Futurism', Lyttelton, op. cit., 212.

[58]Ibid., p.215.

[59]Spengler, O., Spengler Letters, op. cit., A Colsman to Spengler, August 27, 1924, p.167.

[60]Ibid., Hugo Junkers to Spengler, ibid., March 2, 1923, pp.117-118.

importance of German technics among the leading industrialists. It indicates that German economic circles were conscious of a higher calling than their profit-margins, unlike economic cliques in other states. This confusion of the motives of German industrialists and even some bankers, with the self-centred motives of such circles in other Western states, then and now, has resulted in some fundamental errors in seeing the German Right, including National Socialism, as part of an international conspiracy of bankers; a collusion between German industrialists with American and other plutocrats.[61] There was no commonality of interest. German capital saw its mission in nationalist terms; while those in other states were, and are, committed to internationalism or globalisation as it is now called.[62] This difference in attitudes among German business circles is apparent from the success of Spengler's appeal to many of them. Spengler's appeal to German industrialists, and his treatise *Man and Technics*, explaining the philosophy of the matter, indicates that these economic circles were conscious of a national and cultural mission. One of Spengler's lifelong primary supporters was Dr Paul Reusch, head of Gutehoffnungshütte (Good Hope Mill), a leading mining and engineering firm in the Ruhr, and head of the German Chamber of Commerce and Industry.[63]

The closing pages of *Decline* are dedicated to the Machine, as the primary factor of the new – Late – epoch of the West.[64] Faustian Man conquered nature as part of the impulse to assert his Will-to-Power over all that he encounters. Since the Gothic epoch, he has 'thrust himself upon Nature', 'with the firm resolve to *be its master*'.[65] This is the meaning of Faustian 'technique', or 'technics', the conquest of nature and the harnessing of nature to the Faustian will. With the 'alteration of nature', rather than co-existence with it, 'technique becomes more or less sovereign and the instinctive prime-experience

---

[61]Cf. Sutton, A., *Wall Street and the Rise of Hitler* (Suffolk: Bloomfield Books, 1976).
[62]Bolton, K. R., *Revolution from Above* (London: Arktos Media Ltd., 2011), inter alia.
[63]Bolton, K., R., 'Spengler', op. cit., p.63.
[64]Spengler, O., *The Decline of The West*, op. cit., 'the Form World of Economic Life (B) The Machine', pp.499-507.
[65]Ibid., p.501.

changes into a definitely "conscious" prime-*knowing*'. 'Thought has emancipated itself from sensation'.[66]

Spengler was describing a morphological cultural process, whereas the Futurists glorified the process as a cult. The fact-man of the Late West was obliged to accept the realities and act accordingly if the destiny of The West would be fulfilled, Spengler's final lines in *Decline* being:

> We have not the freedom to reach this to or that, but the freedom to do the necessary or to do nothing. And a task that historic necessity has set will be accomplished with the individual or against him.[67]

The alternative was to allow extra-Western forces, or what Spengler referred to as the 'coloured world revolution' under the leadership of Bolshevik Russia, to harness Western technics and defeat The West.[68]

The Futurists seemed not to have been concerned with the *hubris* implicit in the Faustian conquest of Nature. Spengler accepted it as part of the inexorable laws of history, and the most that could be done was to play one's role on the historical stage as time and place had allotted. To the Futurists man was liberated by the Machine, chains unbound, a Faustian outlook without recognising – like the famous Doctor himself – the dangers. Theirs was a youthful exuberance, Spengler's a sceptical acceptance and sobriety. The duty of the Italian Futurist was to be audacious, that of the Faustian to be dutiful to an historical mission.

There was 'the truly Faustian danger of the Devil's having a hand in the game, the risk that he was leading them in spirit to that mountain on which he promises all the power of the earth', listening 'to the law of the cosmic pulse in order to overpower it'. 'The idea of the machine' was created 'as a small cosmos obeying the will of man alone'.[69] That

---

[66]Ibid., p.499.
[67]Ibid., Vol. II, op. cit., p.507.
[68]Spengler, O., *The Hour of Decision*, op. cit. 'The Colored World-Revolution'.
[69]Ibid., Vol. II, op. cit., p.502.

is Faustian technics. Prior to the stream engine 'Nature had rendered services, but now she was tied to the yoke as a *slave*...'[70] This subduing and harnessing of nature had a transformative force upon Work itself, hitherto routine 'muscle-force'. The machine insists that it is 'used and directed'. '*Work* becomes the great word in ethical thinking'. 'The machine works and forces man to co-operate. The entire Culture reaches a degree of activity such that the earth trembles under it'.[71]

The Futurists celebrated what seemed the infinite possibilities that had been opened up by Faustian technics, waxing lyrical about factories, machinery and bridges, 'the gluttonous railway stations devouring smoking serpents; factories suspended from the clouds by the thread of their smoke; bridges with the leap of gymnasts flung across the diabolic cutlery of sunny rivers; adventurous steamers sniffing the horizon; great-breasted locomotives, puffing on the rails like enormous steel horses with long tubes for bridles...'[72]

Spengler, however, saw the intrinsic tragedy in the great Faustian drama. In the 1924 edition of the Christopher Marlowe rendition of the legend of Doctor Faust, Professor R S Knox perfectly describes the implications of the Faustian impulse: 'The Faustus legend becomes for us a symbol of humanity's splendid struggle to reach the stars, the tragedy of infinite aspiration ending in agony and remorse'.[73]

This 'tragedy of infinite aspiration' was clearly forewarned by Spengler, yet he saw the outcome, if The West was to fulfil its destiny, as unavoidable. The demands of the machine epoch had made of man its slave:

Faustian man has become *the slave of his creation*. His number, and the arrangement of his life as he lives it, have been driven by

---

[70]Ibid.

[71]Ibid., p.503.

[72]Marinetti, 'Manifesto of Futurism', Lyttelton, op.cit., p.215.

[73]Marlowe, C., (1604) *The Tragical History of Doctor Faustus* (London: Methuen and Co., 1924), p.7.

the machine on to a path where there is no standing still and no turning back.[74]

'Nothing standing still and no turning back' is precisely what the Futurists demanded, with the self-assurance and rebellion of a Lucifer or an Icarus, or a Prometheus; or, to take the analogies further, Faustian Man was *impelled* to open Pandora's Box, and unleash the consequences.

The Futurists saw man in relation to machine as only the master, and the machine as the tool of mastery in a Nietzschean transcendence, for the individual, for Italy, and for an entire Civilisation. The Futurists were possessed by a youthful optimism and upheld the cult of youth as concomitant with the cult of the machine: speed, energy, the human in perpetual motion. They boasted of their youth, that;

> the oldest among us are not yet thirty years old: we have therefore at least ten years to accomplish our task. When we are forty let younger and stronger men than we throw us in the waste-paper basket like useless manuscripts! They will come against us from afar, leaping on the light cadence of their first pomes, clutching the air with their predatory fingers and sniffing at the gates of the academies the good scent of our decaying spirits, already promised to the catacombs of the libraries.[75]

The doctrine is one of 'eternal youth', and of a Futurist 'permanent revolution', where there would be continual renewal. It seems evident that this was the Futurist means of overcoming the Spenglerian problem of historical morphology: that of stasis and decay. Civilisation would ever be renewed by continually drawing on the younger generations. However, it seems that the problem would not be one of cultural stasis and death but one of constant flux, without the long duration of order necessary for a High Culture to flourish.

---

[74]Spengler, O., *The Decline of The West*, op. cit., Vol. II p.504.
[75]Marinetti, 'First Futurist Manifesto'; Lyttelton, op,. cit., p.214.

Spengler, in contrast, and amidst the Nazi street brawls and the failed Munich Putsch of 1923, called for sober political calculation.[76] That was precisely his message for German youth in his 1924 speech 'The Political Duties of German Youth',[77] and why he remained sceptical about the ability of the National Socialists to accomplish the mission that was required of Germany.[78]

Spengler stated that the peasant, the hand-worker and the merchant had been placed on a path of enslavement from which there is no turning back. 'It forces the entrepreneur not less then the workman to obedience. *Both* becomes slaves, and not masters, of the machine...'[79]

There is one figure, however, that masters the Machine, 'the *engineer*, the priest of the machine, the man who knows it'. It is the engineer who is the machine's 'master and destiny'. Spengler regarded the engineer as being able to solve any problem and refers to the concern during his time that coal was running out,[80] just as there is concern today about oil. He refers to the technician in military terms:

> When, and only when the crop of recruits for this army fails – this army whose thought-work forms one inward unit with the work of the machine –the industry must flicker out in spite of all that managerial energy and the workers can do.[81]

Hence, neither the merchant nor the proletarian are the essential element of the new epoch, contrary to both bourgeois and Marxian economics respectively, but the overlooked third caste in the production process: the engineer who assumed the place of priest of Faustian technics.

---

[76]Bolton, K., R., 'Spengler', op, cit., pp.43-44.
[77]Ibid., p.28.
[78]Ibid., pp.43-49.
[79]Spengler, O., *The Decline of The West*, op. cit., Vol. II, p.504.
[80]Ibid., p.505.
[81]Ibid.

'Money versus Blood': The Final Conflict

There remained a question, however, as to whose service Western technics would function? Spengler held that in the Late or Winter cycle of a Civilisation there emerged a conflict between two forces for the control of the destiny of the Civilisation: Money versus Blood. The rule of Money – or what we might refer to as *plutocracy* - representatives the artificiality of Late Civilisation, materialism, and a lack of cultural élan or service to anything higher than commerce. 'Blood' is symbolic of the return of foundational values and the spirituality and élan of the founding culture of a Civilisation, albeit, according to Spengler, this revival can never be of the same vitality and form as that of the Spring cycle of a High Culture. This revival includes what Spengler called 'Second Religiousness'[82] and 'Caesarism', which places economics in a subordinate position to statecraft.

Spengler pointed out that 'high finance', an intangible that is not bound to anything, controls industry through 'credit-needs'.[83] It is a conflict between 'productive' economics and that 'acquisitive' economics of a speculative and parasitic character. 'This battle is the despairing struggle of technical thought to maintain its liberty against money-thought'.[84]

Because of the intangible character of 'money-thought' its possibilities became exhausted after assuming a period of supremacy over a Civilisation, and there emerges 'the last conflict' within a Civilisation: 'the conflict *between* money and blood'. The 'master will subdues again the plunderer-will'.[85]

Hence, the historical necessity for Western technics to assume its place as a method for the fulfilment of Western Civilisation was *dependent on the freeing of creative forces from that of money*. This subordination

---

[82] Ibid., Vol. II, p.310.
[83] Ibid., p.505.
[84] Ibid., p.506.
[85] Ibid.

of economics to politics Spengler referred to as 'Socialism'[86] or more specifically as 'Prussian Socialism'.[87] This 'Socialism' is antithetical to that of the 'socialism' of Marx and other such 'proletarian' movements, which do not seek to subordinate money to politics but to merely exchange the roles of economic classes.[88]

The Futurists in Italy saw the new epoch as inherently antithetical to bourgeois values and 'money-thinking', which would all become passé. The Futurists adhered to revolutionary politics and actively agitate against the bourgeoisie status quo. They aligned with either Anarchism or the Fascist left-wing, but there revolutionary socialism, like 'Prussian Socialism', was not of the proletarian-based class-politics and money-thinking of the orthodox Left. Spengler wrote of the 'new German outlook upon economics… from beyond all Capitalism and Socialism – both of which were the products of the jejune rationality of the eighteenth century…'[89] This 'Prussian Socialism' was to be the method by which Capital would be overthrown, and Western technics placed at the service of the new Faustian epoch of Caesarism.

While Spengler's 'Prussian Socialism' was drawing interest from industrial, aristocratic and military circles in Germany, who saw it as a means of transcending class conflict for the common interests, in Italy a similar move was taking place, which brought socialistic ideas into the Nationalist Right, and a coalescing of new thinking from Left and Right. The Great War saw a convergence of these forces, as the war was seen by the interventionist wing of the Socialist Party, led by Mussolini, as a means of overthrowing the old order. The Italian Right had, as in France, taken on syndicalism[90] as an alternative to the bourgeoisie order. The Italian Nationalist Association was

---

[86]Ibid., p.504.
[87]Spengler, O., *Prussianism and Socialism*, 1919 (Paraparaumu, New Zealand: Renaissance Press, 2005).
[88]Spengler, O., *The Decline of The West*, op. cit., Vol. II, p.469.
[89]Ibid., p.470.
[90]Corradini, E.,1919; 'Nationalism and the Syndicates', Speech at the Nationalist Convention, Rome, March 16 1919; Adrian Lyttelton (ed.) op. cit., p.138.

thoroughly opposed to the bourgeoisie spirit, Nationalist leader Corradini attacking the liberalism and internationalism of the bourgeoisie as 'the sink into which sentimental socialism drains'.[91] Like the Futurists, Corradini demanded that Italy overcome its sloth of bourgeoisie complacency and enter a new age of dynamism, and like Marinetti referred to Italy's description as the 'land of the dead' being transformed by those who have arisen from the grave 'to a life of industry and work', having been suffocated by the 'net of the deeds of the dying'. [92] The Italian Nationalists, far removed from reaction, regarded Italy as a 'proletarian nation' and viewed the world in terms of a type of 'class struggle' between nations.[93] As early as 1910 they used the term 'national socialism', in a call to war. Like Marinetti's famous axiom that 'war is the world's hygiene', the Nationalists saw war in similar terms and as the means of creating 'national discipline', ending bourgeoisie sentiments, and 'reviving a pact of family solidarity between all classes of the Italian nation'.[94] This was the equivalent Spengler's 'Prussian Socialism' nine years later. The Italian Nationalist temperament was Faustian and Futurist, rejecting reaction and – like Marinetti – contemptuous of the slumber that had been content to maintain Italy on the basis of long past glories, 'led by men left over from her time of bondage, the dregs of traditions, methods and people already decadent and decaying under a regime of tiny, timorous and inept governments'. Coradinni ridiculed, as did Marinetti, the 'patriotism of the perfect good old Italian bourgeoisie', a 'false patriotism' because it was 'inert'.[95]

There was hence, in Italy and Germany, emerging during the same period, and perhaps the result of both nations having been formed about the same late time, ca. 1870, a realisation that bourgeois slumber,

[91]Corradini, E., *Il Regno*, Vol. I, No. I, 1903; Lyttelton, A., (ed.) ibid., p.138.
[92]Ibid., p.140.
[93]'*Principles of Nationalism*', First Nationalist Congress, Florence, December 3, 1910; Lyttelton, A., ibid., p.146.
[94]Ibid., p. 147.
[95]Corradini, E., '*The Proletarian Nations and Nationalism*', 1911; Adrian Lyttelton, ibid., p.150.

cultural decay and the 'money-thinking' of the 19th century, required overcoming if the respective nations were to fulfil their destinies. The Nationalism of Spengler and of Marinetti were consequently 'Socialist' insofar as it was the term – given by Spengler – for the revolt against 'money-thinking'. Hence, much of the Right in Germany, so far from being the bastion of capitalism, as portrayed by Marxist orthodoxy, was in revolt against the dictature of Capital, as it was in Italy.

The Futurist response was to align with the Nationalists and the Fascists, although there was a continual flirtation with Anarchism.[96] However, in demanding the setting in motion of the Faustian impulse at full speed, there was nothing of Marxism in a doctrine that condemned democracy for its pacifism, internationalism, anti-colonialism, and 'lack of racial pride and any idea of race',[97] just as Spengler had condemned democracy as the political weapon of plutocracy.[98] Marinetti's rebuttal of contemporary doctrines established a dichotomy of confrontation between world outlooks, as did Spengler's dichotomy of 'money versus blood'. The character of the Faustian fulfilment of Western destiny would be determined, stated Spengler, by the final conflict between 'blood' (what Marinetti called the 'idea of race') and the forces of money-thinking. In a comment reminiscent of Spengler's final warning in regard to the mechanisation of the coloured world in a struggle against the white, Marinetti repudiated the League of Nations and the allied idea of 'concessions to uncivilised and inferior nations'.[99]

Of particular interest, in Marinetti's attack on pacifism soon after the Great War, he alluded in a very Spenglerian manner to the organic character of politics and ideas:

---

[96]Berghaus, G., *Futurism and Politics: Between Anarchist Rebellion and Fascist Reaction 1909-1944* (Oxford: Berghahn Books, 1996), 'Futurism and Anarcho-Syndicalism', pp.52-59.

[97]Marinetti, F., 'Old Ideas which always go hand in hand must be Separated', *L'Ardito*, March 1919; Lyttelton, A., op. cit., p.216.

[98]Spengler, O., *The Decline of The West*, op. cit., Vol. II, p.506.

[99]Marinetti, F., 1919, op. cit., Lyttelton, op. cit., p.217.

Ideologies are created, dominated and formed by life. Every political idea is a living organism. Political parties are almost always doomed to turn into splendid corpses. The parties with a great past are the ones which now lack vitality. This is a Futurist law.[100]

Marinetti concluded this article with reference to the organic character of a struggle by what Spengler called 'blood' and what the Futurists simply called 'life':

Life against death. Being Futurists means opting for life. The fight against parasitism is the fight against an anti-national tradition that is deeply rooted in the past. Because in Italy tradition is synonymous with defeat.[101]

Similarly, Spengler concluded *Decline* with a clarion call where 'the sword is victorious over the money', in an organic struggle where, *Life* is alpha and omega, the cosmic flow in microcosmic form. It is the fact of facts within the world-as-history.... Ever in history it is life and only life – race-quality, the triumph of the will-to-power – and not the victory of truths, discoveries, or money that signifies'.[102]

CONCLUSION: FAUSTIAN HUBRIS

'Standing on the word's summit we launch once again our insolent challenge to the stars!', stated the Italian Futurists.[103] 'Insolent challenge' connotes *hubris*, but this 'challenge to the stars' is, as previously mentioned, pure Faustianism: the infinity of space, as Spengler defined it.

The fatal flaw in the Faustian and Futurist visions was that The West was not liberated from plutocracy and Western technics remains

[100]Marinetti, F., ibid., p.218.
[101]Ibid.
[102]Spengler, O., *The Decline of The West*, op. cit., Vol. II, p.507.
[103]Marinetti, 'Manifesto of Futurism', Lyttelton, op.cit., p.215.

firmer than ever in the grasp of Money. Both Spengler and Marinetti saw technics as creating a dynamic Civilisation of force and steel, and the domination over Nature according to human will-to-power. This new epoch would proceed by what Spengler called the defeat of 'money' by 'blood' and what Marinetti saw as the repudiation of bourgeois stupor by 'life'. Both saw this as part of an organic process. A significant difference, however, is that Marinetti considered the triumph of technics and the ushering of a new Futurist Civilisation as being one of infinite progress – itself a form of Faustianism – whereas Spengler saw this cycle of Late Western Civilisation as a final great bow on the world stage of history, of limited duration, a dramatic exit, that was no more avoidable in its death than the death of any other organism. Despite the Futurist rejection of *pastism*, the optimism in regard to the unlimited potentialities of technics seems to be still infected by the 19th century optimism engendered by the machine, an optimism that was shared by both the USA and the USSR. This optimism among the highest intellectual circles was cogently expressed for example by the prominent 19th Darwinist Dr A R Wallace in a book aptly titled *The Wonderful Century* (1898):

Not only is our century superior to any that have gone before it but… it may be best compared with the whole preceding historical period. It must therefore be held to constitute the beginning of a new era of human progress. … We men of the 19th century have not been slow to praise it. The wise and the foolish, the learned and the unlearned, the poet and the pressman, the rich and the poor, alike swell the chorus of admiration for the marvellous inventions and discoveries of our own age, and especially for those innumerable applications of science which now form part of our daily life, and which remind us every hour or our immense superiority over our comparatively ignorant forefathers. [104]

There is something about the Futurist enthusiasm for 'progress' and

---

[104]Quoted by Briggs, A., (ed.), *The Nineteenth Century: The Contradictions of Progress*, (New York: Bonanza Books, 1985), p.29.

the incomparable technical superiority of the 20th century expressed by Marinetti et al that had already been enthused over in the prior century by the Victorians Darwinists and merchants. Where Dr Wallace spoke glowingly of 19th century technics, and Marinetti welcomed the dawn of a new age of factories bellowing smoke without interruption and a new rhythm of life that would be one of human perpetual motion, Spengler saw the new epoch for what it was, the Faustian quest that plays out in high drama, but ends in tragedy. While Marinetti was an optimist, Spengler's stark realism is mistaken as 'pessimism'; a misunderstanding of his outlook that he spent much time trying to correct.[105] Spengler foresaw the Faustian end:

> Nature becomes exhausted, the globe sacrificed to Faustian thinking in energies. The working earth is the Faustian aspect of her, the aspect contemplated by the Faust of Part II, the supreme transfiguration of enterprising work – and contemplating, he dies.[106]

The defeat of what Spengler saw in Fascism as a provisional and transient form of the approaching 'Caesarism'[107] that would overthrow Money, was itself overthrown by Money. Technics continues to subdue the Earth in the pursuit of increased profit margins, and despoils everything in its path, until , as Spengler said, 'Nature becomes exhausted'. It serves no greater purpose than as a parasite and like all parasites not only self-destructs but first kills the host; in this instance Western Civilisation. Instead of Caesars the post-War world threw up in cartoonish manner the dictature of American Presidents. Rather than a Western Empire, there is an American Empire masquerading as 'Western' but thoroughly in the service of Money and determined to exterminate any vestige of 'Blood' by its control of Faustian technics. In addition to this, what Spengler warned about regarding the mechanisation of the East, in his final work, *The Hour of Decision*, has been fulfilled.

---

[105]Spengler, O., 'Pessimism?', 1921, op. cit.
[106]Spengler, O., *The Decline of The West*, op. cit., Vol. II, p.505.
[107]Spengler , O., (1934), *The Hour of Decision*, op. cit., p.230.

However, even this ignoble end is a Faustian end; the path of *hubris* that makes the Faustian imperative so dangerous.[108] *Hubris*, defined thus, has – from what we can see on hindsight today – a distinctly Faustian relevance:

> Hubris - arrogance, excessive self-pride and self-confidence. The word was used to refer to the emotions in Greek tragic heroes that led them to ignore warnings from the gods and thus invite catastrophe. It is considered a form of hamartia or tragic flaw that stems from overbearing pride and lack of piety. The word is taken directly from the Greek *hubris*, meaning 'insolence or pride'.[109]

Spengler was under no illusions, and stated:

> Man was, and is, too shallow and cowardly to ensure the fact of the mortality of everything living. He wraps it up in rose-coloured progress optimism, he heaps upon it the flowers of literature, he crawls beneath the shelter of ideals so as not to see anything. But impermanence, the birth and the passing, is the form of all that is actual – from the stars, whose destiny is for us incalculable, right down to the ephemeral concourses on this planet. The life of the individual – whether this be animal or plant or man is as perishable as that of peoples and Cultures. Every creation is foredoomed to decay, every thought, every discovery, every deed to oblivion. Here, there, and everywhere we are sensible of grandly fated courses of history that have vanished. Ruins of the 'have been' works of dead Cultures lie all about us. The hubris of Prometheus, who thrust his hand into the heavens in order to make the divine power subject to man, carries with it his fall. What, then, becomes of the chatter about 'undying achievements?'[110]

---

[108]von Goethe, J. W., *Faust: A Tragedy*, English ed. (London: Frederick Warne & Co., n.d.).

[109]'Guide to Literary Terms', http://www.enotes.com/literary-terms/hubris

[110]Spengler, O., *Man and Technics* (London: European Books Society, 1992), p.17. For a discussion on *Man and Technics* see: Southgate, T., *Spengler: Thoughts & Perspectives Vol. X* (London: Black front Press, 2012), pp.222-262.

The 'Futurism' that must now be discussed, I feel, is not that of the fulfilment of The West's destiny, which has itself become, as the Futurists would say, passé, but that of an as yet unnamed Post-West, the identity of which was occasionally alluded to by Spengler as being centred upon Russia; a collusion of the Faustian and the still vital Russian soul not in pseudomorphosis[111] but in symbiosis.[112]

*****

K R Bolton is a Fellow of the Academy of Social and Political Research (Athens), publisher of the peer reviewed journal *Ab Aeterno*, 'contributing writer' for *Foreign Policy Journal*, and a regular contributor to *The Great Indian Dream* (Indian Institute of Planning & Management) and *New Dawn* (Australia). He has been widely published by the scholarly and broader media. Books include: *Revolution from Above* (London: Arktos Media Ltd., 2011), and *Artists of the Right* (San Francisco: Counter-Currents Publishing, 2012), with several others due out in 2012.

---

[111]Spengler, O., *The Decline of The West*, Vol. II, op, cit, p.189.
[112]Bolton, K. R., 'Spengler and Russian', in Southgate, T., (ed.) op. cit., pp.89-138.

Utopia in Fernando Pessoa
and Emil Cioran

José António Miranda Moreira de Almeida

A brief note about Utopia in the Western world

Talking about utopia implies a mental and intellectual exercise of association, following the establishment of a narrow relation between past, present and the future. The time conjunction that the concept holds within itself makes the conducted dialogue clear, throughout a chronological period around the interpretative variations of a same ideal.

As an attempt of defining a concept for utopia, Gregory Claeys claimed in his book *Searching for Utopia: The history of an idea*, that it grounds fundamentally in three major cornerstones: utopian thinking, literature of utopian nature, and the several practical essays conducted to search and find superior communities far more developed than the existing ones.[1] However, the same author is also quick to stress other aspects which cannot be overlooked, starting with the very concept of definition, as coined by the *vox populis*. As such the author upholds that "the term 'utopia' to be meaningful, it cannot embrace every aspiration to social improvement,[2] as it cannot be reduced to mere psychological impulse, dream, fantasy, projection, desire or wish".[3] The author concludes that there is still a difference between utopia and the search for a perfect life, considering that "'perfection' is essentially a theological concept, which, while historically linked to utopianism,

---

[1]Claeys, G., *Searching for Utopia: The History of an Idea* (London: Thames & Hudson), p.11.
[2]Ibid., p.11.
[3]Ibid., p.11.

115

defines a state that is impossible for mortals to attain in this life."[4]

Providing a specific definition of utopia thus becomes rather complex, bearing in mind its changeable character throughout the course of History, or the vast diversity of categories encompassing positive ideals of better developed societies; its negative oppositions and satire, anti-utopias or dystopias; the several myths about Paradise, golden ages, 'fortunate islands' or simple portraits of primitive people living in communion in a natural state; shipwrecks like Robinson Crusoe's; imaginary voyages through space; forming urban, political, civic or civilizational models, as well as other visions pertaining to the development of the human being, their respective wellbeing and urbanity.

The history of human evolution reveals the way in which utopia, a concept inherent to Man, has contributed from a mythological and religious point of view to the development of the various societies from the very beginning. As defined by Mircea Eliade, the Myth, essential to the affirmation of the archaic or post-modern man, disconnected from a particular time in History is considered to be one of the forerunners of the thought process, and consequently of utopia.[5] Together, in a primal embrace, the myth and utopia feed the embers of History itself – like a lighthouse overlooking the world from its high promontory.

Utopia is a universal phenomenon, common to all cultures and civilizations. If we take the cultures and civilizations of the Western world as an example, cyclical emergence of several works of utopian nature is abundantly evident. These become more pronounced in the way universal questions are approached and ultimately results in the compilation of the most primal conceptions and common collective ideals, preconditioning the path taken by civilizational thinking in view of a better, more perfect future, albeit influenced by models revealed in an imagined and archetypical past. We can, in fact, find

---

[4]Ibid., p.11-12.
[5]In order to further develop this idea, please read: Eliade, M., *O Mito do Eterno Retorno*, Lisboa: Edições 70, 2000), p.153-159.

in ancient times a set of works whose seminal importance from a cultural, civilizational and literary point of view turns them into veritable mythical, archetypical and utopian recompilations. Perfect examples are Homer's *Odyssey*, Virgil's *Aeneid*, or the Holy Scriptures. In this past, formed as a result of a Judeo-Christian and Greco-Roman matrix, tradition and Western thinking have been forged and shaped, offering models and directions to the elites of different peoples, aiming at promoting its own development.

On the subject of the importance of the contribution of the elites, António Marques Bessa sustains that "the history of the Western culture and the analysis of the great political and social transformations suggest that these transformations are usually preceded by intellectual movements, cultural waves which act as gestation periods for the larger systems, revolutions and structural mutations."[6] These essays, which are developed by the elites as an attempt to materialize and operationalize utopia, eventually morph into dystopias, which inherently distort the idyllic character of ideas. This is further confirmed by the failure that accurses various paradigms – amongst others political, economic, historical, social, spiritual – whenever the ethereal domain is abandoned in an attempt to embrace the concrete.

Still bearing in mind Western culture as a reference, it is worth mentioning that following the Ancient times and the advent of the Middle Ages, the periods of change, the breakthroughs and setbacks in the face of the established order were caused by the emergence of new paradigms to attain higher goals; these paradigms kept evolving into new axioms and postulates born from new needs, dreams and utopias. Throughout History the elites are evidently more prominent as the link between the leadership in intellectual problematization and the search for utopia, the main figures of which encompass philosophers and thinkers, theologians, poets, writers, politicians and other men devoted to science and culture.

---

[6]Bessa, A. M., *Utopia – Uma visão da engenharia de sonhos*, (Mem Martins: Publicações Europa-América, 1998), p.9.

From a chronological perspective, it is possible to identify a specific date –fundamentally a date between the Middle Ages and the present day when utopia first became the subject of study. This date is 1516, the year Thomas More's *Utopia* was first published. This was 16th century Renaissance, an age where the Western culture experienced a rebirth and renewed interest. This work is particularly important as this is where the concept of 'utopia' is first defined as a gender. According to Gregory Claeys, "the very title of the work was a pun on two words: eutopia, 'good place' and utopia, 'non-place'",[7] which may explain the title *Eutopia* given to More's book in its Italian first edition.

In this book, among other aspects, the separation between utopia and the idea of perfection is established from the start, through the revelation not of a perfect society but instead of a far more developed one. The reading and exegesis of this work led to a more recurrent conceptualization of the expression 'utopia' itself, by means of the idyllic character of its contents, although the author himself integrates the idea of vice, without eliminating it. Claeys adds that in *Utopia* "Crime and criminals persist, even if, as portrayed by More portraits, the fetters worn by offenders are made of gold."[8] In short, Thomas More's work presents a society which recognizes the possibility of moral decadence and degeneration but is still able to resist it, almost stoically, assuming a metaphorical character that is essential to the understanding of the axiomatic conception of the theoretical meaning of utopia itself.

This work sets a turning point in the conceptualization of the ideas that are nowadays linked to the roots of utopia. It makes a distinction between an archaic conception of the world on one side and a rationally based conception on the other, although it cannot yet be seen as a modern concept. With Thomas More, utopia is for the first time addressed by its proper name and is no longer exclusively associated to sacred and mythical domains, having conquered a place

---

[7]Claeys, G., *Searching for Utopia: The History of an Idea* (London: Thames & Hudson), p.59.
[8]Ibid., p.59.

among philosophical debates.

Understandably, More's work is the result of a particular socio-cultural framework characterized by significant technical and scientific developments. One could argue that the theocentric paradigm had to give way to the newly proposed anthropocentric view. The emergence of a new set of concerns and ambitions fed by new utopias or reinterpretations of old ones which were essentially related to earthly experiences, though sometimes still inspired by things imbued of sacred or fantastic characteristics, led to this focus being shifted back to mankind.

In short, we can denominate a 1st Utopian Revolution Age succeeded by a 2nd Utopian Revolution Age, based on the illusion that with the Discoveries the lost Paradise was found or re-discovered, passing through the near-anarchy of pirate utopia and the desert islands, crossing the idyllic and stereotyped conceptions of the post-Atlantic Revolutions of 18th and 19th century societies. This Revolution was responsible for a significant share of modern society's paradigms, characterized by the emergence of rationalism, positivism, industrialization, technology and modernity now presented as new utopias, liberalism, socialism, communism, anarchism, science fiction, the utopian-dystopian cycle of the 20th century totalitarianisms that culminated in the fatalistic 'lost paradise' of our dystopian 21st century. This century, permanently associated with Pessoa's concept of Fog, preceding a new Renaissance and subsequently a new Age, will compel Man, unable to see the horizon around him, to once again delve deep into his arcane roots, finding in the depths of his cultural and spiritual traditions the new breath for rehabilitating the dream and the utopia of the Western world. In fact, according to Cioran: "We only act under the fascination of the impossible: same is to say that a society unable to give birth and to dedicate itself to a utopia, is threatened with sclerosis and collapse."[9]

---

[9]Cioran, E.M., *História e Utopia* (Venda Nova: Bertrand Editora, 1994), p.149.

FROM PESSOA'S RE-ENCHANTMENT TO THE RETURN OF CIORAN'S DISENCHANTMENT

Although Fernando Pessoa was born in the late 19th century, he should be considered a 20th century author, as should Emil Cioran. The former, born on June 13th 1888 in Lisbon, the capital of the Portuguese Empire, was umbilically separated from his motherland and respective culture, after being taken for family reasons in his early years to Durban, South Africa, where he grew under the influence of the Anglo-Saxon culture, until his final long yearned for return. Contrary to Cioran, a Romanian born on April 8th 1911 in Rășinari, a small Transylvanian village, Pessoa spent the earlier years of his youth away from his motherland's culture but kept the intrinsic need to rediscover his roots even after his return to Lisbon in 1905, from where he would never leave again.

On the other hand, Cioran spent his youth in his homeland in close contact with the surrounding reality and culture, experiencing from an early stage the evolutions and convulsions in the history of his country – firstly internally, in his own country, and at a later stage externally, from his exile. This profound, deep-rooted harmony with the Romanian culture could be construed in no uncertain terms as a result of his father's influence, a nationalist orthodox, supporter of the Romanian self-determination cause, which could potentially explain Cioran's later admiration for Codreanu, as well as the time spent in the Romanian Legionary Movement, also known as Iron Guard.

Still on the subject of Cioran's, Ilinca Zarifopol-Johnson, Cioran's biographer, conveys an image of a young man, very active but also incredibly prone to bouts of depression and melancholic crises. This would eventually worsen when he left Rășinari, "first to Sibiu, then to Bucharest, later to Berlin, and, finally to Paris."[10] The change was

---

[10]Johnson, I.Z., *Searching for Cioran* (Bloomington: Indiana University Press. 2009), p.25.

so sudden and violent for the Romanian author that Cioran himself eventually establishes a comparison between his plight and Adam and Eve's expulsion from Paradise.

By analyzing this biblical allegory a significant difference becomes apparent between the life experiences of Pessoa and Cioran. By returning to his motherland, the Portuguese experiences a moment of reunion with his culture and traditions, a return to a childhood's lost Paradise, while the Romanian is forced to survive an irreversible expulsion from what would have been his Eden. While Pessoa searched the joy of the exiled when returning to his homeland, an inner dream, capable to lead him in the path to create a new universal utopia based on the hope that lays within the cultural and spiritual aspects of the Portuguese tradition, Cioran allowed himself to be dominated by the crudity of the facts and events witnessed or lived, fading away through History – the great human tragedy – and ultimately confining his contact with the imagined world. This confinement made Cioran a historicist author, more so than Pessoa, whose literary and metaphysical spirit, although in the restless and solitude of those who search, communed in the hopeful ambition of the arrival of a new Golden Age.

Pessimism is notwithstanding also very much present in the very typically Pessoan idea of Portugal and the Portuguese. This idea is expressed in many of his writings and António Quadros reminds us by listing some of these aspects: "foreign-facing culture, cultural mimicry, decadence of the creative spirit, denationalization or loss of the higher consciousness of nationality"[11] which, combined with a mythical hypertrophy, prevents the Portuguese Man from fulfilling him - or herself. In this respect and similarly to Pessoa, Cioran also criticized his fellow countrymen, accusing them of perverting Paradise by means of their own historical existence, and comparing them to "petrified larvae, lost in a 'geological dream.'" [12] Nonetheless both

---

[11]Quadros, A., *O Coração do Texto* (Lisboa: Edições Cosmos, 1999), p.83.

[12] Johnson, I.Z., *Searching for Cioran*, p.27.

authors display acute historical awareness of their homeland's role in the defense of the Western culture. Portugal due to its geographical location in the far Western end of Europe and the Portuguese diaspora; Romania as the last pillar of Latinity and Eastern culture at the Eastern end of Europe, where it has from immemorial times served as a buffer against the Muslim and Barbarian invasions. Two peripheral spaces, distant from the great cultural centers and geographically far from each other, but with a common mission: the defense and maintenance of the utopia of a universal West, culturally and spiritually.

Also in *Teatro da vacuidade ou a impossibilidade de ser eu*, Paulo Borges emphasizes the distinct way in which Pessoa and Cioran experienced life, stressing the importance of that set of events that ultimately resulted in bringing the two authors together, in the light of a common flame that nurtured them, stating:

> Thinkers and writers from the outskirts of the dominant European culture and acutely aware of living the end of a cycle of the civilization that was born from it, their strength emanates also from the urge to liberate themselves from the idols of that selfsame civilization and culture, the rules of what is supposed to be mentally correct, not held back by an assumed human limitation, in a titanic and iconoclastic hybris to overcome everything, from the subject and from itself, experiencing nostalgia or a violent 'saudade' – longing – of the unconditioned, perceived and experienced as the instance irreducible from the subject's constitution in the world and the bottomless pit of all possible experience.[13]

As mentioned, both authors lived in a time of transition and the end of a civilizational cycle, where according to Dominique Venner: "Passions were as more intense as it is certain that ideologies have been imposed as substitutes of religion, as immanent religions, of which it was expected to bring here and now a collective 'salvation'."[14]

---

[13]Borges, P., *Teatro da vacuidade ou a impossibilidade de ser eu (Estudos e ensaios pessoanos)* (Lisboa: Verbo, 2011), p.233.

[14]Venner, D., *O século de 1914: Utopias, Guerras e Revoluções na Europa do Século*

The French historian proceeds by explaining the route of this tendency of the Western world and adds:

> The original cause of this substitution has naturally been, in Europe, the dusk, as from 18th century, of Christianity, the 'death of God', the end of hope in 'another world' and the growth of nihilism, another name for the absence of objectives. A great need was therefore born to bridge the emptiness, giving a new sense to life. That was the role assigned to radical political myths, those from revolutions and counter-revolutions. The French revolution was the first transference from religious to political major manifestation [...] It was expected thereafter from it the realization of the identity or justice dreams, which previously were laid on the hope of another world.[15]

That sense of hope, laid on a utopia inspired by libertarian, revolutionary positivist ideas, was in fact one of the main causes of disquiet for an extensive number of Portuguese thinkers, from the 19th century through the 20th century and well into the present time. Portugal, not unlike the vast majority of the Western world, was caught in this wave of convulsion brought about by the arrival of a new, unnatural paradigm. Portugal thus entered a period of degenerative decadence, the climax of which was attained with the establishment of the inorganic, de-spiritualized First Republic. The essence of the First Republic and its positivist ideas, after the failure of the materialization of the republican, revolutionary and socialist utopia, contrary to the Portuguese spiritual tradition, led to some of the more mediatic responses such as the creation of the periodical *A Águia*, and at a later stage the movement *Renascença Portuguesa*, whose main purpose was the re-sacralization of the country and its culture, somewhat similarly to the re-enchantment suggested years later by other European intellectual nuclei, such as the Eranos.

XX (Porto: Civilização Editora 2009), p.14.
[15]Ibid., p.14-15.

Dalila Pereira da Costa wrote that Portugal had been "at the mercy of an escape from itself since the 18th century, in consecutive mimetisms or importations of enlightenment, positivism, materialism: but deep down it will always preserve, secret and untouched, this Western soul, waiting solely to be unmasked and used in thought and in life."[16] This perspective follows the hermeneutics of the Portuguese thinking which, having first seen a ray of light in the 19th century, is eminently evident in the early 20th century in the body of work of Teixeira de Pascoaes and Fernando Pessoa, two of the main heralds of this renewed spiritual utopia, a utopia that is focused on emergence of a new Golden Age. This new Golden Age, inspired by a quasi 'religion' or national spirituality, influenced by a quite particular adaptation of the *Theory of the Three Ages* by Joachim of Fiore, firstly conducted by Father António Vieira and later on by Sampaio Bruno, Teixeira de Pascoaes, Fernando Pessoa himself, among several others.[17]

In a crusade against a certain idea of modernity associated to its time, Pessoa resuscitated old myths, prophesying, not unlike Vieira, the advent of the Fifth Empire, universal and spiritual, successor of the four predecessing empires: "Greece, Rome, Christianity/Europe – the four come to pass".[18]

In the *Myth of the Eternal Return*, Mircea Eliade classifies the transition period from the 19th to the 20th century as a confrontation period between "the 'historical man' (modern), known and wanted as the maker of history, and the man from traditional civilizations, who as we have seen bears a negative attitude towards history."[19] In fact, Fernando Pessoa and Emil Cioran have manifested in their own particular way, through their work and in their personal lives, two militant personalities in search for a new or renewed utopia, able

---

[16]Cioran, E.M., *História e Utopia* (Venda Nova: Bertrand Editora, 1994), p.19.
[17]This trail would link two important elements of the Portuguese spiritual and philosophical tradition: the Fifth Empire and '*Saudade*'.
[18]Pessoa, F., *Mensagem e outros poemas afins (Org. António Quadros)*, Mem Martins: Publicações Europa-América, 1999), p.117.
[19]Eliade, M., *O Mito do Eterno Retorno*, Lisboa: Edições 70, 2000), p.153.

to enlighten the entire civilization once again, hand in hand with a latent conflict between two different conceptions of humanity – a traditional and a modern one. According to Eliade, the first would be defined as archetypical and anti-historical, whilst the second would be characterized by the post-Hegelian axiom, modern and historical.[20] This confrontation between two distinct and opposite realities would lead Cioran to notice that:

> By divinizing History to discredit God, Marxism only succeeded to make God even more strange and besieging. In man it is possible to smother everything except the need for the absolute, which would survive the destruction of temples and even to dispel of religion from the face of the earth.[21]

In his work *Mensagem,*[22] Pessoa wrote that "Myth is the nothing that is all."[23] This suggests that Fernando Pessoa is clearly indicating a way, both individual and collective, that seeks to lead the world towards a new utopia, thus shaking away the traces of a growing decadence rooted in the attempts to operationalize the traditionally materialistic dreams that followed the 'death of God'.

Curiously, Pessoa and Cioran's universes seem to converge once again, when analyzing the Romanian author's perspective regarding the failure of the temporal empires which one day aspired to reach the universal status, as described in History and Utopia. "Charlemagne, Frederick II of Hohenstaufen, Charles V, Bonaparte, and Hitler were tempted, each in his own way, to carry out the idea of a universal empire: they have successfully failed to a greater or lesser extent."[24] After all, according to Cioran, "the West wins by losing itself",[25]

---

[20]Ibid. p.153-154.
[21]Cioran, E.M., *História e Utopia* (Venda Nova: Bertrand Editora, 1994), p.49.
[22]English title translation: *Message.*
[23]Pessoa, F., *Mensagem e outros poemas afins (Org. António Quadros)*, Mem Martins: Publicações Europa-América, 1999), p.100.
[24]Cioran, E.M., *História e Utopia* (Venda Nova: Bertrand Editora, 1994), p.44.
[25]Ibid., p.44.

justifying the Christological sacrifice of D. Sebastião, king of Portugal, as *O Desejado*, the Wanted or Concealed, in the genesis of the Sebastianistic mystic, itself analogous to the Fifth Empire idea.

This idea pursued by Emil Cioran unveils the existence of an immutable cycle which encompasses utopias, ideas and inevitably History itself, suggesting the need for mankind to project itself in the dream and hope of something that does not exist but is nonetheless able to relieve Man from the 'heavy burden of being born'.[26] Together with the end of cycle lived and experienced by both authors and which reveals itself, particularly with Fernando Pessoa, as the proximity of a Renaissance period, this need for mankind's projection into a new dream becomes even more evident when we interpret this reality as a turning point from a moment of crisis, decadence and degeneration to a new reality, idealized and utopically projected in the future. Apparently, Cioran has put aside this possibility, considering his fatalistic look at God's and Man's way to plough mankind's destiny.

However, the idea of Renaissance has always accompanied Pessoa, as well as many Portuguese intellectuals, in a clear tendency that was grounded on the feeling of hope, another archetypical element of the Portuguese culture. António Marques Bessa, José Augusto Seabra as well as Dalila Pereira da Costa all insisted in the issue of the end of the cycle, in the turn of an age and the subsequent arrival to a new Age, all this under the shape of a utopia. António Marques Bessa foresees that moment, dedicating to it his work *Ensaio sobre o fim da nossa Idade*, while José Augusto Seabra published a text in French entitled *Fernando Pessoa et la 'Nouvelle Renaissance' de l'Europe*,[27] but it is in the work of Dalila Pereira da Costa that this possibility seeps more deeply into the root of the problem, defending a traditional and universal perspective which persists perennially. She analyzes the phenomenon of the factual reality of the historical and material world, creating a symbiosis with Pessoa's utopia, sustaining:

---

[26]Reminiscent of Cioran's *The Trouble with Being Born*.
[27]Seabra, J. A., *O Coração do Texto* (Lisboa: Edições Cosmos, 1996), p.163-172.

In our century of imminent turn, marked in the Western civilization (which is now also a worldwide civilization) by disorientation, Babylonian confusion and self-destruction, by loss of soul with its own cultural roots, this nation may emerge towards that West, as an archaic reserve of its tradition, where it may again find his soul and lost or long time denied roots.[28]

There are two undeniable differences between Pessoa's and Cioran's perspective of utopia. The Romanian author's position is more about the way each culture or civilization believes and envisions its ideals and ways of life, trying to convert the world into his own views and idiosyncrasies, in a hidden or expressed form of non-belligerent cultural imperialism.[29] The collision with Pessoa seems inevitable here, in view of the mystic-nationalist character of the Fifth Empire utopic vision, even if usually seen as a universal proposal. To Cioran, utopia is an instrument of manipulation associated with lying, "it is the grotesque pink, the need to associate happiness and therefore the improbable, to the becoming, and to take an optimistic vision, aerial, to the starting point: the cynicism that he wanted to fight back",[30] calling it a "monstrous fairy tale."[31] Contrary to this deceptive utopia vision, Pessoa, sometimes even if pervaded by the most profound sadness or existentialist disbelief, seems likely to believe in Plato's pure ideas. And this leads us to the second issue, regarding the conceptual differences of utopia between both authors, namely to the way that both relate to it and work in their literary and philosophical production. We can in fact state that utopia and dystopia were, in both authors, conditioned by their own experiences and cultural-historical awareness, which influenced their statements and their postulates, in distinct ways, in distinct moments of their lives. Consequently, incorporating

[28]Costa, D. P., "Portugal Arca da Tradição", Seminário de Literatura e Filosofia Portuguesas. Universidade da Misericórdia de Friburgo, June 1988. Fundação Lusíada, Lisboa. p.119-122. (2001: 19).
[29]Cioran, E.M., História e Utopia (Venda Nova: Bertrand Editora, 1994), p.56.
[30]Ibid., p.59.
[31]Ibid., p.59.

Fernando Pessoa's idea that "The poet is a feigned",[32] as shown in the first verse of his poem *Autopsicografia,*[33] adding its demultiplication in several heteronyms, and his markedly creative character as a writer, may lead us to believe that the utopias created by the Portuguese poet and thinker are, as in *O Banqueiro Anarquista,*[34] mere intellectual exercises, derived from literary, poetic and fictional stimulation. With Cioran, the experience of living the disbelief in utopia and Man is real. A narrator participating in his own texts, the Romanian seeks to transmit his painful survival and the world's fatalistic conceptions he feeds as universal truths, being the word for him what it really is, in its most real and concrete value and content.

These differences are revealed by the distinct way in which the two authors expose their literary and philosophical genius which, as stated by Paulo Borges;

> [...] in Pessoa is evidenced in the typically Portuguese baroque and poetic proliferation of shapes – his own as well as others – the heteronym –, other essays pertaining to the escape from the prison that is the birth of individualization and the normality, assumed to be monopsychical in nature. In Cioran however the literary genius serves an obsessively detailed and meticulous struggle with all the fictions of conscience, history and culture fictions, scalped and reduced to ashes by the surgical and caustic aphorism and thinking scalpel, burnt in the vehemence of insomnia, from fever and blasphemy, but from transfiguring and ecstatic enthusiasm as well.[35]

It was the constant failure of utopia and consequently of the History of Man, seen by Cioran as another name for the History of Evil, that

---

[32]Pessoa, F., *Poesia II – 1930-1933 (Org. António Quadros)* (Mem Martins: Publicações Europa-América, 1994), p.54.

[33]English title translation: *Autopsychography.*

[34]English title translation: *The Anarchist Banker.*

[35]Borges, *Teatro da vacuidade ou a impossibilidade de ser eu (Estudos e ensaios pessoanos),* (Lisboa: Verbo, 2011), p.233.

led him to his disenchantment with God and Humanity. According to Cioran, utopias lack the foundations "the more complete (it is), the more it will be based on falsehood, because everything is a menace, including the very principle it emerges from."[36]

One should not forget that Fernando Pessoa wrote as Álvaro de Campos: "Mind the fame and the food/For tomorrow belongs to the fools of today!"[37] Utopian thinkers have throughout History been beyond their own time, often pointed at as fools, however it is thanks to them that mankind is able to develop itself and to progress, as utopia is the engine of hope.

Cioran, as if adding to what Álvaro de Campos wrote, defended: Here as there we find ourselves at a standstill, declining in a similar measure by reference to the ingenuity by which the wanderings about the future are elaborated. Life without utopia becomes unbreathable, at least to the crowd, the world yearns for a new delirium.[38]

We may then conclude that utopia, as suggested by António Marques Bessa, is a fundamental part of the so called 'engineering of dreams', bringing back Henry Corbin's idea that associates the oneiric dimension to the connection between a superior world, unreachable to the concrete plane of the physical and material domain which we inhabit.

---

[36]Cioran, E.M., *História e Utopia* (Venda Nova: Bertrand Editora, 1994), p.27.
[37]Pessoa, F., *Poesia II – 1930-1933 (Org. António Quadros)* (Mem Martins: Publicações Europa-América, 1994), p.271).
[38]Cioran, E.M., *História e Utopia*, p.24-25.

Nicolás Gómez Dávila:
Aphorisms and the Modern World

The reactionary does not extol what the next dawn must bring, nor is he terrified by the last shadows of the night. His dwelling rises up in that luminous space where the essential accosts him with its immortal presence. The reactionary escapes the slavery of history because he pursues in the human wilderness the trace of divine footsteps. Man and his deeds are, for the reactionary, a servile and mortal flesh that breathes gusts from beyond the mountains. To be reactionary is to champion causes that do not turn up on the notice board of history, causes where losing does not matter. To be reactionary is to know that we only discover what we think we invent; it is to admit that our imagination does not create, but only lays bare smooth bodies. To be reactionary is not to espouse settled cases, nor to plead for determined conclusions, but rather to submit our will to the necessity that does not constrain, to surrender our freedom to the exigency that does not compel; it is to find sleeping certainties that guide us to the edge of ancient pools. The reactionary is not a nostalgic dreamer of a cancelled past, but rather a hunter of sacred shades upon the eternal hills.

The Authentic Reactionary, Nicolás Gómez Dávila

Gwendolyn Taunton

Nicolás Gómez Dávila (don Colacho) was born 18 May 1913 in Cajicá, Colombia, into an affluent family. He was a prolific writer and important political thinker who is considered to be one of the most intransigent political theoreticians of the twentieth century. It was not until a few years prior to his death in 1994 that his writing began to gain popularity due the translation of some works into German. At the tender age of six his family relocated to Europe, where they resided for the next seventeen years. During his time in Europe, Gómez Dávila contracted a persistent illness which confined him to his bed for long periods, and as a result of this he had to be educated by private tutors with whom he studied Latin, Greek and developed a fondness for classical literature.

When Gómez Dávila turned twenty-three he moved back to Colombia, residing in Bogotá, where he met and married Emilia Nieto Ramos. Here, with his wife and children Gómez Dávila is reported to have led a life of leisure. Assisting his father briefly in the management of a carpet factory, he spent little time in the office, instead preferring to spend his time at the Jockey Club, where he played polo until incurring an injury (Gómez Dávila was thrown from his horse whilst trying to light a cigar.) Following this, he spent more time reading literature. By the end of his life, he had accumulated a library of approximately 30,000 books, many of which were in foreign languages. In addition to the French, English, Latin and Greek he learnt during childhood, Gómez Dávila could also read German, Italian, Portuguese, and was even reportedly learning Danish prior to his death in order to be able to read Søren Kierkegaard in the original language.

Gómez Dávila was also an eminent figure in Colombian society. He assisted Mario Laserna Pinzón found the University of the Andes in 1948 and his advice was often sought by politicians. In 1958 he declined the offer of a position as an adviser to President Alberto Llera after the downfall of the military government in Colombia, and in 1974 he turned down the chance to become the Colombian ambassador at the Court of St. James. Gómez Dávila had resolved early on during his work as a writer that an involvement in politics would be detrimental to his literary career and thus had decided to politely abstain from all political involvement, despite these tempting and prestigious offers.

During his lifetime, Gómez Dávila was a modest man and made few attempts to make his writings widely known. His first two publications were available only to his family and friends in private editions. Only by way of German (and later Italian as well as French and Polish) translation beginning in the late eighties did Gómez Dávila's ideas begin to disperse. Initially his works were more popular in Germany than in Colombia, and a number of prominent German authors such as Ernst Jünger (who in an unpublished letter defined Gómez Dávila's writing as: "A mine for lovers of conservatism"), Martin Mosebach, and Botho Strauß expressed their admiration for Gómez Dávila's works. His most translated and final work, *El Reaccionario Auténtico* (*The Authentic Reactionary*) was published after his death in the *Revista de la Universidad de Antioquia*.

Gómez Dávila has many unique features that occur within his works, but perhaps the most famous literary feature he is famed for is the aphorism, which remains prominent throughout his writing. Not only is the aphorism used as an aesthetic tool, it is also a purposely deployed technique selected by Gómez Dávila as his method of choice, which he referred to as *escolios* (or *glosses*). This technique was used extensively in the five volumes of *Escolios a un texto implícito* (1977; 1986; 1992).

By definition, an aphorism is an original thought, spoken or written in a concise and memorable form; the term aphorism literally means a distinction or definition, coming from the Greek ἀφορισμός (*aphorismós*). In traditional literature, the aphorism is used as a mnemonic technique to relate wisdom and is found in works such as the *Sutra* literature of India, *The Golden Verses of Pythagoras*, Hesiod's *Works and Days*, the Delphic *Maxims*, and *Epictetus' Handbook*. In more recent times, the aphorism has been used heavily by philosophers such as Nietzsche and Cioran, both of whom share a number of ideas and perspectives with Gómez Dávila. Nietzsche himself used aphorisms heavily and even went so far as to describe why aphorisms are used – naturally in the form of an aphorism itself – "He who writes in blood and aphorisms does not want to be read, he wants to be learned by heart." In regards to Gómez Dávila this is certainly the case, for he himself stated that aphorisms are like seeds containing the promise of "infinite consequences." Thus, with a short but highly memorable sentence, an idea is planted in the mind of the reader, an idea that hopefully sprouts action, and with it consequences. Similarly in *Notas*, he stated that the only two "tolerable" ways to write were a long, leisurely style, and a short, elliptical style - since he did not think himself capable of the long, leisurely style, he opted for aphorisms. As indicated above however, Gómez Dávila's use of the aphorism is not merely a stylistic reference; these short but effective phrases are part of his 'reactionary' tactic, which he hurls like bombs into readers minds – where they either detonate or take root, sprouting into the 'consequences' their author hoped for. In his own words, he describes his use of aphorisms:

> [to] write the second way is to grab the item in its most abstract form, when he is born, or when he dies leaving a pure schema. The idea here is a cross burning, a light bulb. Endless consequences of it will come, not yet but [a] germ, and promise themselves enclosed. Whoever writes well but not touching the surface of the idea, [there] a diamond lasts. The ideas and plays extend the air space. Their relationships are secret, [their] roots hidden. The thought that unites and leads is not revealed in their work, but their fruits [are] unleashed on archipelagos that crop alone in an unknown sea.[1]

According to Gómez Dávila, in the modern era the reactionary cannot hope to formulate arguments that will convince his opponent, because he does not share any assumptions with his opponent. Moreover, even if the reactionary could argue from certain shared assumptions, modern man's dogmatism prevents him from listening to different opinions and ideas. Faced with this situation, the reactionary should instead write aphorisms to illicit a response rather than engaging in direct debate. Gómez Dávila compares his aphorisms to shots fired by a guerrilla from behind a thicket on any idea that dares advance along the road. Thus, the reactionary will not convince his opponent, but he may convert him.[2] Furthermore, the aphorisms themselves are

---

[1]Volpi, F., *An Angel Captive in Time*, http://www.nicolasgomezdavila.com/art%C3%ADculos-y-ensayos-sobre-g%C3%B3mez-d%C3%A1vila/
[2]*Why aphorisms*, http://don-colacho.blogspot.com.au/2010/01/brief-overview-of-nicolas-gomez-davilas.html

not written in isolation – when placed together in their context they are equally as informative as any normally composed text could hope to be.

Another function that Gómez Dávila's aphorisms served was, as their Spanish title (*Escolios a un Texto Implícito*) suggests, as notes on books he had read. The Spanish word *escolio* comes from the Greek σχόλιον (*scholion*). This word is used to describe the annotations made by ancient and medieval scribes and students in the margins of their texts. Many of these aphorisms may therefore be allusions to other works. They constitute the briefest of summaries of books he read and conclusions he had drawn from these works or judgments on these texts.[3]

Gómez Dávila was a truly devout Christian, and his strand of religious thought is deeply entwined with his ideas on politics, democracy and society as a whole. This is a central concept in understanding Gómez Dávila's work. However, not all of his thoughts resonated with other religious thinkers of his era, for he realised that his contemporaries were incapable of revitalising either Christianity or Catholicism and thus were not able to ensure the survival of the church in the modern era. Not only did this aggravate some of his fellow Catholics, they also were wary of Gómez Dávila due to his appreciation of authors such as such as Nietzsche and Heidegger, who are not usually regarded as being affable to Christianity.

In regards to the way religion is combined with his political thought, Gómez Dávila, interprets democracy as "less a political fact than a metaphysical perversion" and is a harsh critic of the ideology. He defines democracy as "an *anthropotheist* religion," which he believes is a methodology that seeks to elevate the common man to a plane above God – which he believes to be a dangerous and unprecedented level of religious anthropocentricism. Though this may sound odd at

---

[3]*Why aphorisms?*, http://don-colacho.blogspot.com.au/2010/01/brief-overview-of-nicolas-gomez-davilas.html

first, Gómez Dávila is by no means the only author who has claimed that democracy incorporates a religious element into it, and even some contemporary political scientists have asserted that democracy functions as a political religion. Gómez Dávila interpreted the vital sign of democracy being a political religion as the modern state's hostility to traditional religions, which he believed was because a true religious authority was capable of challenging a government – thus the power of religion has to be curbed in order for the government to have full, unmediated control of the people – and as a consequence of this a democracy had to replace religion by adopting 'quasi-religious' elements. It is in this light, that contrary to public opinion, Gómez Dávila does not see democracy as a promise of liberation; on the contrary to him democracy represents a loss of freedom. Since democracy has achieved hegemony, spiritual and cultural matters have become secondary to politics, and today when a citizen is branded as a 'heretic' is not because of his rejection of a religion, but because they dare to question the controlling political regime. In this regard, Gómez Dávila questions democracy, but he should be regarded as a critic and not an opponent, for as mentioned earlier Gómez Dávila had no interest in a political agenda. To Gómez Dávila, democracy was a political religion that encouraged the exaltation of the cult of individualism to a dangerous status, which set an individual on a undeserved plateau above God and eroded genuine metaphysical belief but replaced it with nothing substantial. However he was not a blind devotee or fundamentalist either, for Gómez Dávila was also a powerful critic of the Church as well as democracy.

Another feature at play within Gómez Dávila's writing is that he believes equality to be a social construct of modernity – whilst equality levels the playing field for some individuals, for others it hobbles them. Effectively, it creates a mythical average citizen who does not in actuality exist, raising one individual to an elevated position and demoting another. Rather than recognising individual qualities and merits, it removes all hierarchies – not only the negative hierarchies, but also the positive ones. All variation is lost and replaced by the 'myth of the average' – and if Gómez Dávila's interpretation of democracy as a political religion is correct, it then denounces religion and evaluates the mythical 'average citizen' to a theoretical level of freedom wherein the 'average citizen' is a substitute for the very pinnacle of the religious hierarchy – God. Thus, Gómez Dávila criticises democracy because it seeks to replace the sacred with the average and mundane man. And because democracy replaces religion, it is for this reason that criticism of democracy is the taboo of the West, and the modern equivalent to heresy. Thus, the modern ideologies such as liberalism, democracy, and socialism, were the main targets of Gómez Dávila's criticism, because the world influenced by these ideologies appeared to him decadent and corrupt.

In order to critique ideas, Gómez Dávila created the figure of the 'reactionary' as his unmistakable literary mask which he developed into a distinctive type of thinking about the modern world as such. This is explained in *The Authentic Reactionary*, which refers to one of his most well-known works, *El reaccionario auténtico*, originally published in Revista Universidad de Antioquia 240 (April-June 1995), 16–19. By adopting this label, Gómez Dávila is defining himself as one who sits in opposition. This is not simply a matter of placing Gómez Dávila into a neat political pigeon hole for clearly defined and organised policies – because he turned down prestigious political positions, and certainly didn't intend to advocate any political platforms in his literary work. The reactionary is for him not at all a political activist who wants to restore old conditions, but rather a "passenger who suffers a shipwreck with dignity"; the reactionary is "that fool, who possesses the vanity to judge history, and the immorality to come to terms with it."[4] He did not mean to identify himself exclusively with a narrow political position. In several aphorisms, he acknowledged that there is no possibility of reversing the course of history. Rather, the reactionary's task is to be the guardian of heritages, even the heritage of revolutionaries. This certainly does not mean that Gómez Dávila made his peace with democracy; all it means is that he also did not

---

[4] *The Last Reactionary*, http://don-colacho.blogspot.com.au/2010/01/authentic-reactionary.html.

allow himself to be deluded by promises of the restoration of the old order.[5] As we see below;

> The existence of the authentic reactionary is usually a scandal to the progressive. His presence causes a vague discomfort. In the face of the reactionary attitude the progressive experiences a slight scorn, accompanied by surprise and restlessness. In order to soothe his apprehensions, the progressive is in the habit of interpreting this unseasonable and shocking attitude as a guise for self-interest or as a symptom of stupidity; but only the journalist, the politician, and the fool are not secretly flustered before the tenacity with which the loftiest intelligences of the West, for the past one hundred fifty years, amass objections against the modern world.[6]

In this regard Gómez Dávila does not seek to eliminate the concept we know of as 'modernity', which he sees as an impossible task. Instead he provides a criticism of modernity, disputing that it is natural and that it leads to a false conception of progress. The illusionary doctrine of progress, to Gómez Dávila's way of thinking is a myth which has been deployed to help enslave workers to capitalism and industrial society, by effectively manipulating the population to believe that they helping to make the world a better place, when effectively the real event that is taking place is that they are only serving to make capitalism and consumerism more efficient. The illusion of progress acts as a placebo effect to make the citizens feel better about themselves in a world where god and religion has long since perished, replaced by blind faith in the power of the state. "In order to heal the patient, which it wounded in the 19th century, industrial society had to numb his mind [to pain] in the 20th century."[7]

By defending cultural and spiritual heritage, however, Gómez Dávila is not advocating a return to the past – rather he is strategically

---

[5] *What is a reactionary?* http://don-colacho.blogspot.com.au/2010/01/brief-overview-of-nicolas-gomez-davilas.html.
[6] Gómez Dávila, N., *The Authentic Reactionary.*
[7] Ibid.

deploying this as a method to cut ties with the present and create a different future, for in his own words: "To innovate without breaking a tradition we must free ourselves from our immediate predecessors linking us to our remote predecessors".[8] Gómez Dávila believes that "The modern world resulted from the confluence of three independent causal series: population growth, democratic propaganda, [and] the industrial revolution" (*Successive Scholia*, 161). This in turn led to further developments and propaganda which effectively restructured traditional belief and "replaced the myth of a bygone golden age of a future with the plastic age" (*Scholia II*, 88) leading us to a world where consumerism eventually will replace both religion and politics - "The Gospels and the Communist Manifesto pale, the future is in the hands of Coca-Cola and pornography" (*Successive Scholia*, 181).

Therefore Gómez Dávila's stance, through dispersed through an assortment of brief aphorisms, becomes much more perceptible to the casual reader in light of *The Authentic Reactionary*, which for English readers (who as yet are not able to read all of his writing in translation) becomes a pivotal key in understanding Gómez Dávila's work. The reactionary does not act in isolation from history and modernity, rather he seeks to challenge what he perceives as a false doctrine of progress and looks back in retrospect not to recreate the ancient past, but rather to generate ideas which link modernity to tradition, in order to create real progress by offering an alternative to the current regime of mass consumerism, capitalism and other destructive political ideologies. It is incorrect to locate Gómez Dávila in any existing political paradigm, because there is simply nothing which matches his core ideas...and as such he is correctly identified as what he labelled himself – a 'reactionary'. His reactionary stance comes close to touching on the topics at the core of writers such as Guénon and Evola, but in regard to linking spiritual and cultural decline to political origins, he actually goes further beyond their ideas to suggest that as an evitable side product of consumerism, destroying

---

[8]Duke, O. T., <u>Nicolás Gómez Dávila: Passion of Anachronism</u>, in *Cultural and Bibliographical Bulletin*, Issue 40. Volume XXXII, 1997.

belief in a higher power or God would benefit capitalism and help corporations control the people by encouraging self-indulgent attitudes. Thus politics replaces spirituality, and the citizen replaces god with disguised worship of the state, who in turn rewards them with consumerism. The authentic reactionary is someone who is aware of problems like this in society and provides an intellectual critique of the system whilst remaining aloof from it:

> History for the reactionary is a tatter, torn from man's freedom, fluttering in the breath of destiny. The reactionary cannot be silent because his liberty is not merely a sanctuary where man escapes from deadening routine and takes refuge in order to be his own master. In the free act the reactionary does not just take possession of his essence. Liberty is not an abstract possibility of choosing among known goods, but rather the concrete condition in which we are granted the possession of new goods. Freedom is not a momentary judgment between conflicting instincts, but rather the summit from which man contemplates the ascent of new stars among the luminous dust of the starry sky. Liberty places man among prohibitions that are not physical and imperatives that are not vital. The free moment dispels the unreal brightness of the day, in order that the motionless universe that slides its fleeting lights over the shuddering of our flesh might rise up on the horizon of the soul.[9]

The soul of Nicolás Gómez Dávila, the authentic reactionary, departed from his flesh in his beloved library on the eve of his 81st birthday, on May 17, 1994. Though achieving fame in Columbia, where his works are well read today, Gómez Dávila remains largely unread in the Occident. Whilst his writing achieved some popularity in Germany, much of it remains untranslated for English readers, which prevents his writing from reaching a wider audience. Hopefully a new generation of authors will appear to pick up the challenge of translating Gómez Dávila's writing and help him achieve the recognition he deserves as a

---

[9] Gómez Dávila, N., *The Authentic Reactionary*.

thinker and philosopher.

Main Works

Escolios a Un Texto Implicito: Obra Completa. Nicolas Gomez Davila, Franco Volpi.
July 2006.Villegas Editores.
Notas I, Mexico 1954 (new edition Bogotá 2003).
Textos I, Bogotá 1959 (new edition Bogotá 2002).
Sucesivos escolios a un texto implícito, Santafé de Bogotá 1992 (new edition Barcelona 2002).
Escolios a un texto implícito. Selección, Bogotá 2001.
El reaccionario auténtico, in *Revista de la Universidad de Antioquia,* Nr. 240 (April–June 1995), p. 16-19.
De iure, in *Revista del Colegio Mayor de Nuestra Senora del Rosario 81.* Jg., Nr. 542 (April–June 1988), p. 67-85.
Nuevos escolios a un texto implícito, 2 volumes, Bogotá 1986.
Escolios a un texto implícito, 2 volumes, Bogotá 1977.

THE EXALTATION OF FRIEDRICH NIETZSCHE

OTTO HELLER

In these embattled times it is perfectly natural to expect from any discourse on Nietzsche's philosophy first of all a statement concerning the relation of that troublesome genius to the origins of the war; and this demand prompts a few candid words on that aspect of the subject at the start.

The public has been persistently taught by the press to think of Friedrich Nietzsche mainly as the powerful promoter of a systematic national movement of the German people for the conquest of the world. But there is strong and definite internal evidence in the writings of Nietzsche against the assumption that he intentionally aroused a spirit of war or aimed in any way at the world-wide preponderance of Germany's type of civilization. Nietzsche had a temperamental loathing for everything that is brutal, a loathing which was greatly intensified by his personal contact with the horrors of war while serving as a military nurse in the campaign of 1870. If there were still any one senseless enough to plead the erstwhile popular cause of Pan-Germanism, he would be likely to find more support for his argument in the writings of the de-gallicized Frenchman, Count Joseph Arthur Gobineau, or of the germanized Englishman, Houston Stewart Chamberlain, than in those of the "hermit of Maria-Sils," who does not even suggest, let alone advocate, German world-predominance in a single line of all his writings. To couple Friedrich Nietzsche with Heinrich von Treitschke as the latter's fellow herald of German ascendancy is truly preposterous. Treitschke himself was bitterly and irreconcilably set against the creator of Zarathustra,[1] in whom ever since "Unzeitgemässe Betrachtungen" he had divined "the good

---

[1] As is convincingly pointed out in a footnote of J. A. Cramb's *Germany and England.*

European" - which to the author of the *Deutsche Geschichte* meant the bad Prussian, and by consequence the bad German.

As a consummate individualist and by the same token a cosmopolite to the full, Nietzsche was the last removed from national, or strictly speaking even from racial, jingoism. Even the imputation of ordinary patriotic sentiments would have been resented by him as an insult, for such sentiments were to him a sure symptom of that gregarious disposition which was so utterly abhorrent to his feelings. In his German citizenhood he took no pride whatsoever. On every occasion that offered he vented in mordant terms his contempt for the country of his birth, boastfully proclaiming his own derivation from alien stock. He bemoaned his fate of having to write for Germans; averring that people who drank beer and smoked pipes were hopelessly incapable of understanding him. Of this extravagance in denouncing his countrymen the following account by one of his keenest American interpreters gives a fair idea.

No epithet was too outrageous, no charge was too farfetched, no manipulation or interpretation of evidence was too daring to enter into his ferocious indictment. He accused the Germans of stupidity, superstitiousness, and silliness; of a chronic weakness of dodging issues, a fatuous 'barn-yard' and 'green-pasture' contentment, of yielding supinely to the commands and exactions of a clumsy and unintelligent government; of degrading education to the low level of mere cramming and examination passing; of a congenital inability to understand and absorb the culture of other peoples, and particularly the culture of the French; of a boorish bumptiousness, and an ignorant, ostrichlike complacency; of a systematic hostility to men of genius, whether in art, science, or philosophy; of a slavish devotion to the two great European narcotics, alcohol and Christianity; of a profound beeriness, a spiritual dyspepsia, a puerile mysticism, an old-womanish pettiness, and an ineradicable liking for the obscure, evolving, crepuscular, damp, and shrouded.[2]

---

[2]Mencken, H. L., "The Mailed Fist and Its Prophet." *Atlantic Monthly*, November,

It certainly requires a violent twist of logic to hold this catalogue of invectives responsible for the transformation of a sluggish and indolent bourgeoisie into a "Volk in Waffen" unified by an indomitable and truculent rapacity. Neither should Nietzsche's general condemnation of mild and tender forbearance - on the ground that it blocks the purpose of nature - be interpreted as a call to universal militancy. By his ruling it is only supermen that are privileged to carry their will through. But undeniably he does teach that the world belongs to the strong. They may grab it at any temporary loss to the common run of humanity and, if need be, with sanguinary force, since their will is, ulteriorly, identical with the cosmic purpose.

Of course this is preaching war of some sort, but Nietzsche was not in favor of war on ethnic or ethical grounds, like that fanatical militarist, General von Bernhardi, whom the great mass of his countrymen in the time before the war would have bluntly rejected as their spokesman. Anyway, Nietzsche did not mean to encourage Germany to subjugate the rest of the world. He even deprecated her victory in the bloody contest of 1870, because he thought that it had brought on a form of material prosperity of which internal decay and the collapse of intellectual and spiritual ideals were the unfortunate concomitants. At the same time, the universal decrepitude prevented the despiser of his own people from conceiving a decided preference for some other country. He held that all European nations were progressing in the wrong direction, the deadweight of exaggerated and misshapen materialism dragged them back and down. English life he deemed almost irredeemably clogged by utilitarianism. Even France, the only modern commonwealth credited by Nietzsche with an indigenous culture, was governed by what he stigmatizes as the life philosophy of the shopkeeper. Nietzsche is destitute of national ideals. In fact he never thinks in terms of politics. He aims to be "a good European, not a good German." In his aversion to the extant order of society he never for a moment advocates, like Rousseau or Tolstoy, a breach with civilization. Cataclysmic changes through anarchy, revolution,

---

1914.

and war were repugnant to his ideals of culture. For two thousand years the races of Europe had toiled to humanize themselves, school their character, equip their minds, refine their tastes. Could any sane reformer have calmly contemplated the possible engulfment in another Saturnian age of the gains purchased by that enormous expenditure of human labor? According to Nietzsche's conviction, the new dispensation could not be entered in a book of blank pages. A higher civilization could only be reared upon a lower. So it seems that he is quite wrongly accused of having been an "accessory before the deed," in any literal or legal sense, to the stupendous international struggle witnessed today. And we may pass on to consider in what other way he was a vital factor of modern social development. For whatever we may think of the political value of his teachings, it is impossible to deny their arousing and inspiriting effect upon the intellectual, moral, and artistic faculties of his epoch and ours.

*****

It should be clearly understood that the significance of Nietzsche for our age is not to be explained by any weighty discovery in the realm of knowledge. Nietzsche's merit consists not in any unriddling of the universe by a metaphysical key to its secrets, but rather in the diffusion of a new intellectual light elucidating human consciousness in regard to the purpose and the end of existence. Nietzsche has no objective truths to teach, indeed he acknowledges no truth other than subjective. Nor does he put any faith in bare logic, but on the contrary pronounces it one of mankind's greatest misfortunes. His argumentation is not sustained and progressive, but desultory, impressionistic, and freely repetitional; slashing aphorism is its most effective tool. And so, in the sense of the schools, he is not a philosopher at all; quite the contrary, an implacable enemy of the métier. And yet the formative and directive influence of his vaticinations, enunciated with tremendous spiritual heat and lofty gesture, has been very great. His conception of life has acted upon the generation as a moral intoxicant of truly incalculable strength.

All his published work, amounting to eighteen volumes, though flagrantly irrational, does contain a perfectly coherent doctrine. Only, it is a doctrine to whose core mere peripheric groping will never negotiate the approach. Its essence must be caught by flashlike seizure and cannot be conveyed except to minds of more than the average imaginative sensibility. For its central ideas relate to the remotest ultimates, and its dominant prepossession, the *Overman*, is, in the final reckoning, the creature of a Utopian fancy. To be more precise, Nietzsche extorts from the Darwinian theory of selection a set of amazing connotations by means of the simultaneous shift from the biological to the poetic sphere of thought and from the averagely socialized to an uncompromisingly self-centred attitude of mind. This doubly eccentric position is rendered feasible for him by a whole-souled indifference to exact science and an intense contempt for the practical adjustments of life. He is, first and last, an imaginative schemer, whose visions are engendered by inner exuberance; the propelling power of his philosophy being an intense temperamental enthusiasm at one and the same time lyrically sensitive and dramatically impassioned. It is these qualities of soul that made his utterance ring with the force of a high moral challenge. All the same, he was not any more original in his ethics than in his theory of knowledge. In this field also his receptive mind threw itself wide open to the flow of older influences which it encountered. The religion of personal advantage had had many a prophet before Nietzsche. Among the older writers, Machiavelli was its weightiest champion. In Germany, Nietzsche's immediate predecessor was "Max Stirner",[3] and as regards foreign thinkers, Nietzsche declared as late as 1888 that to no other writer of his own century did he feel himself so closely allied by the ties of congeniality as to Ralph Waldo Emerson.

The most superficial acquaintance with these writers shows that Nietzsche is held responsible for certain revolutionary notions of which he by no means was the originator. Of the connection of his doctrine with the maxims of *The Prince* and of *The Ego and His Own*

---

[3]His real name was Kaspar Schmidt; he lived from 1806-1856.

(*Der Einzige und sein Eigentum*)[4] nothing further need be said than that to them Nietzsche owes, directly or indirectly, the principle of "non-morality." However, he does not employ the same strictly intellectual methods. They were logicians rather than moralists, and their ruler-man is in the main a construction of cold reasoning, while the ruler-man of Nietzsche is the vision of a genius whose eye looks down a much longer perspective than is accorded to ordinary mortals. That a far greater affinity of temper should have existed between Nietzsche and Emerson than between him and the two classic non-moralists, must bring surprise to the many who have never recognized the Concord Sage as an exponent of unfettered individualism. Yet in fact Emerson goes to such an extreme of individualism that the only thing that has saved his memory from anathema is that he has not many readers in his after-times, and these few do not always venture to understand him. And Emerson, though in a different way from Nietzsche's, was also a rhapsodist. In his poetry, where he articulates his meaning with far greater unrestraint than in his prose, we find without any difficulty full corroboration of his spiritual kinship with Nietzsche. For instance, where may we turn in the works of the latter for a stronger statement of the case of Power versus Pity than is contained in "The World Soul"?

He serveth the servant,
The brave he loves amain,
He kills the cripple and the sick,
And straight begins again;
For gods delight in gods,
And thrust the weak aside,
To him who scorns their charities
Their arms fly open wide.

From such a world-view what moral could proceed more logically than that of Zarathustra: "And him whom ye do not teach to fly, teach - how to fall quicker"?

---

[4]By Machiavelli and Stirner, respectively.

But after all, the intellectual origin of Nietzsche's ideas matters but little. Wheresoever they were derived from, he made them strikingly his own by raising them to the splendid elevation of his thought. And if nevertheless he has failed to take high rank and standing among the sages of the schools, this shortage in his professional prestige is more than counterbalanced by the wide reach of his influence among the laity.

What might the re-classification, or perchance even the re-interpretation, of known facts about life have signified beside Nietzsche's lofty apprehension of the sacredness of life itself? For whatever may be the social menace of his reasoning, his commanding proclamation to an expectant age of the doctrine that Progress means infinite growth towards ideals of perfection has resulted in a singular reanimation of the individual sense of dignity, served as a potent remedy of social dry-rot, and furthered our gradual emergence from the impenetrable darkness of ancestral traditions.

In seeking an adequate explanation of his power over modern minds we readily surmise that his philosophy draws much of its vitality from the system of science that underlies it. And yet while it is true enough that Nietzsche's fundamental thesis is an offshoot of the Darwinian theory, the violent individualism which is the driving principle of his entire philosophy is rather opposed to the general orientation of Darwinism, since that is social. Not to the author of the *Descent of Man* directly is the modern ethical glorification of egoism indebted for its measure of scientific sanction, but to one of his heterodox disciples, namely to the bio-philosopher W. H. Rolph, who in a volume named *Biologic Problems*, with the subtitle, "An Essay in Rational Ethics,"[5] deals definitely with the problem of evolution in its dynamical bearings. The question is raised, Why do the extant types of life ascend toward higher goals, and, on reaching them, progress toward still higher goals, to the end of time? Under the reason as explained by Darwin, should not evolution stop at a definite stage, namely, when

---

[5] *Biologische Probleme, zugleich als Versuch einer rationellen Ethik.* Leipzig, 1882.

the object of the competitive struggle for existence has been fully attained? Self-preservation naturally ceases to act as an incentive to further progress, so soon as the weaker contestants are beaten off the field and the survival of the fittest is abundantly secured. From there on we have to look farther for an adequate causation of the ascent of species. Unless we assume the existence of an absolutistic teleological tendency to perfection, we are logically bound to connect upward development with favorable external conditions. By substituting for the Darwinian "struggle for existence" a new formula: "struggle for surplus," Rolph advances a new fruitful hypothesis. In all creatures the acquisitive cravings exceed the limit of actual necessity. Under Darwin's interpretation of nature, the struggle between individuals of the same species would give way to pacific equilibrium as soon as the bare subsistence were no longer in question. Yet we know that the struggle is unending. The creature appetites are not appeased by a normal sufficiency; on the contrary, "l'appetit vient en mangeant"; the possessive instinct, if not quite insatiable, is at least coextensive with its opportunities for gratification. Whether or not it be true - as Carlyle claims - that, after all, the fundamental question between any two human beings is, "Can I kill thee, or canst thou kill me?" - at any rate in civilized human society the contest is not waged merely for the naked existence, but mainly for life's increments in the form of comforts, pleasures, luxuries, and the accumulation of power and influence; and the excess of acquisition over immediate need goes as a residuum into the structure of civilization. In plain words, then, social progress is pushed on by individual greed and ambition. At this point Rolph rests the case, without entering into the moral implicates of the subject, which would seem to obtrude themselves upon the attention.

Now to a believer in progressive evolution with a strong ethical bent such a theory brings home man's ulterior responsibility for the betterment of life, and therefore acts as a call to his supreme duty of preparing the ground for the arrival of a higher order of beings. The argument seems simple and clinching. Living nature through a long file of species and genera has at last worked up to the homo sapiens who as yet does not even approach the perfection of his own type. Is it a legitimate ambition of the race to mark time on the stand which it has reached and to entrench itself impregnably in its present mediocrity? Nietzsche did not shrink from any of the inferential conclusions logically to be drawn from the biologic argument. If growth is in the purpose of nature, then once we have accepted our chief office in life, it becomes our task to pave the way for a higher genus of man. And the only force that makes with directness for that object is the Will to Power. To foreshadow the resultant human type, Nietzsche resurrected from Goethe's vocabulary the convenient word Übermensch - "Overman."

*****

Any one regarding existence in the light of a stern and perpetual combat is of necessity driven at last to the alternative between making the best of life and making an end of it; he must either seek lasting deliverance from the evil of living or endeavor to wrest from the world by any means at his command the greatest sum of its gratifications. It is serviceable to describe the two frames of mind respectively as the optimistic and the pessimistic. But it would perhaps be hasty to conclude that the first of these attitudes necessarily betokens the greater strength of character.

Friedrich Nietzsche's philosophy sprang from pessimism, yet issued in an optimism of unheard of exaltation; carrying, however, to the end its plainly visible birthmarks. He started out as an enthusiastic disciple of Arthur Schopenhauer; unquestionably the adherence was fixed by his own deep-seated contempt for the complacency of the plebs. But he was bound soon to part company with the grandmaster of pessimism, because he discovered the root of the philosophy of renunciation in that same detestable debility of the will which he deemed responsible for the bovine lassitude of the masses; both pessimism and philistinism came from a lack of vitality, and were symptoms of degeneracy. But before Nietzsche finally rejected Schopenhauer and gave his shocking counterblast to the undermining action of pessimism, he succumbed temporarily to the spell of another gigantic personality. We are not concerned with Richard Wagner's musical influence upon Nietzsche, who was himself a musician of no mean ability; what is to the point here is the prime principle of Wagner's art theory. The key to the Wagnerian theory is found, also, in Schopenhauer's philosophy. Wagner starts from the pessimistic thesis that at the bottom of the well of life lies nothing but suffering - hence living is utterly undesirable. In one of his letters to Franz Liszt he names as the duplex root of his creative genius the longing for love and the yearning for death. On another occasion, he confesses his own emotional nihilism in the following summary of *Tristan und Isolde*: "Sehnsucht, Sehnsucht, unstillbares, ewig neu sich gebärendes Verlangen - Schmachten und Dursten; einzige Erlösung: Tod, Sterben, Untergehen - Nichtmehrerwachen."[6] But from the boundless ocean of sorrow there is a refuge. It was Wagner's fundamental dogma that through the illusions of art the individual is enabled to rise above the hopelessness of the realities into a new cosmos replete with supreme satisfactions. Man's mundane salvation therefore depends upon the ministrations of art and his own artistic sensitiveness. The glorification of genius is a natural corollary of such a belief.

Nietzsche in one of his earliest works examines Wagner's theory and amplifies it by a rather casuistic interpretation of the evolution of art. After raising the question, How did the Greeks contrive to dignify and ennoble their national existence? He points, by way of an illustrative answer, not perchance to the Periclean era, but to a far more primitive epoch of Hellenic culture, when a total oblivion of the actual world and a transport into the realm of imagination was universally possible. He explains the trance as the effect of intoxication - primarily in the current literal sense of the word. Such was the significance of the cult of Dionysos. "Through singing and dancing," claims Nietzsche, "man manifests himself as member of a higher community. Walking and talking he has unlearned, and is in a fair way to dance up

---

[6]"Longing, longing, unquenchable desire, reproducing itself forever anew - thirst and drought; sole deliverance: death, dissolution, extinction - and no awaking."

into the air." That this supposititious Dionysiac phase of Hellenic culture was in turn succeeded by more rational stages, in which the impulsive flow of life was curbed and dammed in by operations of the intellect, is not permitted by Nietzsche to invalidate the argument. By his arbitrary reading of ancient history he was, at first, disposed to look to the forthcoming Universal-Kunstwerk[7] as the complete expression of a new religious spirit and as the adequate lever of a general uplift of mankind to a state of bliss. But the typical disparity between Wagner and Nietzsche was bound to alienate them. Wagner, despite all appearance to the contrary, is inherently democratic in his convictions - his earlier political vicissitudes amply confirm this view - and fastens his hope for the elevation of humanity through art upon the sort of genius in whom latent popular forces might combine to a new summit. Nietzsche on the other hand represents the extreme aristocratic type, both in respect of thought and of sentiment."I do not wish to be confounded with and mistaken for these preachers of equality," says he. "For within me justice saith: men are not equal." His ideal is a hero of coercive personality, dwelling aloft in solitude, despotically bending the gregarious instincts of the common crowd to his own higher purposes by the dominating force of his Will to Might.

The concept of the Overman rests, as has been shown, upon a fairly solid substructure of plausibility, since at the bottom of the author's reasoning lies the notion that mankind is destined to outgrow its current status; the thought of a humanity risen to new and wondrous heights of power over nature is not necessarily unscientific for being supremely imaginative. The Overman, however, cannot be produced ready made, by any instantaneous process; he must be slowly and persistently willed into being, through love of the new ideal which he is to embody: "All great Love," speaketh Zarathustra, "seeketh to create what it loveth. Myself I sacrifice into my love, and my neighbor as myself, thus runneth the speech of all creators." Only the fixed conjoint purpose of many generations of aspiring men will be able to create the Overman. "Could you create a God? Then be silent concerning

---

[7]Work of all arts.

all gods! But ye could very well create Beyond-man. Not yourselves perhaps, my brethren! But ye could create yourselves into fathers and fore-fathers of Beyond-man; and let this be your best creating. But all creators are hard."

Nietzsche's startlingly heterodox code of ethics coheres organically with the Overman hypothesis, and so understood is certain to lose some of its aspect of absurdity. The will, as we have seen, must be taught to aim at the Overman. But the volitional faculty of the generation, according to Nietzsche, is so debilitated as to be utterly inadequate to its office. Hence, advisedly to stimulate and strengthen the enfeebled will power of his fellow men is the most imperative and immediate task of the radical reformer. Once the power of willing, as such, shall have been - regardless of the worthiness of its object - brought back to active life, it will be feasible to give the Will to Might a direction towards objects of the highest moral grandeur.

Unfortunately for the race as a whole, the throng is ineligible for partnership in the auspicious scheme of co-operative procreation: which fact necessitates a segregative method of breeding. The Overman can only be evolved by an ancestry of master-men, who must be secured to the race by a rigid application of eugenic standards, particularly in the matter of mating. Of marriage, Nietzsche has this definition: "Marriage, so call I the will of two to create one who is more than they who created him." For the bracing of the weakened will-force of the human breed it is absolutely essential that master-men, the potential progenitors of the superman, be left unhampered to the impulse of "living themselves out" (sich auszuleben) - an opportunity of which under the regnant code of morals they are inconsiderately deprived. Since, then, existing dictates and conventions are a serious hindrance to the requisite autonomy of the master-man, their abolishment might be well. Yet on the other hand, it is convenient that the *Vielzuviele*, the "much-too-many," i.e. the despised generality of people, should continue to be governed and controlled by strict rules and regulations, so that the will of the master-folk might the more expeditiously be wrought. Would it not, then, be an efficacious compromise to keep the canon of morality in force for the general run, but suspend it for the special benefit of master-men, prospective or full-fledged? From the history of the race Nietzsche draws a warrant for the distinction. His contention is that masters and slaves have never lived up to a single code of conduct. Have not civilizations risen and fallen according as they were shaped by this or that class of nations? History also teaches what disastrous consequences follow the loss of caste. In the case of the Jewish people, the domineering type or morals gave way to the servile as a result of the Babylonian captivity. So long as the Jews were strong, they extolled all manifestations of strength and energy. The collapse of their own strength turned them into apologists of the so-called "virtues" of humility, long-suffering, forgiveness - until, according to the Judæo-Christian code of ethics, being good came to mean being weak. So people may justly be classified into masters and slaves, and history proves that to the strong goes the empire. The ambitions of a nation are a sure criterion of its worth.

I walk through these folk and keep mine eyes open. They have become smaller and are becoming ever smaller. And the reason of that is their doctrine of happiness and virtue.

For they are modest even in their virtue; for they are desirous of ease. But with ease only modest virtue is compatible.

True, in their fashion they learn how to stride and to stride forward. That I call their hobbling. Thereby they become an offense unto every one who is in a hurry.

And many a one strideth on and in doing so looketh backward, with a stiffened neck. I rejoice to run against the stomachs of such.

Foot and eyes shall not lie, nor reproach each other for lying. But there is much lying among small folk.

Some of them will, but most of them are willed merely. Some of them are genuine, but most of them are bad actors.

There are unconscious actors among them, and involuntary actors. The genuine are always rare, especially genuine actors.

Here is little of man; therefore women try to make themselves manly. For only he who is enough of a man will save the woman in woman.

And this hypocrisy I found to be worst among them, that even those who command feign the virtues of those who serve.

'I serve, thou servest, we serve.' Thus the hypocrisy of the rulers prayeth. And, alas, if the highest lord be merely the highest servant!

Alas! the curiosity of mine eye strayed even unto their hypocrisies, and well I divined all their fly-happiness and their humming round window panes in the sunshine.

So much kindness, so much weakness see I. So much justice and sympathy, so much weakness.

Round, honest, and kind are they towards each other, as grains of sand are round, honest, and kind unto grains of sand.

Modestly to embrace a small happiness - they call 'submission'! And therewith they modestly look sideways after a new small happiness.

At bottom they desire plainly one thing most of all: to be hurt by nobody. Thus they oblige all and do well unto them.

But this is cowardice; although it be called 'virtue.'

And if once they speak harshly, these small folk - I hear therein merely their hoarseness. For every draught of air maketh them hoarse.

Prudent are they; their virtues have prudent fingers. But they are lacking in clenched fists; their fingers know not how to hide themselves behind fists.

For them virtue is what maketh modest and tame. Thereby they have made the wolf a dog and man himself man's best domestic animal.

'We put our chair in the midst'- thus saith their simpering unto me - 'exactly as far from dying gladiators as from happy swine.'

This is mediocrity; although it be called moderation.[8]

The only law acknowledged by him who would be a master is the bidding of his own will. He makes short work of every other law. Whatever clogs the flight of his indomitable ambition must be ruthlessly swept aside. Obviously, the enactment of this law that would render the individual supreme and absolute would strike the death-knell for all established forms and institutions of the social body. But such is quite within Nietzsche's intention. They are noxious agencies, ingeniously devised for the enslavement of the will, and the most pernicious among them is the Christian religion, because of the alleged divine sanction conferred by it upon subserviency. Christianity would thwart the supreme will of nature by curbing that lust for domination which the laws of nature as revealed by science sanction, nay prescribe. Nietzsche's ideas on this subject are loudly and over-loudly voiced in *Der Antichrist* (*The Anti-Christ*), written in September 1888 as the first part of a planned treatise in four instalments, entitled *Der Wille zur Macht. Versuch einer Umwertung aller Werte.* (*The Will to Power. An Attempted Transvaluation of All Values.*)

*****

---

[8] *Thus Spake Zarathustra*, p.243-245.

The master-man's will, then, is his only law. That is the essence of *Herrenmoral*. And so the question arises, Whence shall the conscience of the ruler-man derive its distinctions between the Right and the Wrong? The arch-iconoclast brusquely stifles this naïve query beforehand by assuring us that such distinctions in their accepted sense do not exist for personages of that grander stamp. Heedless of the time-hallowed concepts that all men share in common, he enjoins mastermen to take their position uncompromisingly outside the confining area of conventions, in the moral independence that dwells "beyond good and evil." Good and Evil are mere denotations, devoid of any real significance. Right and Wrong are not ideals immutable through the ages, nor even the same at any time in all states of society. They are vague and general notions, varying more or less with the practical exigencies under which they were conceived. What was right for my great-grandfather is not ipso facto right for myself. Hence, the older and better established a law, the more inapposite is it apt to be to the living demands. Why should the ruler-man bow down to outworn statutes or stultify his self-dependent moral sense before the artificial and stupidly uniform moral relics of the dead past? Good is whatever conduces to the increase of my power, evil is whatever tends to diminish it! Only the weakling and the hypocrite will disagree.

Unmistakably this is a straightout application of the "pragmatic" criterion of truth. Nietzsche's unconfessed and cautious imitators, who call themselves pragmatists, are not bold enough to follow their own logic from the cognitive sphere to the moral. They stop short of the natural conclusion to which their own premises lead. Morality is necessarily predicated upon specific notions of truth. So if Truth is an alterable and shifting concept, must not morality likewise be variable? The pragmatist might just as well come out at once into the broad light and frankly say: "Laws do not interest me in the abstract, or for the sake of their general beneficence; they interest me only in so far as they affect me. Therefore I will make, interpret, and abolish them to suit myself."

To Nietzsche the "quest of truth" is a palpable evasion. Truth is merely a means for the enhancement of my subjective satisfaction. It makes not a whit of difference whether an opinion or a judgment satisfies this or that scholastic definition. I call true and good that which furthers my welfare and intensifies my joy in living; and - to vindicate my self-gratification as a form, indeed the highest, of "social service" - the desirable thing is that which matters for the improvement of the human stock and thereby speeds the advent of the Superman. "Oh," exclaims Zarathustra, "that ye would understand my word: Be sure to do whatever ye like - but first of all be such as can will! Be sure to love your neighbor as yourself - but first of all be such as love themselves - as love themselves with great love, with contempt. Thus speaketh Zarathustra, the ungodly."

By way of throwing some light upon this phase of Nietzsche's moral philosophy, it may be added that ever since 1876 he was an assiduous student of Herbert Spencer, with whose theory of social evolution he was first made acquainted by his friend, Paul Rée, who in two works of his own, *Psychologic Observations*, (1875), and *On the Origin of Moral Sentiments*, (1877), had elaborated upon the Spencerian theory about the genealogy of morals.

The best known among all of Nietzsche's works, *Also Sprach Zarathustra* (*Thus Spake Zarathustra*), is the Magna Charta of the new moral emancipation. It was composed during a sojourn in southern climes between 1883 and 1885, during the convalescence from a nervous collapse, when after a long and critical depression his spirit was recovering its accustomed resilience. Nietzsche wrote his magnum opus in solitude, in the mountains and by the sea. His mind always was at its best in settings of vast proportions, and in this particular work there breathes an exaltation that has scarcely its equal in the world's literature. Style and diction in their supreme elation suit the lofty fervor of the sentiment. From the feelings, as a fact, this great rhapsody flows, and to the feelings it makes its appeal; its extreme fascination must be lost upon those who only know how to "listen to reason." The wondrous plastic beauty of the language, along with the high emotional pitch of its message, render

"Zarathustra" a priceless poetic monument; indeed its practical effect in chastening and rejuvenating German literary diction can hardly be overestimated. Its value as a philosophic document is much slighter. It is not even organized on severely logical lines. On the contrary, the four component parts are but brilliant variations upon a single generic theme, each in a different clef, but harmoniously united by the incremental ecstasy of the movement. The composition is free from monotony, for down to each separate aphorism every part of it has its special lyric nuance. The whole purports to convey in the form of discourse the prophetic message of Zarathustra, the hermit sage, an idealized self-portrayal of the author.

In the first book the tone is calm and temperate. Zarathustra exhorts and instructs his disciples, rails at his adversaries, and discloses his superiority over them. In the soliloquies and dialogues of the second book he reveals himself more fully and freely as the Superman. The third book contains the meditations and rhapsodies of Zarathustra now dwelling wholly apart from men, his mind solely occupied with thought about the Eternal Return of the Present. In the fourth book he is found in the company of a few chosen spirits whom he seeks to imbue with his perfected doctrine. In this final section of the work the deep lyric current is already on the ebb; it is largely supplanted by irony, satire, sarcasm, even buffoonery, all of which are resorted to for the pitiless excoriation of our type of humanity, deemed decrepit by the Sage. The author's intention to present in a concluding fifth division the dying Zarathustra pronouncing his benedictions upon life in the act of quitting it was not to bear fruit.

"Zarathustra" - Nietzsche's terrific assault upon the fortifications of our social structure - is too easily mistaken by facile cavilers for the ravings of an unsound and desperate mind. To a narrow and superficial reading, it exhibits itself as a wholesale repudiation of all moral responsibility and a maniacal attempt to subvert human civilization for the exclusive benefit of the "glorious blonde brute, rampant with greed for victory and spoil." Yet those who care to look more deeply will detect beneath this chimerical contempt of conventional regulations no want of a high-minded philanthropic purpose, provided they have the vision necessary to comprehend a love of man oriented by such extremely distant perspectives. At all events they will discover that in this rebellious propaganda an advancing line of life is firmly traced out. The indolent and thoughtless may indeed be horrified by the appalling dangers of the gospel according to Zarathustra. But in reality there is no great cause for alarm. Society may amply rely upon its agencies, even in these stupendous times of universal war, for protection from any disastrous organic dislocations incited by the teachings of Zarathustra, at least so far as the immediate future is concerned - in which alone society appears to be interested. Moreover, our apprehensions are appeased by the sober reflection that by its plain unfeasibleness the whole supersocial scheme of Nietzsche is reduced to colossal absurdity. Its limitless audacity defeats any formulation of its "war aims." For what compels an ambitious imagination to arrest itself at the goal of the superman? Why should it not run on beyond that first terminal? In one of Mr. G. K. Chesterton's labored extravaganzas a grotesque sort of super-overman succeeds in going beyond unreason when he contrives this lucid self-definition: "I have gone where God has never dared to go. I am above the silly supermen as they are above mere men. Where I walk in the Heavens, no man has walked before me, and I am alone in a garden." It is enough to make one gasp and then perhaps luckily recall Goethe's consoling thought that under the care of Providence the trees will not grow into the heavens. ("Es ist dafür gesorgt, dass die Bäume nicht in den Himmel wachsen.") As matter of fact, the ideas promulgated in *Also Sprach Zarathustra* need inspire no fear of their winning the human race from its venerable idols, despite the fact that the pull of natural laws and of elemental appetites seems to be on their side. The only effect to be expected of such a philosophy is that it will act as an antidote for moral inertia which inevitably goes with the flock-instinct and the lazy reliance on the accustomed order of things.

Nietzsche's ethics are not easy to valuate, since none of their standards are derived from the orthodox canon. His being a truly personalized form of morality, his principles are strictly cognate to his temperament.

To his professed ideals there attaches a definite theory of society. And since his philosophy is consistent in its sincerity, its message is withheld from the man-in-the-street, deemed unworthy of notice, and delivered only to the élite that shall beget the superman. To Nietzsche the good of the greatest number is no valid consideration. The great stupid mass exists only for the sake of an oligarchy by whom it is duly exploited under nature's decree that the strong shall prey upon the weak. Let, then, this favored set further the design of nature by systematically encouraging the elevation of their own type.

*****

We have sought to dispel the fiction about the shaping influence of Nietzsche upon the thought and conduct of his nation, and have accounted for the miscarriage of his ethics by their fantastic impracticability. Yet it has been shown also that he fostered in an unmistakable fashion the class-consciousness of the aristocrat, born or self-appointed. To that extent his influence was certainly malign. Yet doubtless he did perform a service to our age. The specific nature of this service, stated in the fewest words, is that to his great divinatory gift are we indebted for an unprecedented strengthening of our hold upon reality. In order to make this point clear we have to revert once more to Nietzsche's transient intellectual relation to pessimism.

We have seen that the illusionism of Schopenhauer and more particularly of Wagner exerted a strong attraction on his high-strung artistic temperament.

Nevertheless a certain realistic counter-drift to the ultra-romantic tendency of Wagner's theory caused him in the long run to reject the faith in the power of Art to save man from evil. Almost abruptly, his personal affection for the "Master," to whom in his eventual mental eclipse he still referred tenderly at lucid moments, changed to bitter hostility. Henceforth he classes the glorification of Art as one of the three most despicable attitudes of life: Philistinism, Pietism, and

Estheticism, all of which have their origin in cowardice, represent three branches of the ignominious road of escape from the terrors of living. In three extended diatribes Nietzsche denounces Wagner as the archetype of modern decadence; the most violent attack of all is delivered against the point of juncture in which Wagner's art gospel and the Christian religion culminate: the promise of redemption through pity. To Nietzsche's way of thinking pity is merely the coward's acknowledgment of his weakness. For only insomuch as a man is devoid of fortitude in bearing his own sufferings is he unable to contemplate with equanimity the sufferings of his fellow creatures. Since religion enjoins compassion with all forms of human misery, we should make war upon religion. And for the reason that Wagner's crowning achievement, his Parsifal, is a veritable sublimation of Mercy, there can be no truce between its creator and the giver of the counsel: "Be hard!" Perhaps this notorious advice is after all not as ominous as it sounds. It merely expresses rather abruptly Nietzsche's confidence in the value of self-control as a means of discipline. If you have learned calmly to see others suffer, you are yourself able to endure distress with manful composure. "Therefore I wash the hand which helped the sufferer; therefore I even wipe my soul." But, unfortunately, such is the frailty of human nature that it is only one step from indifference about the sufferings of others to an inclination to exploit them or even to inflict pain upon one's neighbors for the sake of personal gain of one sort or another.

Why so hard? Said once the charcoal unto the diamond, are we not near relations?

Why so soft? O my brethren, thus I ask you. Are ye not my brethren?

Why so soft, so unresisting, and yielding? Why is there so much disavowal and abnegation in your hearts? Why is there so little fate in your looks?

And if ye are not willing to be fates, and inexorable, how could ye conquer with me someday?

And if your hardness would not glance, and cut, and chip into pieces - how could ye create with me some day?

For all creators are hard. And it must seem blessedness unto you to press your hand upon millenniums as upon wax,

Blessedness to write upon the will of millenniums as upon brass -harder than brass, nobler than brass. The noblest only is perfectly hard.

This new table, O my brethren, I put over you: Become hard![9]

The repudiation of Wagner leaves a tremendous void in Nietzsche's soul by depriving his enthusiasm of its foremost concrete object. He loses his faith in idealism. When illusions can bring a man like Wagner to such an odious outlook upon life, they must be obnoxious in themselves; and so, after being subjected to pitiless analysis, they are disowned and turned into ridicule. And now, the pendulum of his zeal having swung from one emotional extreme to the other, the great rhapsodist finds himself temporarily destitute of an adequate theme. However, his fervor does not long remain in abeyance, and soon it is absorbed in a new object. Great as is the move it is logical enough. Since illusions are only a hindrance to the fuller grasp of life which behooves all free spirits, Nietzsche energetically turns from self-deception to its opposite, self-realization. In this new spiritual endeavor he relies far more on intuition than on scientific and metaphysical speculation. From his own stand he is certainly justified in doing this. Experimentation and ratiocination at the best are apt to disassociate individual realities from their complex setting and then proceed to palm them off as illustrations of life, when in truth they are lifeless, artificially preserved specimens.

Encheiresin naturae nennt's die Chemie, spottet ihrer selbst und

---

weiss nicht wie.[10]

Nietzsche's realism, by contrast, goes to the very quick of nature, grasps all the gifts of life, and from the continuous flood of phenomena extracts a rich, full-flavored essence. It is from a sense of gratitude for this boon that he becomes an idolatrous worshiper of experience, "der grosse Jasager," - the great sayer of Yes - and the most stimulating optimist of all ages. To Nietzsche reality is alive as perhaps never to man before. He plunges down to the very heart of things, absorbs their vital qualities and meanings, and having himself learned to draw supreme satisfaction from the most ordinary facts and events, he makes the common marvelous to others, which, as was said by James Russell Lowell, is a true test of genius. No wonder that deification of reality becomes the dominant - motif - in his philosophy. But again that onesided aristocratic strain perverts his ethics. To drain the intoxicating cup at the feast of life, such is the divine privilege not of the common run of mortals but only of the elect. They must not let this or that petty and artificial convention, nor yet this or that moral command or prohibition, restrain them from the exercise of that higher sense of living, but must fully abandon themselves to its joys. "Since man came into existence he hath had too little joy. That alone, my brethren, is our original sin."[11] The "much-too-many" are doomed to inanity by their lack of appetite at the banquet of life:

> Such folk sit down unto dinner and bring nothing with them, not even a good hunger. And now they backbite: "All is vanity!"

> But to eat well and drink well, O my brethren, is, verily, no vain art! Break, break the tables of those who are never joyful![12]

The Will to Live holds man's one chance of this-worldly bliss, and supersedes any care for the remote felicities of any problematic future

---

[10]Goethe's *Faust*, II, ll. 1940-1. Bayard Taylor translates: Encheiresin naturae, this Chemistry names, nor knows how herself she banters and blames!
[11]*Thus Spake Zarathustra*, p.120.
[12]Ibid., p.296, sec. 13.

state. Yet the Nietzschean cult of life is not to be understood by any means as a banal devotion to the pleasurable side of life alone. The true disciple finds in every event, be it happy or adverse, exalting or crushing, the factors of supreme spiritual satisfaction: joy and pain are equally implied in experience, the Will to Live encompasses jointly the capacity to enjoy and to suffer. It may even be paradoxically said that since man owes some of his greatest and most beautiful achievements to sorrow, it must be a joy and a blessing to suffer. The unmistakable sign of heroism is *amor fati*, a fierce delight in one's destiny, hold what it may.

Consequently, the precursor of the superman will be possessed, along with his great sensibility to pleasure, of a capacious aptitude for suffering. "Ye would perchance abolish suffering," exclaims Nietzsche, "and we - it seems that we would rather have it even greater and worse than it has ever been. The discipline of suffering - tragical suffering - know ye not that only this discipline has heretofore brought about every elevation of man?" "Spirit is that life which cutteth into life. By one's own pain one's own knowledge increaseth; knew ye that before? And the happiness of the spirit is this: to be anointed and consecrated by tears as a sacrificial animal; knew ye that before?" And if, then, the tragical pain inherent in life be no argument against Joyfulness, the zest of living can be obscured by nothing save the fear of total extinction.

To the disciple of Nietzsche, by whom every moment of his existence is realized as a priceless gift, the thought of his irrevocable separation from all things is unbearable. "'Was this life?' I shall say to Death. 'Well, then, once more!'" And - to paraphrase Nietzsche's own simile - the insatiable witness of the great tragi-comedy, spectator and participant at once, being loath to leave the theatre, and eager for a repetition of the performance, shouts his endless encore, praying fervently that in the constant repetition of the performance not a single detail of the action be omitted. The yearning for the endlessness not of life at large, not of life on any terms, but of this my life with its ineffable wealth of rapturous moments, works up the extreme optimism of Nietzsche to its stupendous a priori notion of infinity, expressed in the name *die ewige Wiederkehr* ("Eternal Recurrence"). It is a staggeringly imaginative concept, formed apart from any evidential grounds, and yet fortified with a fair amount of logical armament. The universe is imagined as endless in time, although its material contents are not equally conceived as limitless. Since, consequently, there must be a limit to the possible variety in the arrangement and sequence of the sum total of data, even as in the case of a kaleidoscope, the possibility of variegations is not infinite. The particular co-ordination of things in the universe, say at this particular moment, is bound to recur again and again in the passing of the eons. But under the nexus of cause and effect the resurgence of the past from the ocean of time is not accidental nor is the configuration of things haphazard, as is true in the case of the kaleidoscope; rather, history, in the most inclusive acceptation of the term, is predestined to repeat itself; this happens through the perpetual progressive resurrection of its particles. It is then to be assumed that any aspect which the world has ever presented must have existed innumerable millions of times before, and must recur with eternal periodicity. That the deterministic strain in this tremendous *Vorstellung* of a cyclic rhythm throbbing in the universe entangles its author's fanatical belief in evolution in a rather serious self-contradiction, does not detract from its spiritual lure, nor from its wide suggestiveness, however incapable it may be of scientific demonstration.

From unfathomed depths of feeling wells up the pæan of the prophet of the life intense.

O Mensch! Gib Acht!
Was spricht die tiefe Mitternacht?
Ich schlief, ich schlief,
Aus tiefem Traum bin ich erwacht:
Die Welt ist tief,
Und tiefer als der Tag gedacht.
Tief ist ihr Weh,
Lust - tiefer noch als Herzeleid:

Weh spricht: Vergeh!
Doch alle Lust will Ewigkeit -
Will tiefe, tiefe Ewigkeit!

O man! Lose not sight!
What saith the deep midnight?
"I lay in sleep, in sleep;
From deep dream I woke to light.
The world is deep,
And deeper than ever day though! it might.
Deep is its woe,
And deeper still than woe - delight."
Saith woe: "Pass, go!
Eternity's sought by all delight,
Eternity deep - by all delight.

A timid heart may indeed recoil from the iron necessity of reliving
ad infinitum its woeful terrestrial fate. But the prospect can hold no
terror for the heroic soul by whose fiat all items of experience have
assumed important meanings and values. He who has cast in his lot
with Destiny in spontaneous submission to all its designs, cannot
but revere and cherish his own fate as an integral part of the grand
unalterable fatality of things.

*****

If this crude presentment of Friedrich Nietzsche's doctrine has not
entirely failed of its purpose, the leitmotifs of that doctrine will have
been readily referred by the reader to their origin; they can be subsumed
under that temperamental category which is more or less accurately
defined as the romantic. Glorification of violent passion - quest of
innermost mysteries - boundless expansion of self-consciousness,
visions of a future of transcendent magnificence, and notwithstanding
an ardent worship of reality a quixotically impracticable detachment
from the concrete basis of civic life - these outstanding characteristics

of the Nietzschean philosophy give unmistakable proof of a central, driving, romantic inspiration: Nietzsche shifts the essence and principle of being to a new center of gravity, by substituting the Future for the Present and relying on the untrammeled expansion of spontaneous forces which upon closer examination are found to be without definite aim or practical goal.

For this reason, critically to animadvert upon Nietzsche as a social reformer would be utterly out of place; he is simply too much of a poet to be taken seriously as a statesman or politician. The weakness of his philosophy before the forum of Logic has been referred to before. Nothing can be easier than to prove the incompatibility of some of his theorems. How, for instance, can the absolute determinism of the belief in Cyclic Recurrence be reconciled with the power vested in superman to deflect by his autonomous will the straight course of history? Or, to touch upon a more practical social aspect of his teaching - if in the order of nature all men are unequal, how can we ever bring about the right selection of leaders, how indeed can we expect to secure the due ascendancy of character and intellect over the gregarious grossness of the demos?

Again, it is easy enough to controvert Nietzsche almost at any pass by demonstrating his unphilosophic onesidedness. Were Nietzsche not stubbornly onesided, he would surely have conceded - as any sane-minded person must concede in these times of suffering and sacrifice - that charity, self-abnegation, and self-immolation might be viewed, not as conclusive proofs of degeneracy, but on the contrary as signs of growth towards perfection. Besides, philosophers of the métier are sure to object to the haziness of Nietzsche's idea of Vitality which in truth is oriented, as is his philosophy in general, less by thought than by sentiment.

Given his obvious connection with significant contemporaneous currents, the author of "Zarathustra" has altogether too much sui generis to be amenable to any crude and rigid classification. He may plausibly be labelled an anarchist, yet no definition of anarchism will

167

wholly take him in. Anarchism stands for the demolition of the extant social apparatus of restraint. Its battle is for the free determination of personal happiness. Nietzsche's prime concern, contrarily, is with internal self-liberation from the obsessive desire for personal happiness in any accepted connotation of the term; such happiness to him does not constitute the chief object of life.

The cardinal point of Nietzsche's doctrine is missed by those who, arguing retrospectively, expound the gist of his philosophy as an incitation to barbarism. Nothing can be more remote from his intentions than the transformation of society into a horde of ferocious brutes. His impeachment of mercy, notwithstanding an appearance of reckless impiety, is in the last analysis no more and no less than an expedient in the truly romantic pursuit of a new ideal of Love. Compassion, in his opinion, hampers the progress towards forms of living that shall be pregnant with a new and superior type of perfection. And in justice to Nietzsche it should be borne in mind that among the various manifestations of that human failing there is none he scorns so deeply as cowardly and petty commiseration of self. It also deserves to be emphasized that he nowhere endorses selfishness when exercised for small or sordid objects.

> I love the brave. But it is not enough to be a swordsman, one must also know against whom to use the sword. And often there is more bravery in one's keeping quiet and going past, in order to spare one's self for a worthier enemy: Ye shall have only enemies who are to be hated, but not enemies who are to be despised.[13]

Despotism must justify itself by great and worthy ends. And no man must be permitted to be hard towards others who lacks the strength of being even harder towards himself.

At all events it must serve a better purpose to appraise the practical importance of Nietzsche's speculations than blankly to denounce

---

[13] *Thus Spake Zarathustra*, p.304.

their immoralism. Nietzsche, it has to be repeated, was not on the whole a creator of new ideas. His extraordinary influence in the recent past is not due to any supreme originality or fertility of mind; it is predominantly due to his eagle-winged imagination. In him the emotional urge of utterance was, accordingly, incomparably more potent than the purely intellectual force of opinion: in fact the texture of his philosophy is woven of sensations rather than of ideas, hence its decidedly ethical trend.

The latent value of Nietzsche's ethics in their application to specific social problems it would be extremely difficult to determine. Their successful application to general world problems, if it were possible, would mean the ruin of the only form of civilization that signifies to us. His philosophy, if swallowed in the whole, poisons; in large potations, intoxicates; but in reasonable doses, strengthens and stimulates. Such danger as it harbors has no relation to grossness. His call to the Joy of Living and Doing is no encouragement of vulgar hedonism, but a challenge to persevering effort. He urges the supreme importance of vigor of body and mind and force of will.

> O my brethren, I consecrate you to be, and show unto you the way unto a new nobility. Ye shall become procreators and breeders and sowers of the future. Not whence ye come be your honor in future, but whither ye go! Your will, and your foot that longeth to get beyond yourselves, be that your new honor![14]

It would be a withering mistake to advocate the translation of Nietzsche's poetic dreams into the prose of reality. Unquestionably his Utopia if it were to be carried into practice would doom to utter extinction the world it is devised to regenerate. But it is generally acknowledged that "prophets have a right to be unreasonable," and so, if we would square ourselves with Friedrich Nietzsche in a spirit of fairness, we ought not to forget that the daring champion of reckless unrestraint is likewise the inspired apostle of action, power, enthusiasm, and aspiration, in

---

[14] *Thus Spake Zarathustra*, p.294.

fine, a prophet of Vitality and a messenger of Hope.

Guenon Against the World

The Difference Between Primordial and "Enlightened" Metaphysics

Alexander Shepard

René Guénon was without a doubt one of the most enlightened and insightful luminaries of the 20th century. His rich writing style and original philosophy stood against the unquestioned dogma of progress, materialism, and so-called "rationalism". His task was to uncover, or rather, rediscover the primordial truth of Metaphysics, in a literal sense of the word. True Metaphysics is the study of what exists beyond the natural world, the worlds that exist in the medium between God and the material world. The philosophy that arose in the modern and post-modern period, roughly dating between the 15-21st centuries, demonstrates the futility of attempting to establish a philosophy and civilization without a Metaphysical basis. Baruch Spinoza, David Hume, and Friedrich Nietzsche were three thinkers who made significant changes to western understanding, and shall be examined in juxtaposition with René Guénon. Spinoza's pantheism at least partially resonates into the post-modern era and influenced the development of a materialistic perspective. David Hume, one of the most important philosophers of the Scottish Enlightenment, contributed significantly to the modern understanding of the self. The curious case of Friedrich Nietzsche shall be looked at last, for Nietzsche represents an interesting paradox in his views. He certainly agrees with Guénon about the dismal state of modernity. He leveled devastating attacks against progress and scientism, yet he suffers from the same error as the vast majority in post-medieval philosophy. The contradictions of Spinoza, Hume, and Nietzsche shall all be examined in their own right.

GUENON'S RELATIONS TO OTHER PHILOSOPHERS

While Guénon shall be compared here to Spinoza, Hume, and Nietzsche, this by no means exhausts the topic. There are many other philosophers to choose from of course, who represent the errors of the western civilization. Those familiar with Guénon are aware that Guénon engaged in scorched earth refutations of Rene Descartes, father of modern philosophy, in *The Reign of Quantity and Signs of the Times*, *Symbolism of the Cross*, *Crisis of the Modern World*, and multiple other works. He also engaged in scorched earth refutation of Madam Blavatsky and the "New Age" phenomenon in *Theosophy: History of a Psuedo-Religion* and *The Spiritist Fallacy*. In his works he also made criticisms of other representatives of the modern error. He made sharp critiques of Kant, who helped further seal the door to the Metaphysical world by arguing that it lay beyond the capability of human understanding. He made occasional references to Spinoza and Nietzsche, as well as William James, Einstein, Freud, Pascal, Leibniz and several others. The attacks against all of the aforementioned thinkers were with the same method he used to critique Descartes. The charge being that they all in their own way, reduced the Metaphysical to the physical, and closed the West's spiritual eye. While the similarity and differences between Guénon and each of the aforementioned philosophers is a Pandora's box itself, the cases of Spinoza, Hume, and Nietzsche are among the most pressing for the reasons referenced at the beginning of this paper.

THE ONTOLOGY OF SPINOZA

Seventeenth century writer Spinoza is perhaps best known for his popularization of pantheism. Pantheism is the belief that the universe is God, or at least part of God, or more simply put, everything that exists, exists in the oneness of God. Pantheistic conceptions can be attributed to certain readings of various eastern philosophies. In reality, the world-view of Spinoza and the world-view of non-western spirituality is quite different. In order to understand the depth and complexity of eastern spirituality, the works of René Guénon shall be used as the authority and source. Once a difference in understanding has been established, a critical evaluation of Spinoza's ontological system shall be undertaken, and the paradoxes that arise in his work shall prove its logical impossibility.

Spinoza used the qualifiers in what he saw as the order and structure of the universe to come to his understanding of God. Spinoza rested primarily on his understandings of the concepts of "substance," "affliction," and "attribute" to build his philosophical beliefs. He defined substance as what can be perceived as existing necessarily, of which it is impossible to conceive something greater.

> That which is in itself and is conceived through itself; that is, that which does not need to come under the concept of another thing, from which concept it must be formed.[1]

Spinoza defined attribute as that which is perceived of the substance, or, in other words, the substance's essence. The "affliction" of the substance is, quite simply, the actions of the substance.[2] He theorized that God must exist because it would be impossible for him not to exist. The first premise of Spinoza's argument is that something either exists or does not exist by its nature; a triangle, square and circle all exist from the virtue of their natures; the numbers one, three, and four all exist, as does the side. A square circle on the other hand does not exist from the fact that it cannot, by its own nature, exist. According to Spinoza, things necessarily exist unless they have a reason not to exist.

> There can be no reason or cause which hinders God from existing, or which negates his existence, then it must be inferred that God exists necessarily.[3]

---

[1] de Spinoza, B., *The Ethics* (New York: Oxford University Press, New York, 2000), p.175.
[2] Ibid.
[3] Ibid. p.81-82.

Spinoza demonstrates the absurdity of denying the existence of God. For example, when one says that God does not exist, one has to say that non-existence is part of God's nature, which is a blatant contradiction. On the other hand, should one attempt to point to a substance outside of God to try to confirm or deny one's beliefs, the substance would have very different attributes from God, and would not be able to confirm, or deny, God's existence.[4]

Building on the last point, Spinoza makes it very clear that besides God, there is no existence, and that all things exist within the oneness of God. Therefore, God is an infinite corporeal substance. Individual finite manifestations of the infinite differ in their amount of reality.[5]

> There cannot exist two separate substances because one distinguishes between different things by the attributes and afflictions that things possess. If there were two substances, one would have to know them by different attributes and afflictions, yet this is not the case; all things possess all the same identifiers, be they size, shape, color, smell, taste, weight, and distance.[6]

Spinoza clarifies his thesis in his responses to the numerous objections that were raised against it. Some people objected to Spinoza's association of the infinite with the material universe on the basis that the application of the infinite created paradoxes. For instance, if a quantitative body could be cut in half, then the following paradox would ensue; either the bodies are finite, or they are infinite. The halves cannot be finite because the infinite is not a countable number, and the bodies cannot be infinite because that would mean there is "twice" the infinity that there was beforehand. Similarly, if there is an infinite line, then one could measure it with an infinite amount of twelve inch rulers, which would make an infinite line of both infinite feet and infinite inches. Another argument against Spinoza's ontology was the perceived limitation of perfection. God is ultimately perfect, and

[4]Ibid.
[5]Ibid.
[6]Ibid.

cannot be harmed, manipulated or divided, yet corporeal substance is something that people harm, manipulate and divide all the time.[7]

Spinoza believed these arguments to be red herrings. The first two arguments fail because he never once argued that substance can be divided, or that infinite quantity can be measured. The argument of perfection fails because even though many things consisting of substance are destroyed and brought into existence, the actual substance remains unmolested.[8]

Guénon was quite critical of all post-medieval philosophy, especially pantheism and the distortion of eastern philosophy through so-called "spiritual" groups like Theosophy that had become prevalent at the time of his writing.[9] Guénon did use the terms "Manifestation" quite a bit when referring to nature and did write extensively on the nature of God and the universe from the point of view of eastern mysticism. Guénon brought several arguments against pantheism. One argument consisted of the perfection of the divinity. As Spinoza frequently wrote, the corporeal substance that makes up the universe is God. Although Spinoza already dealt with arguments regarding the perfection of the divinity, Guénon aptly pointed out that corporeal substance is contingent upon space and time, thus imperfect. Guénon also protested that if a being were to "emanate" physically from the infinite, then there would be parts and limits assigned to it, which would make the infinite then in turn, finite. If it is only the "Being" from which the material universe emanates, there is still the same problem in that manifested beings would not be beings at all.[10] Even though the latter point is in agreement with Spinoza, what makes René Guénon's view of God quite different than Spinoza's is that Guénon refuses to say that God exists. Existence is derived from the Latin root "ex stare" which means dependent on. God then, is "beyond" what

---

[7]Ibid. p.89.

[8]Ibid.

[9]Early 20th century.

[10]Guénon, R., *Insights into Islamic Esoterism and Taoism* (Hillsdale: NY, Sophia Perennis Press, 2001), p.44.

should be considered "existence" because God is the only thing that is necessary and other things are mere contingents.[11]

Spinonza's Metaphysics is incoherent; on one hand he insists that all is one; and that everything is a part of God, yet at the same time, he argues that God does not possess human emotions. He even scoffs at those who believe God has human emotions:

> Some people imagine God in the form of a man, consisting of body and mind, and subject to passions. But it has been satisfactorily established, from what has already been proved, how far these people stray from a true knowledge of God. But I pass them by; for all who have in any way contemplated the divine nature deny that God is corporeal.[12]

If God does not possess human emotions, then where in the world did humanity derive its emotions? It could not have been from another substance because that is impossible according to Spinoza. Besides, even if there were an exception to this rule; and all laws of Spinoza's ontology were broken and humanity obtained its emotions through a different substance, the emotions exist in us now, and thus, are part of our corporeal bodies. This means they exist as part of God.

Spinoza's ninth proposition creates yet another paradox, which is "The more reality or beings each thing has, the more attributes belong to it."[13] While in principle, I agree with this statement, it is not possible to say that God is part of the inferior levels of being. Spinoza's system requires this view however, for it would mean that God is both greater and lesser then himself. Even though Spinoza explained how substance is never created, destroyed, or defiled, God is still a contingent entity in his system; for corporeal substance is still subjected to shape; and dependent on time, making God not perfect, and not the greatest

---

[11]Guénon, R., *The Symbolism of the Cross*, Sophia Perennis Press (Hillsdale: NY, Sophia Perennis Press, 2001), p.9.
[12]Spinoza, p.86.
[13]Ibid. p.81.

thing in existence.

Spinoza would likely respond to the objections to his thesis by claiming that I do not have an adequate understanding of God, and so all the alleged paradoxes and contradictions that have been pointed out are red herrings. He would correct me by saying God is not an incorporeal spirit who dwells 'wholly' within each individual object, but simply everything in nature. So thus God is able to exist as both greater and lesser forms of being. In regards to the contingency, Spinoza would likely argue that this falls under the same misconception; contingent entities which compromise God do not have the "whole" of God in them.

Spinoza's presumed defense creates a paradox in his definition of God. The contingent entities must assume one of two roles; either they are God, which makes God imperfect, or they are not God, which makes God and nature not the same thing. Take for example the paper on which this essay is written; it is a contingent imperfect entity. For its substance, the paper and the ink that it comprises cannot exist with out shape. Shape has no necessary substance yet is a necessary predicate for the existence of any physical object. Shape is thus superior to God within Spinoza's ontological system. Another variable that is superior to God in Spinoza's system is time. This essay could not have been written unless it was written with in a span of time. Similarly, unless the computer on which this essay was typed occupied a certain amount of space, it could not have been written. The variables of shape, time, and space are superior to the substance that comprises God. Should Spinoza still insist that he is still misrepresented, he must deny that things in the natural world exist in God, which appears to be the opposite of his pantheism. So thus, it seems that an imperfect nature is incompatible with a perfect God.

THE METAPHYSICS OF THE SELF

The belief in an abstract Self is one of the most crucial elements of Traditional society. However with the coming of the so-called "enlightenment" the sense of the self became regulated to a so-called "subconscious". With the rise of the discipline of "psychology" the conception of a spiritual, metaphysical self was no longer taken seriously. The Traditional Self that exists as a reflection of the Ultimate Reality was forgotten. This was not true of all psychologists, as some psychologists like William James and Carl Jung, had great respect for religious belief. Freud, the founder of psychology however, and many of his successors dismissed the idea of God and of the abstract Self as a regurgitation of "repressed urges".

To understand the deviancy of the notion of psychology, one must understand the error of the concept of the "subconscious". René Guénon, in *The Reign of Quantity and Signs of the Times*, leveled a criticism against psychology. He argued that it was the only so-called "science" in modernity that could have access to the superior levels of being. Yet, instead of embracing this gift, as the Mystics have always done, the psychologists seek to disprove and destroy this connection. What is described as the subconscious: dreams, visions, beliefs, and the like; is actually the bridge between the natural and supernatural world or in Guénon's terms, a "super" consciousness.

> There is certainly something more than the mere question of vocabulary in fact, very significant in itself, that present-day psychology considered nothing but the 'subconscious', and never the 'super conscious,' which ought logically to be its correlative.[14]

To further and fully understand the notion of the Self,[15] in the abstract Metaphysical sense, Hindu Metaphysics has to be explored. The only thing that exists according to René Guénon is Brahma, the Hindu word for God. Guénon's terminology came mostly from Hinduism because he saw it as the world's oldest Tradition. What can be called Brahma

---

[14] Guénon, R., p.228.
[15] As much as it can be elaborated on here, a full study is far greater a project than the task at hand.

is the Beyond-Being that transcends the universe and all degrees of manifested existence. The projected universe consists entirely of Atma, which is Being reflected from Brahma; because the Atma is a direct reflection of Brahma, there is no real qualitative difference between the two. Between God and the corporeal world, there are multiple degrees of existence. Each world with in the multiverse contains a greater level of Atma depending on its proximity to God and distance from the corporeal world. Once the spiritual pilgrim ascends these levels, his or her self is fully realized and obliterated at the same time, for it is replaced by the essence of God. This prompted Guénon to write on several occasions that humanity is simultaneously so much more and so much less than it is generally assumed to be; so much more, because in modern ways of thinking only the "exterior" or corporeal manifestations are considered, and people dismiss the ability to ascend and to be annihilated in the face of God. One is so much less however, because one is just that, a reflection, absolute nothingness in face of the Real. The Mystics of all religious traditions know this truth; to discuss the universal spiritual path is a task too expansive for a single paragraph or paper. All Mystics whether they exist as Christians, Muslims, Buddhists, Jains, or practitioners of indigenous religions, experience the same journey through the realms of Atma that the Hindu goes through.[16]

While David Hume was writing well before the days of Sigmund Freud, his denial of the Metaphysical Self inevitably paved the way for such a quantitative discipline. Hume was a leading Skeptic of the 1800's; he was the opposite of Guénon in that he based his philosophy first and foremost on a rejection of the idea of God. Subsequently, Hume's theories on self and the world were divorced from Traditional notions of the world being God's creation and/or emanation, and humankind existing in the image of God. His system of ethics was grounded in an empirical study of human psychology and sociology, rather than on a model of accountability to God.[17] Hume was highly critical of the

---

[16]Ibid.

[17]Hume, D., *A Treatise of Human Nature* (Mineola: NY, Dover Publications, 2003), p.179-80.

concept of a "Self" on the basis that he saw no real evidence for it. He believed that whenever the issue of a "Self" was in place, there was always a perception and/or emotion. Hume argued that it was these perceptions, emotions and experiences that constitute the so-called 'Self' and nothing more.

> After what manner do they belong to the self; and how are they connected with it? For my part, when I enter most intimately into what I call *myself*, I always stumble on some particular perception of other, of heat or cold, light or shade, love or hatred, pain or pleasure. I never catch *myself* at any time without a perception, and never can observe any thing but a perception. When my perceptions are remov'd for any time, as by sound sleep; so long am I insensible of *myself*, and may truly be said not to exist.[18]

In other words, not only is one defined by simple perceptions and emotions, but the perceptions and emotions that our so-called "self" experience are at opposite ends of the spectrum. The perceptions attached to the so-called 'Self' are too different to have originated from the same source.[19] Hume's objections are founded on a seemingly rigid and un-imaginative thesis. A basic observation one can make in regards to Hume's objections to the idea of the self is that his examples "love and hate" "pain and pleasure," etc., all fall under the same category of emotion. Hume claims that they are "contradictory" when in fact, they are both manifestations of the same archetype of emotion. More precisely, in the examples he brings up: love and hatred, pain and pleasure, heat and cold, light and shade, one "exists" only as the absence of the other. Hatred only exists inasmuch as it is the absence of love, human beings are born and dependent on love as small infants, they naturally love until they have a reason to abandon it, that is, to hate. Pleasure and pain is the same concept, we seek what we call pleasure to avoid what we call pain. Pain only appears as pleasure dissipates. The same is true, for his last conception of light and shade.

---

[18]Ibid.
[19]Ibid.

Shade is the absence of light, wherever light shines, it illuminates, and shade is created as a byproduct of the light. Light itself, does not take into account the shade that it produces, it shines irrespectively of the objects that create the shade in what ever way they are positioned to. Cold is every bit as much an illusion as hatred, pain, and shade, for it exists only as the absence of heat. Heat naturally speeds things up and is defined by the faster vibration of molecules. Only as molecules lose their momentum are they considered "cold".

There is a bigger problem inherent in the paragraph; he claims "I never catch myself at any time without a perception". This essentially contradicts his entire thesis about the non-existence of Self. If there is no Self, then who is doing the perceiving? The act, the power of perception, the agent through which it is accomplished is not perceived. The agent of feeling is not felt. What ever it is that feels the love and the hate, the heat and the cold, the pain and the pleasure is not felt. So then, what is it that is doing the "Catching"? It should be clear that this itself, the power of perception, feeling, and emotion proves the existence of some kind of self.[20] Of course, as it has already been demonstrated, the Self in Traditional thought transcends the mere perceiver. In Traditionalist Metaphysics, God is the only thing real, and all else is a fluidic illusion.[21]

All the rest (besides God) is, no doubt, real also, but only in a relative way, by reason of its dependence upon the Principle and in so far as much as it reflects It in some degree, as the image reflected in a mirror derives all its reality from the object it reflects and could enjoy no existence apart from it; but this lesser reality, which is only participative, is illusory in relation to the supreme Reality, as the image is also illusionary in relation to the object.[22]

---

[20]Self here in the lower case to signify a difference between "Self" as a manifestation and any other interpretation.

[21]Guénon, R., *Man and his Becoming according to the Vedanta* (New Delhi: Oriental Books Reprint Corporation. 1981), p.36-8.

[22]Ibid.

In light of the earlier points about love, light, pleasure, and heat, this is how the self is constructed, as a projection of God's attributes mixed with non-being or nothingness. Humankind can safely be said to be murky reflections of the Absolute. The extent of the human condition is too lengthy a thesis to be defended here, but it can be safely said that of all of humanities attributes, they can be said to either be Godly, in which case they retain what was imprinted by the Almighty, or they are ungodly, in which case they are deformed imposters of the True attributes. These examples being love as the godly attribute while hate exists as its deformed imposter, the same formula can be applied to romantic attraction and lust, friendship and animosity, respect and bitterness, justice and malice, lawful and chaotic, etc.

Hume would likely respond to my critique by arguing that there is no evidence for the Self, let alone God on any rational principle. In his view, my arguments are likely poetic at best, and are devoid of any kind of rational or empirical evidence. Hume after all, spent most of his career questioning the existence of God and challenging traditionally held proofs for the existence of God. If God cannot be proved, then how can the existence of a "Self" be argued to exist?

The experience of God is not felt or discovered by reason; the ascension through the chains of being is achieved by inner mystical experience. Such an action is unbelievable to those who cannot understand and to those who have not experienced the ascension. The experience of God is felt and proved as with any other passion or impression, by feeling. For moderns and post-moderns to denounce the existence of it just because they have not seen it or observed it, is like a blind person telling others they cannot see.[23]

In terms of 'empirical evidence' however, there is something that absolutely cannot be ignored, that being the nearly identical descriptions of God found in multiple mystical texts. Take for example

---

[23]Nasr, S., *The Essential Seyyed Hossein Nasr* (Bloomington: World Wisdom, 2007), p.91.

this Hindu text:

> The *Atma* which dwells in the heart, is smaller than a grain of rice, smaller than a grain of barley, smaller than a grain of mustard, smaller than a grain of millet, smaller than the germ which is the grain of millet; this *Atma*, which dwells in the heart, is also greater than the earth, greater than the atmosphere, greater than the sky, greater than all the worlds together.[24]

Notice the emphasis on the 'heart' as the dwelling place of God. This is because the ascension to God is done by the way of the heart and not the mind, and the power of the heart, the experience of God, is the most powerful emotion. Now compare that saying with this quatrain by the famous Sufi Muslim poet Rumi, who also puts emphasis on the 'heart' of the believer, and the need to enter/explore it in order to ascend to God.

> Consider the breast as the cave/ the spiritual retreat of the Friend/ if thou art the companion of the cave/ enter the cave, enter the cave.[25]

The symbolism of the heart as the dwelling place for God is elaborated upon in the *Quran* itself many times. Whenever it is referenced, it always is in reference to being the spiritual center of the human person. It has given the attributes of sight and understanding. Consequently, blasphemy and disbelieve are associated with diseases of the heart.

> And their hearts are sealed, so that they apprehend not.[26]
> These are they into whose hearts He has impressed faith and strengthened them with a spirit from Him.[27]
> And as for those who believe not in the Hereafter there hearts

---

[24]Guénon, R., *The Essential*, p.173.
[25]Nasr, p.91.
[26]*Quran*, 9:87.
[27]*Quran*, 58:2

refuse to know, for they are proud.[28]

The Bible, in both the Old and New Testament, speak of the heart as the vehicle in which the human beings experiences God. Just like the Quran, the heart is ascribed to the attributes of the body and mind, such as speaking, joy, listening, and rest. The Book of Samuel describes this phenomenon in several people. Hannah and Saul are both described as having the heart commune with the Divine. In the case of Hannah:

> Now Hannah, she spake in her heart; only her lips moved, but her voice was not heard: therefore Eli thought she had been drunken.[29]

> And Hannah prayed, and said, My heart rejoiceth in the lord, mine horn is exalted in the Lord: my mouth enlarged over mine enemies; because I rejoice in thy salvation."[30]

Later, Saul is described as having his heart replaced. This replacement of the heart is a distinct Mystical symbol, as Mystics, in any Tradition, once they complete their levels of spiritual realization, are described as having their hearts, and often, their whole bodies, cut out and replaced with a new heart by God.

> And it was so, that when he had turned his back to go from Samuel, God gave him another heart: and all those signs came to pass that day. [31]

The Book of Ezekiel contains a very similar passage, one that speaks with more clarity to the process of spiritual rejuvenation. "Cast away from you all of your transgressions, whereby you have transgressed; and make you a new heart and new spirit: for why will ye die, O

---

[28]*Quran,* 16:22.
[29]Samuel 2:11, *King James Bible.*
[30]Samuel 3:1, *King James Bible.*
[31]Samuel 10:9, *King James Bible .*

house of Israel?"[32] Further in the Book of Samuel, the place of the heart as the dwelling place of God is clearly established in describing a confrontation that took place between Saul and King David. The reference in this case, clearly gives the example of the heart existing as the recipient of God, housing His Divine Manifestation. It is specifically references the heart has punishing King David, an attribute properly ascribed only to God.

> And it came to pass afterward, that David's heart smote him, because he had cut off Saul's Skirt, And then he said unto his men, The Lord forbid that I should do this thing unto my master, the Lord's anointed, to stretch forth mine hand against him, seeing he is the anointed of the Lord.[33]

The New Testament is also quite adamant about the heart as a manifestation of the Metaphysical world. Throughout all of it, the parts recounting the life of Christ and the letters of Paul and the rest of the Apostles, the heart is spoken of as the vehicle in which the human being experiences the Divine. St. Paul writes:

> But as it is written, Eye hath not seen, nor ear heard, neither have entered into the heart of man, the things which God hath prepared for them to love him.[34]

The references to the heart as the dwelling place of God could be elaborated on for eternity. For only through what has been presented has only been a sampling of references, it should prove enough to discredit Hume's denial of the Self and of the Supernatural. To conclude upon this point, one last quotation shall be brought, that of the famed poet and counter-enlightenment philosopher William Blake. The quote is brought from his magnum opus, *The Marriage of Heaven and Hell,* one of the greatest treatises of mystical philosophy

---

[32]Ezekiel 18:31, *King James Bible.*
[33]Samuel 24, *King James Bible*
[34]Corinthians 2:9, *King James Bible*

in the English language, although commonly not identified as such.[35] The ancient Poets all animated all sensible objects with Gods or Geniuses, calling them by the names and adorning them with the properties of woods, rivers, mountains, lakes, cities, nations, and whatever their enlarged and numerous senses could perceive. And particularly they studied the genius of each city and country, placing it under its mental deity. Till a system was formed, which some took advantage of and enslav'd the vulgar by attempting to realize or abstact the mental deities from their objects; thus began Preisthood. Choosing forms of worship from poetical tales. And at length they pronounc'd that the Gods has order'd such things. Thus men forgot that All deities reside in the human breast.[36]

The Metaphysics of the Modern Crisis

Far better known than Guénon is the great intellectual Friedrich Nietzsche. He is generally well remembered as one of the worlds most profound, original, and insightful philosophers. Nietzsche was born in Germany in the mid 19th century and died towards the beginning of the 20th century. He challenged many of the assumptions and pre-conceptions regarding science, philosophy, and religion. He coined the famous term "God is Dead" which is today seen on many bumper stickers, billboards, and T-shirts. Nietzsche believed that the death of the idea of God had resulted in much purposelessness and restlessness in the modern spirit. Guénon, essentially, came to the same conclusion a generation later making many of the same criticisms against science that Nietzsche made. Guénon addressed modernity from a completely

---

[35]His Wikipedia page identifies him as a "poet, painter, and printmaker" with "philosophical and mystical undertones within his work". While immensely popular among the deconstructionists within the English departments, he unfortunately does not seem to be recognized as a philosopher or a theologian within his own right. An analysis of Blake as a Traditional philosopher, more specifically, a thinker in the fashion of the "Radical Traditionalists" of Evola and his sub-school is a thesis far too vast for this paper.

[36]Blake, W., *The Marriage of Heaven and Hell* (New York, Dover Publications Incorporated), p.34.

different perspective however. Nietzsche directed his criticisms from a subjective, emotional, and essentially anti-rational standpoint. While Guénon was by no means a rationalist or a positivist, he critiqued modern society for its deviation from Metaphysical principles. A juxtaposition of Nietzsche's and Guénon's Metaphysics shall be undertaken and so shall their social critiques. Just as with the cases of Spinoza and Hume, Guénon will then be demonstrated to have the superior Metaphysics; thus once again showing the necessity of a solid Metaphysical basis when trying to establish any sort of philosophy. The case of Friedrich Nietzsche demonstrates the most important and peculiar case, for indeed it seems that most would agree today there is something deeply wrong with our state of affairs.

A lot of ink from a great many perspectives has been spilled to account for the perceived insanity of the (post)-modern condition. The Marxists, racial theorists, constitutional libertarians, neo-luddites, existentialist atheists, and religious fundamentalists have all elaborated on why they believe our society exists in such a reprehensible condition. The explanations and solutions that have been purposed to solve these problems have all failed because of their ignorance of higher Metaphysics. To explain the inconstancy of each and every one would take far too long, by focusing on Nietzsche, however it will be sufficient to prove why any kind of moral system or solution, founded on anti-Metaphysical principles, is insufficient.

Guénon defines Metaphysics as literally meaning what is beyond nature, from the Greek terminology of the word "Meta" meaning "beyond" and the word "physics" meaning "nature". Guénon wrote prolifically on what lay beyond the material world and God, that being a string of Metaphysical worlds in the intermediary between God and the material world.[37]

Gradually the material world shrinks in its proximity to the superior

---

[37]Guénon, R., *The Symbolism of the Cross* (Hillsdale: NY, Sophia Perennis, 2004), p.15.

levels of manifestation. Thus society becomes more and more concentrated on quantification and society becomes less and less concerned with quality. This process is cyclical; in Hinduism it is referred to as a "Manvantara". There are four ages, or "Yugas" which exist within the Manvantara, each age existing in a certain proximity to God. Within each of the four ages, the doctrine repeats itself on a miniature scale. The modern world is thus the darkest of the Dark Age, for the Kali Yuga, or age of vice, which began, according to Hinduism, 6,000 years ago. In the modern world, we are trapped and confined within the miniature age of vice within the grand age of vice. Once the overall shift to quantification is completed, the Cycle thus starts over once again as there is no more quality to be drained. To use Guénon's words directly:

> In the most general sense of the term, a cycle must be considered as representing the process of development of some state of manifestation, or the case of minor cycles of one of the more or less restricted and specialized modalities of that state. Moreover, in virtue of the law of correspondence which links all things in universal Existence, there is necessarily and always a certain analogy, either among different cycles of the same order or among the principal cycles and their secondary divisions.[38]

Friedrich Nietzsche did not believe in a concrete system of Metaphysics. He saw the ideas as mere projection of the psychological need to feel like a conqueror. He describes the belief in the Metaphysical world as "an escape remains: to pass sentence on this whole world of becoming as a deception and to invent a world beyond it, a *true* world".[39]

Nietzsche did not believe in metaphysical cyclical law. Instead he believed that if humanity had an end result, it would have been achieved by now. Nietzsche postulated the idea called "eternal return"

---

[38]Guénon, R., *The Essential René Guénon* (Hillsdale: NY, Sophia Perennis and World Wisdom Inc, 2009), p.117.
[39]Nietzsche, F., *The Will To Power* (New York, Vintage Books, 1968), p.13.

which is quite simply, the universe has always been infinite, and shall always be infinite. So therefore, everything that has happened has happened an infinite amount of times before and will happen an infinite amount of times in the future.[40]

Despite their differences in Metaphysics, Guénon and Nietzsche agreed on the state of modern science. Guénon saw the materialistic view of modern science as a consequence of dissipation of Divine quality in the modern world. Modern scientists are like the prisoners in Plato's cave, only focused on the material/relative. This was in contrast to the "Sacred" or "Traditional" scientists of old who based their work first and foremost on Metaphysical principles. It is arrogance and ignorance on the part of modern science to assume the reality of only the physical world.[41]

Nietzsche was critical of the Nihilism that seemed to be overtaking Europe. He believed (at least he seems to indicate in some of his aphorisms) that society was superior when it believed in God. For he believed that it provided people with values and purpose. He was particularly critical of science for he believed that all it could measure was things that can be quantified. Attaining quantified measurements is undoubtedly important, and thus, science is quite useful in this respect. Science itself however fails to answer the most essential questions in life, that being what constitutes the nature of ethics and value. A life where everything is quantified would be "dead, stiff, motionless. The reduction of all qualities to quantities is nonsense: what appears is that the one accompanies the other, an analogy."[42]

Nietzsche's arguments for an infinite universe are rather unconvincing, for he is premature in saying that the universe would have ended by now if it had a fixed end. The world has passed through many

---

[40]Deleuze, G., *Nietzsche and Philosophy* (New York: Colombia Classics, 2006), p.28-32.

[41]Guénon, R., *The Reign of Quantity and the Signs of Times* (Hillsdale: NY, Sophia Perennis. 2004), p.1-11.

[42]Nietzsche, p.304.

important historical and scientific changes. Some that come to mind are the creation of the earth, the creation of humanity, the coming and going of many great historical figures, etc. Who is to say that the end of the world and the rejuvenation of a new golden age are not at hand? For Guénon demonstrated the striking similarities between the predicted anti-Christ and modern society. Modern society and now, even more so the post-modern, fits the definition of the Anti-Christ, who is generally perceived to be a mockery or parody of God. Things in the Post-modern world resemble Traditional society in a quantified parody. For example, the concept of a community, or brotherhood, which had been largely decimated by industrial era technology and the advent of rugged, isolated individualism has made a return in an inverted fashion with social networking. Communities and family relations have certainly made a strong comeback with the advent of Myspace, Facebook, and Twitter. Despite all practical purposes, it is inferior to traditional social structure in quality. Religious "fundamentalism" which was not a problem in the time of the first generation Traditionalists certainly has made a sweeping surge within the last several decades within the Abrahamic Traditions. To use René Guénon's words directly, "There are even some who gladly profess a religious faith, and whose sincerity is not in doubt; but their scientific attitude does not differ significantly from that of the avowed materialists."[43]

The infinite, in the material world, is a logical impossibility. Nietzsche claims that the world would have ended already if it were suppose to run on a finite course. But Nietzsche does not seem to be able to account for the classic problem of the infinite, which has been elaborated on by a great many philosophers, from Plato to Al-Ghazali to Thomas Aquinas. If the universe is infinite, it makes no sense for anything to be in existence now, for it is impossible to take any finite quantity and multiply or add it up to the infinite amount. Due to the fact that time consists of a finite amount of intervals, the time which exists now, should not be in existence for the finite intervals of time

---

[43]Guénon, p.29.

should never had elapsed up to this point.[44]

Additionally, the sense, the knowledge of the perfection, is within the mind of every human being. Nietzsche himself admits that all our knowledge comes from what actually exists, so then, as Descartes has noted before, how can the perfection exist, how can the conception of the Metaphysics exist, with out an actual perfection? Nietzsche would argue it is to create a sense of feeling of superiority. However if this were the case, the sense of superiority easily could have been created without the drive to seek the perfection. For if perfection does not exist, it could not have been conceived.[45]

Nietzsche is brilliant in his criticisms of science and his demonstrations of the pointlessness of modern life when science strips things of their quality down to the simply quantified level. His Metaphysics however is inconsistent with his criticism; he strangely admits to believing in a world governed by chance and one that lacks any intrinsic value. For the sake of consistency and responsibility, the Metaphysics of Guénon prove to be the superior argument. For René Guénon provides a detailed critique into not only the nature of the universe, but how her great cyclical laws have created the modern reign of quantity.

CONCLUSION

The emptiness of modern and post-modern life is inevitably the end result of a materialistic world-view. The pantheism of Spinoza sets the stage for believing in Materialism, or believing that no reality exists outside the physical substantial universe. The denial of an abstract metaphysical "Self" by David Hume paves the way for the development of a reduction of all things spiritual and of a higher principle order to the "subconscious repressions." These views are both self-contradictory and morally irresponsible. The materialistic ontology creates a sense of emptiness, rightly diagnosed as spiritual sickness

---

[44]Deleuze, p.28-31.
[45]Nietzsche, p.140-41.

by Friedrich Nietzsche. However the Existentialism of Nietzsche suffers from internal inconstancy. Only Primordial Metaphysics, rediscovered and re-illuminated by the late great René Guénon, illuminates the Truth that binds together the ontology of the world, misunderstood by Spinoza, the abstract Self that is a manifestation of the Absolute, misunderstood by Hume, and a criticism of modernity, misunderstood by Nietzsche.

The Return Of Myth

Boris Nad

Translated by Zinka Brkic

The contradictory processes of de-mythologization and re-mythologization are not unknown to ancient civilizations, in which the old myths are sometimes destroyed (de-mythologization) and replaced with new myths (re-mythologization). In other words, herein are the processes of de-mythologization and re-mythologization mutually caused and interdependent processes. They do not call into question the very basis of traditional mythical community; moreover, they are maintaining it at current and keeping it alive.

Myth, namely - except in special cases of extreme degradation and secularization of tradition and culture - for us, is not a fiction of primitive people, a superstition or a misunderstanding, but a very concise expression of the highest sacred truths and principles, which are "translated" to a specific language of earthly reality, to such an extent as is practically possible. The myth is sacral truth described by popular language. Where the presumptions for its understanding are disappearing, the mythical content must be discarded to let in its place another one.

The Dangerous Intuitions

Myth is, in traditional cultures, a great antithesis as well, where, as it was shown in the capital work of J. J. Bachofen, *Mother Right: An Investigation of the Religious and Juridical Character of Matriarchy in the Ancient World*, the two major and irreconcilable principles are confronted: uranic and chthonic, patriarchal and matriarchal, and this is projected to all second modalities of state and social order through to the arts and culture.

With the advent of Indo-Europeans, patriarchal invaders on the soil of the old, matriarchal Europe started the struggle of two opposite principles that are highlighted in Bachofen's study. In the given case, the old matriarchal myths and cults turn patriarchal, through the parallel and alternating processes of de-mythologization and re-mythologization, and traces of this struggle are also found in some mythic themes, which can be understood as a very brief religious-political history, the way Robert Graves interpreted them, in his book *The Greek Myths*.

In contrast, in Greece, a process of demythologization which reaches its peak after Xenophanes (565-470) is complete and radical. This is not followed by any process of re-mythologization, it is a consequence of a total process of de-sacralization and profanization of the culture, which results in the extinguishing of the mythical and the awakening of a historical consciousness, when man stops seeing the self as mythical and begins to understand the self as a historical being instead. This is a phenomenon that has analogies with two moments in history: first, with a process of de-mythologization brought by early Christianity.

To the first Christian theologians, myth was the opposite of the Gospel, and Jesus was a historical figure, whose historicity the church fathers proved and defended to the unbelieving. As a contrast there is the actual process of re-mythologization of the Middle Ages, with a whole series of examples of revitalization of the ancient mythical content, often conflicting and irreconcilable, from the Graal myths and the myth of Friedrich the Second, to eschatological myths in the epoch of Crusades and various millennium myths. It is, without doubt, a much older re-actualization of mythic content and its "dangerous intuition", which surpasses its causes and it serves as evidence of the presence of mythic forces in the historical world, which no process of de-mythologization is able to destroy or extinguish.

THE CONSUMER MYTHOLOGY. THE MIDNIGHT OF HISTORY

Another example of the radical process of de-mythologization is de-mythologization that begins with the epoch of enlightenment to its peak experienced in the "technological universe". It is (as above) the direct expression of the degradation and decline of modern man, who is no longer a mythical or historical being, but a mere "consumer" within the "consumeristic and technocratic civilization" or simply a plug to the technological universe. The heroic impulse of man as a mythical, and historical being, was burnt out. Destructive forces of de-mythologization constantly clean and remove the mythical ingredients from the area of consumeristic civilization and human memory in general, exterminating "dangerous intuitions" that are contained in them. Within the technological universe, which is only a final stage of the fall of (modern) man, the human horizon is finally closing, because here man has only one power and only one freedom: power to spend and freedom to buy and sell. This freedom and this power, testify about the death of man (known by the myth and history), because within the universe of technology and consumer civilization, anything that transcends this "animal of consumption" simply can not exist. "The Death of Art" spoken about by the historical avant-garde is a simple consequence of the death of man, first as a mythical, then as a historical being.

Of course, the process of de-mythologization can never be completed, for the simple reason that destruction does not touch the very mythical forces. They continue to appear and return through history, whether under the guise of the "historical", or as something that is opposed to history. This is also true for the one-dimensional universe of a technocratic utopia. As a result, in the consumer civilization real mythical contents are replaced by the mythical simulacrum: wild-growing sub-cultural ideologies and myths, or consumer mythology, whose heroes are comic figures such as Superman.

But the exhaustion of the long and destructive processes of de-mythologization does not mean a return to the mythical time.

> We are standing in the midnight of history, the clock struck twelve and we look ahead into the darkness where we see the contours of future things. This view is followed by fear and heavy premonition. Things we see or think that we can see still do not have a name, they are nameless. If we address them, we do not affect them accurately and they escape the noose of our governing. When we say peace it could be a war. Plans of happiness turn into murderous ones, often through the night.

In short: "Rough incursions, which in many places convert historical landscapes into elementary ones, hide subtle changes but of the more aggressive kind" (Ernst Jünger: *At the Wall of Time*).

AT THE DAWN OF HISTORY

The writing *At the Wall of Time* by German author Ernst Jünger conveys much about the transition of myth into history, and about the moment in which the mythical consciousness was replaced by the historic one. History, of course, does not exist as long as man: historical consciousness rejects as non-historic the vast spaces and epochs ("prehistory"), and peoples, civilizations and countries, because "a person, an event must have very specific characteristics that would make them historic". The key to this transition, according to this author, provides the work of Herodotus, through which man "passes through a country illuminated by rays of dawn":

> Before him (Herodotus) there was something else, the mythical night. That night, however, was not darkness. It was more of a dream, and it knew about a different way of connecting people and events of historical consciousness and its selective forces. This brings rays of dawn into Herodotus' work. He stands on top of the mountain that separates day from night: not only the two epochs, but also two types of epochs, the two types of light.

In other words, it is the moment of the transition from one way of existence into something quite different, that we call history. This is the time of the shift of two cycles, which we can not identify with the change of historical epochs - the issue in question is the profound change in the existence of man. The sacral in the manner of previous epochs retreats, ancient cults disappear and into their place come religions, which soon after, by themselves become historical or anti-historical, even when they trigger events and historical plots. Crusader wars, called on by the Western Church, deepened divisions and schisms and eventually gave birth to the Reformation, which began with religious enthusiasm and desire to return to "biblical beginnings", and then end with the historical movement which opens the way to unhampered development of industry and technology - unconstrained by the norms of (Christian) tradition, and free of human hopes and desires.

THE GRIMACE OF HORROR

World of History, outlines of which we can find in Homer, which were shaped by Thucydides, and which experienced its zenith somewhere at the end of XIX and at the beginning of XX century, with unclear boundaries in time and space, but with a clear consciousness of its laws and regulations, started to collapse; and the vast edifice of history becomes unstable, as a sign of penetration of the hitherto unknown foreign forces. These forces have a titanic, elementary character, first seen in technical disasters, which affected hundreds of thousands of victims and then, in the cataclysmic events of XX century, in the world wars and revolutions, millions were killed and crippled. The release of nuclear energy, radiation and the environmental destruction that enormous areas were exposed to, the daily toll in blood, whether it is sacrificed to "progress" in peacetime conditions, whether as a direct consequence of military intervention and conflict, is something that comes out of the framework established by the historical world. Of course, history does not end there, as expected, by Marx or by Fukuyama. What is more noticeable is the acceleration of historical time, which concentrates events and reduces the distance between the key turning points of history. What we are talking about is, however, that here there are not only forces operating that we call historical, and that the role of man in these events is fundamentally changed: he is no longer able to operate equally with the gods, or to follow them, to stand against them or to even subjugate them, as was represented by myth. He (man) is no longer an active participant in history, guided by the passions or his own will, as happens in a mature historical epoch. He becomes the plaything of something unknown, involved in events that surpass him, against his will and outside of his ideas.

The expression of cheerful confidence is gradually replaced by a grimace of horror. Man, who until yesterday considered himself a sovereign and master, acknowledges his weakness. The means that man is shown as weak or in the decisive hour turned against his creator. Technological systems and social orders have his other sides, his automatic schemes, which do not restrain but encourage destruction, which place man in the position of the sorcerer's apprentice, who release uncontrollable forces. Corruption, crime, violence and terror are rather results than the causes. Political responses, regardless of colour and sign, do not offer solutions but rather increase disintegration. If he had not have found himself in this time of panic, man might gain at least an awareness of his own decline.

All this was unthinkable in the ripe age of history because then, man was still ruled by himself, and thus history as well, and therefore history could have no sense of direction other than the one given by man himself, his own deeds and thoughts.

Each concept of the "meaning of history" is the concept of the beginning of man, while in the classical historical time man is not created *but he is*. The question about the "meaning of history" was a meaningless question, and it is indeed not found in classical writers, from Herodotus onward. The question about the "meaning of history", which is always found outside of man, becomes possible only when the history and the focus moves out of man, either in the social sphere, or in the sphere of technological relations.

Modern man is too late to reveal his own weakness, but his breakdown does not accuse myth or history, but precisely the weakness and cowardice of modern man. The world of "civilized values", the historical world in general, which he himself had created, is showing itself much weaker than we used to believe - structurally weak, spiritually and ethically. At the first sign of alarm, he begins to shatter, exposing, in fact, internal readiness to capitulate modern man.

This is the "midnight of history", which will soon be replaced by something different, and that moment is marked by the spread of titanic forces, requiring the sacrifice of blood.

Towards Post-History: The Awakening of Myth

History, should we repeat it again, does not last as long as man on Earth. But the consciousness of it occurs late in history, perhaps only at its end, when the boundaries of time and space are changing: on one side, by discovering the distant past of man, with lost civilizations, then the past of the planet and the universe, and on the other side, with the exploration of the cosmos, the depth of the ocean, or the interior of Earth itself, through the archaeological and geological layers, in an almost Verne like manner. New perspectives cause dizziness. Prehistory and post-history gain in importance only when history becomes a crumbling edifice. But turning man from history to something that he has not been able to determine yet or clearly perceive, is now reminisce of the flight.

In one way or another, the technological universe and the consumer civilization will come to an end, in the same way a classic historical epoch ends with technocracy and with a totalitarian order in its complete form, which arises neither from courage nor strength but from cowardice, weakness and fear. It is impossible to say how long this will take. It is irrelevant whether this will happen due to an internal attrition, an overstrain or a disaster, or with all of these together. But in each of these cases, the collapse is only a consequence of man's inability to further dwell within the historical world, and to rule it as a sovereign-supreme being.

The return to myth, however, is not possible in terms of a return to the state of "pre-history." Mythological forces remain present, as they were during the entire historical period, but they can not establish a previous state because they lack the preconditions in the first place, the missing "substrate", a fertile ground. Modern man is too weak for that, in the spiritual, psychological and even "physiological" sense.

Together with history, culture gradually disappears as well, in its current meaning, which is basically just an instrument of social engineering. In a technocratic utopia (as opposed to the culture in the historical period), mass culture is just one of the ways that channels the energy to drive their utopian fantasies and desires of the masses; the elite culture, which constantly wanders between conformism and negation, between skepticism and denial, between skepticism and irony, and back to conformism, essentially remains a tool of de-mythology (or deconstruction of mythology) and destruction of dangerous intuitions contained in myth, which allows for more or less seamless integration into the technological universe, with the illusion of free will. The appearance and the awakening of dangerous intuitions and sleeping archetypes, on the margins of the technocratic social mechanism, creates a situation of conflict and leads to delays in its functioning.

In the region beyond the technocratic utopia, culture will need to take a more traditional role than the one it has in the consumer civilization. The disintegration of the historical world in its late stage, which we are just witnessing, allows us to see something of it.

For much of the historical period, culture is a privileged area of sacred and mythical powers. This is one of the ways in which mythical forces again penetrate into the world historically, realizing themselves in history, unlike the technological universe, where they usually manifest themselves through the uncontrolled elements of folklore subcultures, and are often distorted to the unrecognizable simulacra of the mythical, and not as credible expressions. They testify more about the eternal and unquenched need of man for mythical content, than they represent a sign of their real presence.

Culture in the post-technocratic era will be very closely related to the reestablishment of mythology, in terms of recognition and the awakening of true mythical content, marked by innovation and the revitalization of the ancient and traditional form, rather than, as hitherto, their exorcism. Meaning and purpose of the process of de-mythology, by contrast, must be limited to the one it had in traditional societies: the cleaning of degenerate "folklore" mythical forms, as to let into their place those who credibly represent the tradition.

THE PRIMORDIAL TRADITION

Remember that I have remembered / and pass on the Tradition.
- Ezra Pound, *Cantos*

GWENDOLYN TAUNTON

The Primordial Tradition is an obscure and widely misunderstood term, and though used repeatedly in the works of René Guénon and Frithjof Schuon, it still remains largely undefined. Perhaps the clearest description of the Primordial Tradition can be found in a more recent author, Huston Smith, a professor of comparative religion who was the first to utilize the Primordial Tradition as a substitute term for perennial philosophy. Smith justifies his replacement of perennial philosophy with the new title of the Primordial Tradition at the start of his major work *Forgotten Truth: The Primordial Tradition* in the introduction.

> The reader will recognize the affinity of this thesis with what has been called "the perennial philosophy." I am not unhappy with that phrase, but to bring out the fact that this particular philosophy nowhere originated, nor has it succeeded in maintaining itself operatively, save in a cultic context – a context that works to transform lives as well as minds – I prefer the less exclusively intellectual designation "the primordial tradition" (primordial: existing...from the beginning; fundamental. (*Oxford English Dictionary*)[1]

Smith's motivation in adopting this premise is all too easily comprehensible – from it's current standpoint of existing purely as a school of philosophy, the perennial philosophy sets itself apart from

---

[1] Smith, H., *Forgotten Truth: The Primordial Tradition*, (New York: Harper Row, 1976) p.x.

mundane daily existence, instead manifesting as a purely intellectual phenomenon – the adaptation of the designated title 'Primordial Tradition' provides this school of thought with a worldly and tangible presence, no longer purely existent in a cerebral content; Tradition as espoused by Huston Smith becomes accessible to the mainstream. Though the above quotation from Smith immediately explains that the Primordial Tradition is a substitute name for perennial philosophy, if we were to ask the common man on the street if he could explain to us the meaning of perennial philosophy, we would most likely receive a garrulous 'no' as a response, accompanied by a blank stare. Therefore, to discover the meaning of the Primordial Tradition, we must as a point of necessity, first explain the nature of perennial philosophy.

Perennial Philosophy, also known as '*philosophia perennis*' (Latin: Eternal Philosophy) was utilized by Gottfried Leibniz to designate the common, eternal philosophy that underlies all religions, and in particular the mystical or esoteric components – in this way it is also similar to the Hindu idea of *Sanatana Dharma*. As such, the *philosophia perennis* is an intellectual transmission of gnosis, based on the study of the religions, not in isolation from each other, but rather in a conjunction wherein the underlying ideas converge, independent of the concept of *communitas* (as defined by Victor Turner as the social aspect in religion). Normally, because of the cultural boundaries exerted by the principle of communitas 'religions are cut off from one another by barriers of mutual incomprehension'.[2] Schuon elaborates on the nature of this cultural barrier further by stating that "There is no metaphysical or spiritual difference between a truth manifested by temporal facts and a truth expressed by other symbols, under a mythological form for example; the modes of manifestation correspond to the mental requirements of the different groups of humanity."[3] Here we see expressed the notion that the symbols found in religion have been equated as truth values – what lies at the root of mutual miscomprehension and mistranslations

---

[2]Schuon, F., *Gnosis: Divine Wisdom*, (Middlesex, Perennial Books, 1990), p.11.
[3]Ibid., p.18.

between cultures is not that some religions are inherently wrong or different to others, but rather that the principle of communitas, the social and communal mode of religious behaviour actually serves to distort and hide the essence of the symbols themselves. The same ties of communal religious behaviour that serve to bind a community together as a distinct cultural group can also hinder the process of understanding different religious traditions.

This is quite similar to Kant's interpretation of how religious solidarity is defined; it is not the universal meaning of the symbol (or in this case the Primordial Tradition) but rather how symbols are interpreted and applied to social behaviour within a specific community or culture.

> As Kant sees it, genuine religious solidarity does not rest on the confession of a uniform symbol or creed anyway; Kant suspects such creedal formulas of contributing more to a spirit of hypocrisy within people and between them than to anything else. What unites believers in rational religion is not the content of their beliefs but the morality of their dispositions and their propensity to associate their moral vocation with the thought of God.[4]

According to Schuon the link that connects the many different cultural strands of religious thought, is gnosis, or the philosophia perennis (which has already been explained as homologous with the Primordial Tradition). Therefore, to fully ascertain how there can be a 'fluid' transmission of gnosis occurring between different communities and social groups, and to fully understand what the Primordial Tradition actually is requires, as an a priori, a lucid and working definition of how gnosis is to be understood in this context. Returning again to the writings of Schuon, it is an important aspect of his philosophy that he draws a distinction between gnosis and sacred scripture, the latter of which Schuon regards as static and permanent.

---

[4]Wood, A. M., Kant's Deism in *Kant's Philosophy of Religion Reconsidered*, ed Rossi, P. J., and Wreen, M., (Indiana: Indiana University Press, 1991) p.9 - 10.

The mode of manifestation of gnosis is 'vertical' and more or less 'discontinuous'; it is like fire and not water, in the sense that fire arises from the invisible and can disappear into it again, whereas water has a continuous existence; but the sacred Scriptures remain the necessary and unchanging basis, the source of inspiration and criterion of all gnosis.[5]

What is immediately apparent in this extract is that Schuon is ascribing to gnosis an intangible and erratic character, by comparing its qualities to fire. Though teaching and scripture provide fuel and sustenance for gnosis, ultimately the driving power and modus operandi of gnosis is the philosophia perennis and the Primordial Tradition which is the language of the symbol, contained in the interpretation of both scripture and sacred art. Symbols, images, semiotics – despite the wealth and plethora of the records of the exploration of man's inner world through the medium of myth and legend, the science of the sub-conscious has long fallen into disregard, only being revitalized in comparatively recent times through the work of Carl Jung (Analytical Psychology), James Hillman (Archetypal Psychology) and Mircea Eliade (History of Religions). It has taken science almost 2,000 years to reclaim the knowledge and potency inherent in the discourse of myth – an almost irrefutable proof that empirical methods cannot quantify the core of any religious belief; namely wisdom. To quote René Guénon;

> Truths which were formerly within reach of all have become more and more hidden and inaccessible; those who possess them grow fewer and fewer, and although the treasure of 'nonhuman' (that is, supra-human) wisdom that was prior to all the ages can never be lost, it nevertheless becomes enveloped in more and more impenetrable veils, which hide it from men's sight and make it extremely difficult to discover. This is why we find everywhere, under various symbols, the same something which has been lost – at least to all appearances and as far as the outer world is concerned

---

[5]Schuon, F., *Gnosis: Divine Wisdom*, p.23.

– and that those who aspire to true knowledge must rediscover.[6]

Lost to consumerism, the oblivious masses, the meaning of the symbol, the interpretation of gnosis itself, is now obfuscated – the exoteric shell remains, binding teachings together, but the inner heart, the esoteric tradition that veiled the highest mysteries in the tapestry and garlands of symbol have dissolved, crumbling from within to leave behind only the exterior corpus of teachings. To know, to understand – this is the core of gnosis, and it is the loss of this elusive element of religion that causes René Guénon to despair. The *Modern World* is truly one where *God is Dead* – yet curiously, this famous catch phrase of Nietzsche's is not as atheistic as many would claim it to be. When Zarathustra uttered his grand proclamation, Nietzsche knew well its consequences. The phrase is itself an inversion of the value tables of the society of his day – it is the *devaluation of the highest value.* Nietzsche knew the void this would create in the spiritual life of man, and it is here that it becomes paramount that he must be recognized as an important thinker on religion as well as philosophy, for he postulated a number of concepts which are far from being purely atheistic in sentiment. His rejections and attitudes to religion are a reaction to the Christian doctrine of his day – to which end it is no mere coincidence that he chose *Dionysus* as the adversary of the 'Crucified'. Even without considering Nietzsche's fondness for Pagan Greece, a number of his thoughts are of deep significance to our understanding of the Primordial Tradition, such as the *"Ur-Eine."*

The Ur-Eine - the primal oneness of things [...] Later the Ur-Eine is another kind of phenomenal world, one which is not knowable to us." But whatever is interpretational of different stages of Nietzsche's development may be, the Ur-Eine represents his tortured longing to reach the deeper dimensions of being "which are not known to us".[7]

---

[6] Guénon, R., *The Crisis of the Modern World* (New York: Sophia Perennis 2004), p.7.
[7] Smith, H., *Forgotten Truth: The Primordial Tradition*, p.40.

The concept of the Ur-Eine is also similar to the vast and great *Collective Unconscious*, as was theorised by Carl Jung, a past pioneer in the then emerging field of psychology. In terms of Jung's hypothesis concerning the Unconscious and the influence of dreams and symbols upon man's waking life, it is well known that Jung drew heavily upon mythological sources, applying cross-cultural interpretations to phenomena occurring within the psyche, such as the archetypes. The archetypes are a type of universal (in a similar manner to that espoused by Plato), which on the one hand can be said to contain a purely abstract truth, and yet on the other one can also infer that as an absolute occurrence of a tautological value, the archetypes in question are also possessed of a metaphysical existence. Jung himself was quite aware of the fact that his theory placed archetypes in a very liminal boundary region between the material and immaterial, and himself referred to the archetypes as '*psychoids*'.

> The archetypes seemed close enough to the patterns he saw emerging in the theories and experiments of twentieth-century physics for him to conclude that archetypes are psychoids. By this he meant that they shape matter (nature) as well as the mind (psyche). They transcend the split between these two and are neutral toward it favouring neither one side nor the other.[8]

The archetypes, functioning as what Jung terms as psychoids, are in fact operating also on the level of 'God-Forms' in that they themselves are symbols and/or representations of the respective deities. Elaborating on this in relation to his own system of belief, Jung expresses the following train of thought.

> We know that God-images play a great role in psychology, but we cannot prove the [actual] existence of God. As a responsible scientist, I am not going to preach my personal and subjective convictions which I cannot prove...To me, personally speaking, the question whether God exists at all or not is futile. I am

---

[8]Smith, H., *Forgotten Truth: The Primordial Tradition*, p.40.

sufficiently convinced of the effects man has always attributed to a divine being. If I should express a belief beyond that...it would show that I am not basing my opinion on facts. When people say they believe in the existence of God, it has never impressed me in the least. Either I know a thing and then don't need to believe it; or I believe it because I'm not sure that I know it. I am well satisfied with the fact that I know experiences which I cannot avoid calling numinous or divine.[9]

From this passage it is amply illustrated that Jung did not base any of his theories on the archetypes or psychoids from a belief in the divine; his ideas were, at least to Jung's line of reasoning, based on verifiable facts that he knows to exist. In this regard, the current dogmatic line of argument drawn between science and religion crumbles – for the study of religion as archetypes and symbols provides empirical evidence of recurrent ideas outside the regions of that which would be expected through the medium of normal cross-cultural contact. Therefore, the symbols of religion and myth are transformed from mere metaphor to a system of universal truths that will occur within all genuine religious traditions. The symbol then, becomes much more than a pictorial representation of an incident or 'God-Form'; rather it is lesser manifestation of the subject/object represented, and this is the core foundation to the understanding of all sacred art. In the words of Frithjof Schuon, "the understanding of some symbol is enough to consider the nature of its form, secondly its doctrinal, and so traditional, definition, and finally the metaphysical and spiritual realities of which the symbol is the expression."[10] It is precisely for this reason, that religion and art will always be linked in ways which to many appear inexplicable. It is extremely common in both the philosophy of art and in the philosophy of religion, to explain both topics in terms of lacking a definable sense of purpose – hence the age old question, "What is art?" or "What is religious experience?" Science and logic will always fail to explain both art and religious

---

[9]Cottingham, J., *The Spiritual Dimension: Religion, Philosophy and Human Value*, Cambridge, (Cambridge University Press, 2005) p.72.

[10]Schuon, F., *Spiritual Perspectives and Human Facts*, trans. Matheson, M., (London: Perennial Books, 1969) p.63.

belief, for both lie outside of the sphere of scientific evidence and mathematical truths. It is commonly accepted by academics studying the philosophy of religion today that a purely empirical attitude to explaining religious belief will always meet with failure.

> Bernard Williams, perhaps the most distinguished analytic moral philosopher writing at the turn of the twentieth century, once speculated that there might be something about ethical understanding that makes it inherently unsuited to be explored through the methods and techniques of analytic philosophy alone. If that is true, the point may apply a fortiori to religion, in so far as religious attitudes, even more than moral ones, often seem to encompass elements that are resistant to logical analysis.[11]

Neither the value of art nor the value of religion can be explained by recourse to logic and empirical systems of thought alone. Rather, the two subjects, sharing a common origin in the Primordial Consciousness, are more kindred than they are in opposition. The function of art and the function of the religion both operate on a level of subliminal aesthetics – a successful piece of art captures the same experience as a successful experience of the divine – it raises the mental state to what I will now refer to as a state of *pathos* or an appeal to emotion that strives to recapture the original state of either the artist or priest. It is this altered state of emotive pathos which is replicated in the observer though the transmission of a meme or the medium of thought that determines the success or failure of a both a piece of art and a sacred or ritual act. This is what the Tantric philosopher Abhinavagupta also sought to express in his theory of aesthetics, and correlates to his *rasa* theory. Notably we can also find the importance of the "flavour" expressed in the art theory of the Western philosopher David Hume. Similarly, Nietzsche also noted the similarity between aesthetic and religious experience, concluding that the current path of religion (meaning that which is derived from the relatively modern Judeo-Christian current) was *only one form* which spirituality could have taken, for Nietzsche says that "Art and not morality is the true

---

[11]Cottingham, J., *The Spiritual Dimension: Religion, Philosophy and Human Value*, p.1.

metaphysical activity of man."[12] John Cottingham elaborates further on the links between moral and aesthetic experience in his work the *Spiritual Dimension.*

> Our religious (and moral and aesthetic) experience involves transformative ways of perceiving reality. And this points, incidentally, to something of a paradigm shift when we look, for example, at some of what have been considered traditional arguments for God's existence. Every standard textbook in the philosophy of religion mentions the arguments 'from religious experience', or 'from moral [aesthetic] experience', as if what was involved was a kind of inference from one sort of act – roughly a fact about a certain kind of subjective occurrence – to a conclusion about a supposed objective correlate or external cause for the relevant experience.[13]

The topic of the connection between the art of symbols and religious expression is also dealt with at length by Frithjof Schuon.

> In speculations about formal elements it would be a handicap to lack this aesthetic function of intellect. A religion is revealed, not only by its doctrine, but also by its general form, and this has its own characteristic beauty, which is reflected in its every aspect from its "mythology' to its art. Sacred art expresses Reality in relation to a particular spiritual vision. And aesthetic intelligence sees the manifestations of the Spirit even as the eye sees flowers or playthings.[14]

This study of symbols is by no means a simple topic – to Schuon it is a precise science. Nor is it limited purely to symbolism – Schuon, like others authors before him, is connecting the mystic experience of the sacred to aesthetics, which he is defining as a unique type of

[12]Pfeffer, R., *Nietzsche: Disciple of Dionysus* (New Jersey: Associated University Presses, Inc. 1977),p.206.
[13]Cottingham, J., *The Spiritual Dimension: Religion, Philosophy and Human Value*, p.85.
[14]Schuon, F., *Spiritual Perspectives and Human Facts*, p.133.

intelligence, distinct from the more earthly and aspects of cognition. When attempting to explain the science of symbols, Schuon's definition is likewise complex; the interpretation of a symbol as a singular object is not deemed sufficient to understand its inherent qualities - rather what must be dwelt upon by the translators of religious semiotics is the relation of the symbol to other qualities, properties, objects and individual contexts.

> The science of symbols – not simply a knowledge of traditional symbols –proceeds from the qualitative significances of substances, forms, spatial directions, numbers, natural phenomena, positions, relationships, movements, colours and other properties or states of things; we are not dealing here with subjective appreciations, for the cosmic qualities are ordered in relation to Being and according to a hierarchy which is more real than the individual; they are, then, independent of our tastes, or rather they determine them to the extent that we are ourselves conformable to Being; we assent to the qualities to the extent we ourselves are 'qualitative.'[15]

What defines the Primordial Tradition as a potential major current in religious belief and philosophy lies in its use of the symbol and its advocacy of the *aesthetic experience* – belief in the potency of any specific symbol relies upon the most basic human aspect of belief. Belief in a sentient god or creator is not even required, and by this explanation of religious belief and symbolism it is possible for even the most ardent 'atheist' to be a believer in the Primordial Tradition. In such regards, it is similar to the thoughts once espoused by Kant on Deism:

> Essential to any deism is the view that there is such a thing as rational or natural religion, religion based on natural reason and not on supernatural revelation [...] Kant is emphatic that there need not be any special duties to God in order for there to be religion; he also denies that theoretical cognition of God's existence is required

---

[15]Schuon, F., *Gnosis: Divine Wisdom*, p.92-93.

for religion – naturally enough he thinks that no such cognition is available to us.[16] [...] this faith needs merely the idea of God...only the minimum cognition (it is possible that there is a God) has to be subjectively sufficient"[17]

A symbol is of course, only a picture to those who cannot ascertain a deeper meaning. To those who are capable of learning this difficult code, it is reasonable to apply the following quotation: *ex magna luce in intellectu sequitur magna propensio in voluntate* ('from a great light in the intellect there follows a great inclination in the will).[18] It is not satisfactory to develop a rudimentary knowledge of the numinous – this alone is not sufficient to produce gnosis, which in its full manifestation must be grasped at both the level of the theoretical and the practical; the Primordial Tradition being composed of absolute ideals from different traditions and pathways, does not advocate a strict system of practice, but rather takes a philosophical stance in regards to practice that can be applied by any religious tradition. What is advocated in regards to the practical element is similar to that which is found in the Stoic school of thought. There were many Stoic treatises entitled '*On Exercises*', and the central notion of *askesis*, found for example in Epictetus, implied not so much 'asceticism' in the modern sense as a practical program of training, concerned with the 'art of living'.[19] The primacy of praxis, the vital importance that is placed on the individual's embarking on a path of practical self-transformation, rather than (say) simply engaging in an intellectual debate or philosophical analysis.[20]

The general aim of such programmes was not merely intellectual enlightenment, or the imparting of abstract theory, but a transformation of the whole person, including our patterns of emotional response. *Metanoia*, a fundamental conversion or change

---

[16]Wood, A., M., Kant's Deism in *Kant's Philosophy of Religion Reconsidered*, p.7.
[17]Ibid., p.8.
[18]Cottingham, J., *The Spiritual Dimension: Religion, Philosophy and Human Value*, p.14.
[19]Ibid., p.4.
[20]Ibid., p.5.

of heart, is the Greek term; in the Roman Stoic Seneca it appears as a 'shift in one's mentality' (*translatio animi*) or a 'changing' (*mutatio*) of the self. 'I feel, my dear Lucilius,' says Seneca, 'that I am being not only reformed but transformed (*non tantum emendari sed transfigurari*)'.[21]

The relevance here is of course part of the problem Huston Smith grasped earlier in his work *The Forgotten Truth* – perennial philosophy, in the forms which it had existed previously, was in danger of becoming over intellectualized, to the point where it was in peril of divulging from the point of being a system of religion to existing as a philosophy alone. Thus his purpose by recommending that perennial philosophy be renamed as The Primordial Tradition, was an attempt to revitalize what he saw as a failing system of ideology – the time of the great Traditionalists such as Julius Evola and René Guénon was over, and Huston Smith realized that a new tactic needed to be deployed in order for the philosophy to extend beyond the reach of an intellectual elite into the main stream culture. In a sense, he elected to effect a change within the nature and the delivery of Tradition itself. Here, we must also bear heed to Guénon's warnings that Traditions can disappear:

> It is evident that all traditional forms do not proceed directly from the primordial tradition and that other forms must have sometimes played the role of intermediaries; but the latter are most often traditions that have entirely disappeared, and those transmissions in general go back to epochs far too distant for ordinary history – whose field of investigation is really very limited – to be capable of the slightest knowledge of them, not counting the fact that the means by which they were effected are not among those accessible to its methods of research.[22]

This passage also exemplifies the interpretation of the Primordial

---

[21]Ibid., p.5.

[22]Guénon, R., *Traditional Forms & Cosmic Cycles*, (New York: Sophia Perennis 2004) p.42.

Tradition even further – it is not a single specific Tradition, but rather an underlying layer of universal truth which acts as a foundation for Traditions to evolve from, and at times dissolve back into. It is the substratum of human conscious itself and defines the nature of and the direction of history, *whether man professes to believe in its existence or not.* Thus far, interest in religion is on swift decline – it stands at the apex of a descent and interior degeneration that has been unparalleled in history; aided by the concurrent deterioration in the academic quality of the arts and the humanities, the material sciences have ascended to point of total domination. Under such an aegis, religion, the science of the spirit needs to be rethought, reshaped, and reconstructed from the very foundations of thought itself to survive in this era. As such, the Primordial Tradition delivers what should rightly be termed a *sui generis* argument for religion and spirituality from which there is no defense short of an outright denial of the fundamental concepts of the social sciences as we know them today – it applies the study of the translation of symbols as a logical argument, and manifests itself as a rational system of human belief, as opposed to the more traditional arguments from a religious perspective, such as the teleological model or the more commonly resorted to argument from religious experience which occur frequently in philosophical discourse on religion. From this perspective, it should be apparent that the concept of the Primordial Tradition has far more in common with the comparative mythology of Georges Dumézil or the study of the History of Religions as espoused by the author Mircea Eliade than it has with the currently accepted philosophical models for religious debate. In general, however the study of religion at an academic level is in rapid decline, which is echoed throughout the modern world – religion, the science of the soul, is facing oblivion. As it stands religion and spirituality must either take a stand or face total extinction as modernity further encroaches into man's private world of the spirit; the only methodology by which to promote any religious or spiritual thought in this age, is to restructure it, to change people's most basic and rudimentary understanding of *what religion is.* To quote Huston Smith there is but one way left to achieve this in the current sociological and political climate, "Short of a historical breakdown which would render routine ineffectual and force us to attend again to things which matter most, we wait for art: for metaphysicians, who imbued with that species of truth that is beauty in its mental mode, are (like Plato) concomitantly poets".[23]

[23]Smith, H., *Forgotten Truth: The Primordial Tradition*, p.36.

Confrontation with Nothingness:
The Amorality, Nihilism and Isolation of a Leader

"It can never be," those wise modern people said, hoping to make their prediction true through your obedient credulity to what *they* claim will be true. And yet like the tiny purple fishes of modern lore, you slipped laughing through their fingers...

Brett Stevens

Among the wisest and stupidest people of our time it is equally accepted that the aristocratic principle will never return. We are now a government of laws, and of equality, not of human beings.

We trust the solidity of laws, regulations, measurements and money. It is unlike the organic measure of the "quality" of a human being, because that requires us to judge them as exceptional or not and exclude those who are not equal enough.

At the same time they trumpet this great innovation, people in our society are careful to be self-loathing and to loathe their civilizations. They like to point out how "we" are fat, lazy, stupid and undeserving. Some of the wiser people in our time see this as a result of our lack of purpose.

The thinking goes that we have crucified God again and he stayed dead this time, and as a direct result of that deicide, our society has slipped into the warm fatal bath of nihilism. We are too far underwater to hear the cries of our rescuers, or even heed common sense.

It is this nihilism, we are told, that is responsible for our lack of values in this modern time. No meaning exists: life is finite, death is permanent, and there is no divine authority to give any one outcome priority over any other.

Thus we return to an ancient hypothesis. We live in the garden of Eden, except for the fatal serpent called nihilism. What is nihilism?

> Nihilism is the belief that all values are baseless and that nothing can be known or communicated.

It is often associated with extreme pessimism and a radical scepticism that condemns existence. A true nihilist would believe in nothing, have no loyalties, and no purpose other than, perhaps, an impulse to destroy. While few philosophers would claim to be nihilists, nihilism is most often associated with Friedrich Nietzsche who argued that its corrosive effects would eventually destroy all moral, religious, and metaphysical convictions and precipitate the greatest crisis in human history.

> In the 20th century, nihilistic themes – epistemological failure, value destruction, and cosmic purposelessness – have preoccupied artists, social critics, and philosophers. Mid-century, for example, the existentialists helped popularize tenets of nihilism in their attempts to blunt its destructive potential. By the end of the century, existential despair as a response to nihilism gave way to an attitude of indifference, often associated with antifoundationalism.[1]

In this view, nihilism is not just an absence of values, but a rejection of all values. However, much like the difference between amorality and immorality, this constitutes an acknowledgment of those values, and then a conscious decision to disregard them through extreme scepticism.

---

[1] Nihilism, *The Internet Encyclopaedia of Philosophy*, retrieved from http://www.iep.utm.edu/nihilism/.

However, popularly we treat nihilism as an erosion of values. Very few have stopped to think that, if we're already drowning in corrupt logic, that this very thought - that without God we die of nihilism - is itself a product of that same corrupt logic.

Corruption in thinking happens most profoundly when the thoughts themselves are left unchanged, but the underlying assumptions are subtly and devastatingly altered. Change the meaning of a symbol, or the assumed positive goals of a society, and the unchanged thought takes on an entirely different direction.

When our assumptions are tainted, the only solution is to go lower, to a less-advanced level of thinking. Bring it all back to square one: go so low that we debride the assumptions along with the bad concepts from which we flee.

If, as said above, we assume that we are in a dying time when popular notions are illusory, it is safe to say that they are all illusory. We must go further than "tune in, turn on, and drop out" - we must drop *away* from civilization entirely, and go back to our human origins, to discover the reality that is now buried under layers of social judgment.

Friedrich Nietzsche created a parable of man as a bridge between beast and a new state, the overman. In this view, the concepts of a dying civilization are not bridges, but targets in themselves; to get past them, a person must "go under" these higher concepts, because to try to rise above them is to build upon them and thus incorporate the misgiven assumptions into the "new" idea.

What is great in man is that he is a bridge and not an end; what can be loved in man is that he is an *overture* and a *going under.*

> I love those who do not know how to live, except by going under, for they are those who cross over.
> I love the great despisers, for they are the great reverers and arrows

of longing for the other shore.[2]

We consider ourselves above reality because we have invented the platform we call morality. Morality is not found in nature and does not exist except in the minds of humans. But we apply it as if it were inherent to the universe, and without it, we claim we will be lost.

Nihilism suggests that morality is not inherent. It is at best one choice among many others. There is no universal reason to pursue it, especially since in its common form it is little more than social logic.

"Play nice with others," says the nagging teacher, threatening us with disciplinary reports that can follow us for the rest of our lives. "Share your toys. Include everyone. Give each person the same amount of time to talk."

Those who fear nihilism tell us that without inherency, we lose morality and every choice beyond the immediate pleasures of a distracted, self-pitying citizenry. However, by losing those things, we also lose the assumptions of morality.

Going under means rejecting socialization, the morality it brings, and all things above reality itself. Our society considers pure self-interest to be evil, and finds it dubious that we would judge by outcomes, and not what other people think. Those are higher values.

Lower values on the other hand are less separated from reality itself. A caged animal wants to escape; a predator must find, kill and consume prey; a person who is exceptional must break away from the herd, amass wealth to be independent, and then do their real work, periodically assaulted by the chaotic, schizoid and neurotic masses who essentially destroy anything they touch.

---

[2]Nietzsche, F., trans. Kaufmann, W., Thus Spoke Zarathustra, *The Portable Nietzsche*, (Penguin: 1976), p.4.

Insanity in individuals is something rare - but in groups, parties, nations and epochs, it is the rule.[3]

To understand what is below, we must escape the herd and its assumptions and use our brains again as the powerful instruments for analysis that they are. We must escape socialization, morality and the controlling symbols (of carefully altered meaning) of others.

This requires a confrontation that mirrors the last great evolution of humankind, in which the lone hunter-gatherer and his inconsistent ad hoc tribal unit confronted settled civilization, in which almost every task of survival is a delegation and not a singular task. A hunter-gatherer finds his own food, shelter, tools and medical care; a fixed civilization puts each person in a specialized role, and has them delegate all others tasks to other specialized workers in exchange for money, goodwill or both.

As the lone creatures of the steppes went from being isolated hunters who met to mate, trade and tussle only to being humans who lived together in constant contact, a new magical science arose in the human condition: socialization. With it came manipulation, sycophantism, flattery, deception, self-aggrandizement, narcissism and just about every other human evil.

Indeed, what we know of as the early days of human civilization could be described as a process of *holding back* the influence of socialization. Like any tool, it seeks to become the master of its master by forcing him to see the world in terms of the tool - "when you have a hammer, everything looks like a nail" - and thus to become dependent on it. This inverse parasitism relationship defines many human interactions.

At this point, something interesting happened: our ability to deceive ourselves became the ability to deceive others, by sharing images that we had in our own heads through the symbolic code of language, so

---

[3]Nietzsche, F., trans. Kaufmann, W., <u>Aphorism 156</u>, *Beyond Good and Evil*.

that the other shared the symbol and with it, its imprecision. This was a form of manipulation that since that time has been impolite to mention, because it sort of - well, mostly -invalidates the notion of society:

> Once upon a time, in some out of the way corner of that universe which is dispersed into numberless twinkling solar systems, there was a star upon which clever beasts invented knowing. That was the most arrogant and mendacious minute of "world history," but nevertheless, it was only a minute. After nature had drawn a few breaths, the star cooled and congealed, and the clever beasts had to die. One might invent such a fable, and yet he still would not have adequately illustrated how miserable, how shadowy and transient, how aimless and arbitrary the human intellect looks within nature. There were eternities during which it did not exist.

And when it is all over with the human intellect, nothing will have happened. For this intellect has no additional mission which would lead it beyond human life. Rather, it is human, and only its possessor and begetter takes it so solemnly - as though the world's axis turned within it. But if we could communicate with a gnat, we would learn that he likewise flies through the air with the same solemnity, that he feels the flying center of the universe within himself. There is nothing so reprehensible and unimportant in nature that it would not immediately swell up like a balloon at the slightest puff of this power of knowing.[4]

To Nietzsche, "knowing" is how human beings create a thought-object that refers to outside reality, and then treat that thought-object as reality itself:

> Just as it is certain that one leaf is never totally the same as another, so it is certain that the concept "leaf" is formed by arbitrarily

---

[4]Nietzsche, F., trans. Kaufmann, W., On Truth and Lies in an Extra-Moral Sense, *The Portable Nietzsche*, p.1.

discarding these individual differences and by forgetting the distinguishing aspects. This awakens the idea that, in addition to the leaves, there exists in nature the "leaf": the original model according to which all the leaves were perhaps woven, sketched, measured, colored, curled, and painted - but by incompetent hands, so that no specimen has turned out to be a correct, trustworthy, and faithful likeness of the original model. We call a person "honest," and then we ask "why has he behaved so honestly today?" Our usual answer is, "on account of his honesty." Honesty! This in turn means that the leaf is the cause of the leaves.[5]

The human mind creates a layer of illusion in which it mistakes its recognition of parts of reality for that reality itself, and assigns to objects properties that are the result of complex chains of cause-effect reasoning.

Plato attempted to point this out with his metaphor of the cave, and Schopenhauer tried to reveal it through his admonition that human reality consists of "representations of representations." Neither were successful because for most people the will to deny this is so strong.

Yet it is the source of our error. Our independent representations are like branches of nature itself, and continue evolving on their own. With each thought we touch to them, they become changed in recollection or gain new dimension of our musing.

For the most part, we are able to tolerate this view because as individual humans we live without goals. We have goals within life, but these are more accurately described as preferences; we want promotions, so we attend work to that end, but we are not questing in a situation where victory is survival and defeat is death.

In fact, the ordinary person probably welcomes this view, because it enables them a type of stability in the modern world. With science

---

[5]Ibid.

claiming to debunk all but materialism, and no actual structure to society except a tendency against hierarchy, people have no center to their lives. Their nihilism is the result of being cut off from any connection to the essence of "real," whether nature, reality, meaning, wisdom, transcendence or even dubstep.

On the other hand, a leader - one who leads, one who influences others, or one who invents direction-changing ideas - studies consequences, because a goal is a consequence yet to come. He then studies the rules of his world so that he can predict the method of achieving that goal. Finally, he purges distractions from his mind.

That moment of confrontation illustrates the role of the leader, which is to go where others are afraid to go, and to find in those desolated places the same meaning others claim to find in the warm and fuzzy places they are afraid to leave.

The leader must confront emptiness, and triumph, or the tribe is lost in a kind of heat-death caused by a lack of will to make choices. Without purpose, all choices are potential obligations or penalties. Better to do as little as possible, and not risk being wrong.

A leader is the one who rises above those fears to confront the nothingness eye-to-eye, and yet who does not blink. He or she has a simple but effective weapon: if inherency is removed, all outcomes are choices, and the leader is the one with a nose for optimum choices. A leader thrives in a nihilistic state because for a leader, what matters is not meaning but outcomes.

Meaning is assumed because there can only be one meaning, and it is derived from the process of leadership itself. The goal is a consequence, a victory over the infinite other possible directions that could have ensnared events. To see this with clarity is to understand the relationship between the universe and thought itself.

Paradoxically, such thought requires nihilism. Leaders require nihilism: a lack of belief in belief, a lack of truth, a lack of an inherent goal.

*****

Nihilism does not exist.

At least, we should acknowledge that it rejects itself. A true nihilist, having no belief in anything, would wither away. Our nihilists on the other hand seem to be sceptical about everything except *themselves*, and in fact invent a morality around those selves. Thus it is unlikely that they are nihilists. Further, nihilism reduces itself to nothing. Those who believe in no truth are in turn going to reject even that belief in no truth, and the belief in no communication, because these beliefs and communications are part of the human thought process and are themselves necessary even to formulate nihilism. A non-thinking object like a rock might have true nihilism, but anyone else is putting a nihilistic veneer on what is essentially *radical self-interest*.

Modern nihilists are very much moralists, only moralists of meaningless, muteness and destruction - except for themselves. And their friends. And their pleasures. That's not very nihilistic; they are as pious as the church-goer, but with a different set of gods. Their gods are the self and its pleasures, and since these are empty gods, they must be appeased with constant sacrifice.

This behaviour pattern is a subset of a larger type of mental outlook which we might call *fatalism*. Fatalism is the belief that different actions do not change (ultimate) consequences. One form of it is express in the vernacular: "oh well, we're just going to rot away and die anyway, so nothing matters." There is no point struggling against the void, only degrees of acquiescence, and thus how cool you look while acquiescing is of primary importance.

A fatalist sees the world as an insoluble problem, which leaves only himself. He can then please himself, and justify his apathy toward the world at large with his fatalism, and presuming that he lives in a society and time which allows him to be so lazy, have a pleasant obligation-free life. By casting aside the possibility of meaning, he frees himself from the obligation to do something about it.

What undoes the fatalist is the possibility of better outcomes. Contentment exists so long as there is not a bad outcome, but the instant there is a possibility of a better one, contentment is gone. This is the same principle behind "keeping up with the Joneses": you feel good about your car until the exact moment your neighbour drives up in a new or better one.

> Even before I left graduate school I had come to the conclusion that virtually all people live by what I think of as a "fiction-absolute." Each individual adopts a set of values which, if truly absolute in the world - so ordained by some almighty force - would make not that individual but his group...the best of all possible groups, the best of all inner circles. Politicians, the rich, the celebrated, become mere types. Does this apply to "the intellectuals" also? Oh, yes... perfectly, all too perfectly.[6]

The leader is the person who does not wait for the Joneses to show up in a new car. The leader knows that new cars exist, and the possibility that his opponents, adversaries or hostile parasite-predators have access to such vehicles. He is not surprised when it shows up; he is merely calculating how to effect the most positive consequences in light of this new information.

Where an ordinary person might assess themselves according to whether or not they have a new car as well, the leader has no time to waste mental cycles on such things. He is concerned only with his goal: does this car get me closer to my goal? If yes, acquire one; should

---

[6]Wolfe, T., *The Human Beast* - lecture given to the Jefferson Institute in 2006. Retrieved from http://www.neh.gov/about/awards/jefferson-lecture/tom-wolfe-lecture.

I steal this one, attempt to purchase one, make one, or what?

For this reason, fatalism is incompatible with leadership. It is also incompatible with ordinary people, but they don't realize this until they have seen the inverse of a better possibility; that inverse is a life looked on rearward, as the waning days of consciousness approach. At that point, it dawns on them that something better might have come out of their lives.

Leaders never have that problem.

*****

A leader must always *know* that his cause is necessary, just or excellent. A leader cannot be infected with a tendency to shrug things off and ignore them. There cannot even be the possibility of nothingness, which makes sense to a leader as when one has a goal, all of life is reduced to data which either calculates to achieve that goal, or is of the ambiguous and possibly hostile combinations that do not achieve it.

This is not a "with-us-or-against-us" calculus, but a sense of knowing that some acts achieve a result and everything else is irrelevant.

In this mode of thought, nothingness itself does not exist. What exists are probabilities and, as time passes, certainties; these must be managed so that the goal is achieved. A leader thinks of nothing else, and does not require the goal to be inherent. It is better than inherent, it is necessary, whether by mandate for survival or from an aesthetic need.

Another way to express this is that, in a relative universe, nothingness cannot exist without somethingness to delineate its borders, which makes nothingness a form of somethingness:

Bertrand Russell (1985) laboured mightily to reduce negative truths to positive truths. Russell tried paraphrasing 'The cat is not on the mat' as 'There is a state of affairs incompatible with the cat being on the mat'. But this paraphrase is covertly negative; it uses 'incompatible' which means not compatible. He tried modelling 'Not p' as an expression of disbelief that p. But 'disbelief' means believing that something is not the case. Is it even clear that absences are causally inert? Trapped miners are killed by the absence of oxygen. In the end Russell gave up.[7]

"The cat is not on the mat" can be phrased as "the cat is elsewhere than on the mat" or "something else occupies the mat" in lieu of the cat. But lest we fall into the gross modern error of assuming that linguistic constructions define the world, which is a reversed causal flow as language is derived from the world but in a Goedelian sense does not necessarily fully mirror it, it is important to look at the more basic struggle he encounters.

If all that existed were nothingness, then there would be no concept of somethingness or any distinction from nothingness. There would be nothing other than the condition itself, because with an absence of positive truths or existence, it would have no observer-agents to hypothesize whether it was nothingness or not. Nothingness is a state of absence *of something* and without that something, nothingness itself is not clear.

Nothingness, like nihilism, either reduces itself to a nonsense definition (negating a negative) or by the necessity of being a referent and having a logical boundary in a relative universe, elevates itself into being non-nothing. Either way, this human concept of non-existence seems to fall before us in the same way many things are obliterated by William Blake's statement, "If the doors of perception were cleansed everything would appear to man as it is, infinite."

---

[7]Sorensen, R., Nothingness, *Stanford Encyclopaedia of Philosophy2009*, retrieved from http://plato.stanford.edu/entries/nothingness/.

The idea of nothingness either being a non-definition or a form of somethingness suggests an infinite structure, or at least a very large circular one, such that the most extreme definitions converge on their opposites. This suggests a world where limitations and distinctions are imposed from within. This further suggests that nihilism itself is equally self-reducing, or even *affirming*.

In the hands of a leader, who takes for granted that his cause is right and that he must only accomplish it, nihilism is a natural state. There is no inherent value to anything; there are only choices. With the decision made to strive for the goal, the only mathematic of the mind is to balance these choices for favourability. Which gets me closest to the goal? Elect that and then face the consequent next array of choices.

In this state of mind, the leader is closest to the workings of his own mind - pure idealism - and thus free of the materialist/idealist tension that mars human existence. There may be a reason for choosing this form of active nihilism:

One who is detached from pleasure and from desire, from predilection and from thirst, from fever and from craving is called "void." Elsewhere the texts speak of a "superior man" dwelling principally in the state of "real, inviolable, pure voidness" - it is in this state that Prince Sidhatta receives and speaks to kings. He has said that the perceptions no longer cling to those who know, who are troubled by nothing in the world, who ask no more questions, who have rooted out every loathing, and who crave neither existence nor nonexistence. As one who is detached he experiences every kind of perception or sensation or feeling. With particular reference to the triad "void," "signless," "without tendency," all this is associated with the form of experience - either internal and psychological or of the outside world - of one who continues to live with the centre of his own being in the state of *nibbana* or in one or other of the higher contemplations...[8]

Parallels to Nietzsche's overman have been drawn here, confused mainly by the tendency of Western New Age interpretations of Eastern religions to view "detachment" as meaning a lack of purpose outside the individual, when in fact as indicated above it refers to a state of disconnected from biased toward certain behaviours, including appetites, tendencies, habits and other extraneous matter to the question of achieving the goal. When the goal is in sight, the regular ways a person might behave are meaningless; all that matters is discipline of the self toward acting so that the goal is achieved.

A leader can elect to use nihilism as a gateway toward this state. This inverts the fatalist equation, in which the world is negated and the self is preserved as an ideal. In the nihilist view, both world and self are deprecated in favour of a focus to task. One is not aware of the world in a constant presence, but only insofar as it is relevant to the task, and the self is seen as an implement and given no further significance.

Most people enter this state when they concentrate intensely. The world recedes, their heartbeat is present and then forgotten, they breathe deeply and rhythmically and descend into a state where they become their own focal point and exist only through their actualization in the task as a means toward the goal. This is the state of a leader.

It is not threatened by nihilism because it does not need inherent value, since it has the goal, and does not need inherent obsession with self or standard behaviours, as it is narrowed to the task. This is the state in which a leader exists, and the mode from which decisions must be made. We might in fact call this the "aristocratic state" because it belongs to only the most intellectually mature citizens.

*****

---

[8] Evola, J., *The Doctrine of Awakening*, (USA: Inner Traditions, 1996), p.212.

The leader knows, from his exalted state of nothingness, several things that would shatter the psyche of the ordinary person.

First, he realizes that control is an illusion. A group can be controlled through fear and reward, but it can break that control at any time the illusion of uniformity is shattered. This is why crowds, mobs and vigilante posses are retributive toward *any* deviation from orthodoxy, because as soon as one escapes to the non-orthodox the ranks are shattered.

The leader is aware that a liberal movement will emerge. This is the mob formed of individuals that decide to flatter each other, and by extending approval and inclusion without demanding people prove anything, they can form a movement based around negativity. They know what they don't want: standards, which they can fail to attain; values, which they can be shown to be in violation of; quality, which isn't accessible to everyone. They want equality as a result, which means *equal approval* more than any state of political or economic stature. The negative movement creates an external ideology so that its few rules are spelled out clearly and made so simplistic that everyone can participate, and it derives its power from the number of dissatisfied people who want to join such a group, and the fact that as it develops it will create chaos and produce more rootless, dissatisfied, neurotic and paranoid people. It is like a cancer cell, growing without a goal except itself, which is a more complex way of saying that "if you *are* a hammer, you'd better make everything look like a nail."

Such groups immediately set about trying to prove what is "inherent." They depend on the idea that certain things are inevitable for their control, because since they do not have a goal, they need fixed standards - tendencies, preferences, habits, etc. in essence - to become assumptions. They create assumptions by claiming these things are absolutely true, which requires them to deconstruct, reduce to the material level, and translate into social terms the basis of these assumptions. They call it inherent, but what they really mean is "inherent" to their ability to remain in power.

This in turn translates to a need for ahierarchicalism. Equality requires that all are accepted equally; this tautological mental virus further requires these inherent values so that someone can remain in control. The result is that complex hierarchies are instead distilled into an endless flat field of options. Instead of a tree structure, which at its top has five options, each of which then have five options, and each of those options have five options below leading toward a fan-like structure, the ahierarchicalism produces a giant linear structure of if-then statements. Each possible situation has a fixed slot, like a preference or habit, into which it slides and activates a response. This is a substitute for thinking and critical analysis; the successful power structure will even produce *ersatz* versions of thought and critical analysis to turn its citizens into vigilantes against "bad" or nonconforming thought.

What this does is create the worst type of world, which is a consensual reality that operates by cognitive dissonance making people look for a compensation against a threatening reality, and through a one-dimensional dogma projecting themselves onto it. In this strange world, symbol becomes reality, as perception becomes reality, because each individual is viewed as a confirmation of reality through the principle of equality. Since this view is hostile not only to reality, but to *any* central idea or goal, these civilizations tend to fall apart. Because the reality is consensual, and based in cognitive dissonance, its victims re-enforce it whenever it fails by insisting that the dogma get more and more extreme. Eventually the civilization reaches a state of being either a corrupt open market, or a corrupt open market hidden within an ideological state. Neither can adapt to change or even sustain itself owing to the vast amount of internal confusion.

*****

The nihilist as leader faces this process as his or her primary enemy because such narcissistic societies obstruct the leadership principle. The leadership principle is that reality comes first, achievements occur in reality and thus require study of reality, so individuals including the leader become means to this end.

The decadent principle on the other hand is that people are the goal, not the implement, and thus that symbolic perception of reality is adjusted to be convenient for the people involved. In order to support this, the false inherency of the narcissistic society becomes a control mechanism; nihilism is the opposite principle which breaks down this false inherency and allows the leadership principle to return, because the only person who can operate under nihilism is a leader with a goal supreme to all else.

A leader recognizes, using nihilism, that Machiavelli and Kautilya were right; there is no morality inherent to life. Most people live in illusion and most groups form by deluding each other and re-enforcing this delusion, thus making all their members co-dependent on one another for reinforcement of their view of existence. The moralistic viewpoint is created to avoid allowing people to break ranks. So long as the illusion of inherency holds, the political group holds together.

This conceals the fact that politics is self-serving. The political process, like a parasite, grows atop a human colony and siphons away energy and time for its own use. It does not provide better leadership, but in fact provides horrible leadership so that more energy must be given to it. Similarly to the free market forces that reward those who provide inefficient services with high margins over those who are efficient and solve problems, politics like economy is an extraneous force that by becoming a discipline in service to inherency, becomes an essential part of the daily lives of many.

Although many claim to be leaders, they tend to either be authoritarians or permissivists. The former attempt direct control in the way North Korea currently does, while the latter more resemble the open societies of the West, in which decadence is embraced is a form of positive value. In both cases, the sleight-of-hand is to redirect the population including its thinkers from the actual task toward a second task, like equality, economy or politics.

Shattering the boundary of morality and equality is necessary to transcend this illusion. On the other side of the boundary, the tools of leadership await and like all tools, suggest the hand of their creator.

*****

Is it true that the more people that are in a group, the less of the burden of a bad decision falls on an individual? Would it be too outlandish to wonder if that lessened burden did not correspond to a lessened concern, since most of the burden now falls on someone else?

From that, is it too strange to presume that the more issues faced by a group, the less likely it is to unite? And that any group as time goes on forgets its issues, and succumbs to takeover from those who have "simpler solutions"?

Could the same apply to individuals? Namely that the more issues they produce, the less they care about any one, and that thus any time a simpler explanation of the world comes along, the individual opens the gates of the castle to a new conqueror?

*****

The modern view of tradition forgets one of its most important and baffling concepts, mythic imagination.

Through this method, the imagination projects mythological imagery to symbolize real-world situations, and uses this symbolic set to derive meaning from them and to show a way to apply values, much as novels by recontextualizing our own concerns as those of enigmatic characters, force us to reinterpret our values.

To a nihilist, in a world without nothingness, there are no boundaries between thought and reality; if the information in a thought influences reality, or vice-versa, the crossover will impregnate the seemingly opposite medium. Underneath the everyday there is a vaster existence in which thought and matter are formed of the same substrate.

In this view, mythic imagination is not projection so much as creation. It takes the metaphorical form of the information found in matter, creates an ideal counterpart, and in doing so joins the world of idealism with the mental world of idealism of the individual. If structured in a way that corresponds to that world, and shared among many, it is possible the mental world not only symbolizes, but brings into existence that which is mythologized.

The secret of ancient nihilism is here: religion is not something external, but a union, and thus has no fixed form. It is a vocabulary of imagination joined to perception that creates its goal through a clear mind which, in the state of void, escapes the illusions of human reality and replaces them with an understanding of reality as a whole.

It is the universe joining to itself, like the middle finger joining the thumb, and with that union, creating that which is both logical (non-arbitrary) and new.

It alone is for the aristocrat of the soul, the person who has disciplined his or her mind to be pure void, and by removing the artefacts of existence and personality, can focus alone on the construct of ideals which both correspond to reality and like a gardener pruning, shape it toward greater health.

This state is both transcendence in the material, meaning that it allows us to see a greater meaning behind the material existence we lead, and a transcendence of the material through the idealistic and infinite.

It is odd that it requires nihilism, or the erosion of all that is, to see this - or is it? Nihilism removes all to nothingness and destroys the split between something and nothing, freeing the mind to see the unending.

This is the essence of tradition and the nihilism of the leader. It is the forbidden science that the crowd fears, and as humanity tumbles toward the inevitable collision between its grandiose notions and the reality it denies, this is the foundation of its salvation.

Political Aspects of Crowley's Thelema

Dr K R Bolton

B ritish occultist Aleister Crowley scandalised early 20th Century Britain and further a field as he sought to create an image for himself as the "Great Beast 666" while a sensationalist media obligingly took up his aim. The image seems likely to have adversely affected Crowley's potential role as a serious thinker in the perennial tradition in comparison to such personalities as Julius Evola and René Guénon, whose social and political thoughts have been gaining interest over the past decade.[1]

Colin Wilson, himself a Crowley biographer,[2] aptly sums up Crowley's predicament in his Foreword to Sandy Robertson's pictorial biography: "The key to Aleister Crowley's life is simple: from childhood to the end of his life he was in the grip of a ravenous, unsatisfied appetite for recognition."[3]

Wilson alludes to Crowley as having compared himself in greatness to Shakespeare, as one of England's two greatest poets. Wilson explains:

---

[1]Many of Evola's books have been published in English in recent years, and these include not only his occult books, but his works on politics and cultural criticism. Inner Traditions International has for e.g. published over the past ten years Evola's *Revolt Against the Modern World, Men Among the Ruins, The Mystery of the Grail, Meditations on the Peaks*, and *The Hermetic Tradition*. Integral Traditions has recently (2009) published Evola's autobiography *The Path of Cinnabar*. Many of René Guénon 's books have been published in English translation by Sophia Perennis Books, New York, www.sophiaperennis.com/.../Ren%E9%20Gu%E9non%20Series. html.

[2]Wilson, C., *Aleister Crowley: The Nature of the Beast* (Northamptonshire: The Aquarian Press, 1987).

[3]Wilson, C., Foreword to Sandy Robertson in Robertson, S., *The Aleister Crowley Scrapbook* (W. Foulsham & Co., Berks, 1988).

But fate was to play Crowley an extremely unkind trick. For the first forty years of his life he made tremendous efforts to achieve recognition. He published his 'collected works' in his early twenties; he persuaded someone to write a book declaring him to be the greatest man of his generation; he indulged in every possible self-advertisement. And the British public remained unaware of his existence. Then quite suddenly he became a household name when the magazine *John Bull* dubbed him 'the wickedest man in the world', and ran headlines like THE KING OF DEPRAVITY, A HUMAN BEAST, and A MAN WE'D LIKE TO HANG....[4]

The scandal involved Crowley's Abbey of Thelema at Sicily where he reportedly held satanic type rituals of quite depraved character, and where shortly one of his acolytes died apparently from bad water. Wilson continues:

At first Crowley was delighted by this 'fame' then it gradually dawned on him that nothing he could ever do could now make the British take him seriously. The world had finally noticed his existence – and reacted with a cry of disgust, as if it had trodden on a slug. And so for the last twenty years of his life, Crowley remained, in effect, as 'unknown' as he had ever been. He died a tired and disappointed man.[5]

While there has been a surge of interest in Crowley as a magician and mystic,[6] few of the many books or articles written about Crowley

---

[4]Ibid.

[5]Ibid.

[6]His literary executor John Symonds wrote the first post-mortem biography of Crowley, published in 1949, two years after Crowley's death. His staring and eyes shaven head appear on The Beatle's *Sergeant Peppers'* album cover. Many of the sub cultural Metal and Industrial music genres refer to Crowley, with such band names as "*Current 93*" for e.g. In film his devotee Kenneth Anger has produced movies with Crowleyite themes, including *Inauguration of the Pleasure Dome* (1953), *Invocation of My Demon Brother* (1969), and *Lucifer Rising* (1970-1980). A large number of Crowley's books have been published by such relatively major occult publishers as Samuel Weiser. The autobiography, *The Confessions of Aleister Crowley*,

have so much as touched upon the political and sociological aspects of Thelema. Yet Crowley also advocated a metaphysical critique of modernity and a revival of the eternal wisdom from which it derives, as did Evola and Guénon. Crowley was also a product of the turbulent era of post World War I Europe that manifested mass political movements such as Bolshevism and Fascism and Wilsonian globalist democracy, all three systems competing for mastery of the world ideologically and morally. Many of the literati and cultural establishment turned to one of the extremes of Bolshevism or Fascism, although the rejection of most of those who took up the latter was the result of their general distrust for all 'mass movements', as they came to regard Fascist elitism and hierarchy as too crassly materialistic to serve as a practical expression of their metaphysics. Among those who turned to the Right, based on a metaphysical and/or cultural outlook included Evola, D.H. Lawrence, Ezra Pound and W.B. Yeats.[7] The Italian poet D'Annunzio was also a man of action and a veteran of World War I. Commanding popular respect not only among the literati and the veterans of Italy, but among the general populace. He attempted a short-lived but highly interesting revival of a Renaissance City State when occupying Fiume and claiming it for Italy directly after World War I.[8] As for Crowley, his initial impressions of Fascism were positive, if particularly brief, as will be described herein.

While Crowley, Evola, Guénon and others of the perennial tradition, represented a cultural and metaphysical counter current to what they considered the levelling creeds of democracy and attendant materialism, rationalism and liberalism; those very concepts were championed by an oppositional stream among secret societies that can broadly be considered masonic, and themselves propagated cults of Deism, Reason and Nature which were heralded as a new 'rationalistic' religion in similar manner to the way which communism became a religion with its own saints, martyrs, holy wars, dogma, ritual and

---

was published in 1979, 1983 and 1986 by Routledge & Kegan Paul.
[7]Bolton, K., *Thinkers of the Right*, (Luton: Luton Publications, 2003).
[8]Ibid. p.23-30.

liturgy, despite its materialistic intentions.[9]

These secret societies with mystical symbols and initiatory structure, yet advocating naturalistic and materialistic revolutionary doctrines, have been identified as 'counter traditions' by Guénon and Evola. In *The Reign of Quantity and the Signs of the Times* Guénon wrote of this anti-tradition as paving the way for the establishment of a counterfeit 'counter-tradition'.[10]

It is therefore possibly a paradox that Crowley included Adam Weishaupt, founder of the 19th century crypto-masonic conspiratorial *Illuminati* in his list of 'Saints for his Thelemite Gnostic Mass.[11] Weishaupt was clearly a part of the anti-tradition in his advocacy of revolutionary, proto-communistic and naturalistic doctrines.[12] His inclusion among the Thelemite 'Saints' can perhaps be understood by his having been in dramatic conflict with the Catholic Church.

While Weishaupt sought to shape a new world order along communistic egalitarian lines as part of an 'anti-tradition' leading to a 'counter-tradition' as Guénon saw it, other occultists and mystics rejected democracy and liberalism as innately contrary to what they considered the elitist foundations of metaphysics maintained by a hierarchy atop which stood magician-priests and priest-kings.

Hence Eliphas Levi, one of the most influential of occult theorists of the late 19th Century, wrote of the anti-democratic and anti-egalitarian character of magic and occult doctrine, in terms later characteristic of Crowley:

---

[9]Note for e.g. the embalming of Lenin and his entombment at an edifice reminiscent of the stepped pyramids of ancient priest-kings.
[10]Guénon, R., 2002.
[11]Crowley, *Liber XV OTO Ecclesiae Gnosticae Catholicae Canon Missae, Magick*, 1984, Appendix VI, *The Saints*, p.430. First published privately 1911.
[12]Robison, J., *Proofs of a Conspiracy* (Boston: Western Islands, 1967). First published 1798.

Affirmation rests on negation; the strong can only triumph because of weakness; the aristocracy cannot be manifested except by rising above the people... The weak will ever be weak... the people in like manner will ever remain the people, the mass which is ruled and which is not capable of ruling. There are two classes: freemen and slaves; man is born in the bondage of his passions, but he can reach emancipation through intelligence. Between those who are free already and those who are as yet not here is no equality possible.[13]

Crowley rejected democracy for the same reasons as Levi and other occultists such as Evola and Guénon. In the Thelemic 'bible' *Liber Al Legis*, Crowley writes of democracy: "Ye are against the people, o my chosen."[14] To which Crowley commented: "The cant of democracy condemned."[15]

Having rejected democracy and other mass movements as innately alien to the Royal Art, Crowley sought to develop the political and social aspects of Thelema, the bible *Liber Legis*[16] of which is explained with uncharacteristic clarity by Crowley in *The Law is for All: An Extended Commentary on the Book of the Law*.

CROWLEY AS 'PROPHET OF THE NEW AEON'

Crowley was part of the occult revival of the late 19th and early 20th Centuries, as were many other budding and established literary figures such as W B Yeats, Arthur Machen, Algernon Blackwood, and Sax Rohmer.[17]

Crowley began his initiation in the primary organisation responsible for the occult revival in Britain was the Hermetic Order of the Golden

---

[13]Levi, E., *The History of Magic* (London: Rider, 1982), p.44.
[14]*Liber Legis* 2:25 (Main: Samuel Weiser Inc., 1984).
[15]Crowley, *The Law Is For All* (Arizona: Falcon Press, 1985), p.192.
[16]*The Book of the Law*.
[17]Robertson, *Crapulous Contemporaries?*, 1988, p.43.

Dawn, which he joined in 1898.[18] He shortly fell out with the leadership however.

Crowley spent the next few years travelling. In 1904 Crowley and his wife Rose were in Egypt. Here an event occurred which according to Crowley was of Aeonic significance. Crowley claims to have received a scripture for the 'New Aeon', channelled from the 'God's' through a supernatural entity called Aiwass from whom Crowley claimed to have received *Liber Legis*, via automatic writing over the course of three days. This became the bible of Thelema, the name of Crowley's new religion, derived from the Greek word Will.

What was written by Crowley over the course of three days became the bible of Thelema, a Greek word meaning Will, the word *Thelema* being prescribed in *Liber Legis* as the name of the doctrine.[19]

Liber Legis reads in parts like a mystical rendering of Nietzsche, with a strident rejection of 'herd' doctrines including Christianity and democracy. That Nietzsche was a major influence on Crowley is seldom stated, but is strongly implied in Nietzsche being listed as a 'saint' in Crowley's Gnostic Mass.[20]

Under Thelema all doctrines and systems that restrict the fulfilment of the 'will' or the 'True Will', whether social, political, economic or religious, are to be replaced by the Crowleyite religion in a new aeon, the Aeon of Horus, The Conquering Child.[21]

---

[18]Wilson, C., *Aleister Crowley: The Nature of the Beast*, (Northamptonshire: The Aquarian Press, 1987), p.45.

[19]For an account of Crowley's occult career and the so-called 'Cairo Working' where *Liber Al Legis* was written, see Colin Wilson, 1988, p.71.

[20]Crowley, A., *Liber Legis* (Main: Samuel Weiser Inc., 1984), op.cit., p.430.

[21]Part 3 of *Liber Legis* is the revelation of Horus as the God of the New Aeon following that of Isis (matriarchy), and the present Aeon of Osiris, the religious of the sacrificial god, including Christianity. Horus is described as the god of war and vengeance, *Liber Legis* 3:3.

"*Do what thou wilt*" is the foundation of Thelema.[22] It does not mean a nihilistic 'do what you want' but 'do your will' that is, your 'true will' which must be discovered by the rigorous processes. Crowley states that the dictum "*must not be regarded as individualism run wild.*"[23]

Reflecting the individual 'true will' Thelemic doctrine describes "*every man and every woman [as] a star*".[24] That is, each individual is a part of the cosmos but with its own orbit.[25]

Liber Legis states "*the slaves shall serve.*"[26] Again this is Nietzschean in the sense that many individuals - probably to Crowley the vast majority - will not have the will to fulfil their 'true will'; that while everyone is a 'star' some will shine brighter than others.

In *The Star Sponge Vision*, an astral revelation,[27] Crowley explained this inequality as reflecting the "*highly organised structure of the universe*" which includes stars that are of "*greater magnitude and brilliance than the rest.*"[28]

The mass of humanity whose natures are servile and incapable of what Nietzsche called 'self-overcoming'[29] will remain as they are, their true wills being to being to serve those who are of – again in Nietzschean terms – those with a 'master morality',[30] or those whom *Liber Legis* described as being "*Kings of the Earth*", those whose starry will's are that of rulers.[31]

---

[22]"There is no law beyond do what thou wilt." *Liber Legis* 3: 60.
[23]Crowley, A., *The Law Is For All*, (Arizona: Falcon Press, 1985), p.321.
[24]Crowley, A., *Liber Legis* 1:3.
[25]Crowley, A., *The Law Is For All*, p.72-75.
[26]Crowley, A., *Liber Legis* 2: 58.
[27]Crowley, op.cit., p.143-145.
[28]Ibid., p.145.
[29]Nietzsche, F., *Thus Spake Zarathustra* (Middlesex: Penguin Books, 1969), *Of Self-Overcoming*, p.136-138.
[30]"There is a master morality and slave morality…" Nietzsche, F., *Beyond Good and Evil*, (Middlesex: Penguin Books, 1984), p.175 (260).
[31]Crowley, A., *Liber Legis,* 2:58.

Such a doctrine is individualistic but neither anarchistic, nihilistic nor even liberal. It is revival of castes. More here is implied than classes, which are an economic and materialistic debasement; castes reflecting a metaphysical order where each individual fulfils his or her function according to their true will, as manifestations of the cosmic order. Inequality to such followers of the perennial tradition is a manifestation of the divine order, and not merely some economic division of labour for crass exploitation. This was far better explained by Evola[32] than by Crowley.

However Crowley (or Aiwass) does explain the fundamental anti-democratic and anti-egalitarian doctrine of Thelema in these terms, which are again more reminiscent of Nietzsche:

> We are not for the poor and sad: the lords of the earth are our kinsfolk. Beauty and strength, leaping laughter, and delicious languor, force and fire are of us... we have nothing to do with the outcast and unfit. For they feel not. Compassion is the vice of kings; stamp down the wretched and the weak: this is the law of the strong; this is our law and the joy of the world...[33]

New Aristocracy

This hierarchical social order, while in accord with the perennial tradition, postulates a *new* aristocracy, the old having become debased and beholden to commerce. This again reflects the cultural decline that is the basis of the historical cyclicity of the perennial doctrine.[34] Under the Aeon of Horus[35] the new aristocracy would form from those who in a Nietzschean type self-overcoming will seek and fulfil their 'true will'. Crowley specifically refers to the Nietzschean influence:

---

[32]Evola, J., *Revolt Against the Modern World*, (Vermont: Inner Traditions, 1995), p.89-100.
[33]*Liber Legis*, 2: 17-21 (Main: Samuel Weiser Inc., Main, 1984).
[34]Evola, op.cit., The Regression of the Castes, p.327-337.
[35]"I am the Hawke-headed god of silence and of strength." *Liber Legis* 3:70.

The highest are those who have mastered and transcended accidental environment... There is a good deal of the Nietzschean standpoint in this verse.[36]

However, in contradistinction to Nietzsche, as well as to others of the perennial tradition, Crowley clearly draws on social Darwinism which seems more akin to the mercantile Free Trade School of his time than to any aspect of either Nietzsche or traditionalism. After referring to the 'Nietzschean standpoint" Crowley states in social-darwinesque terms:

It is the evolutionary and natural view... Nature's way is to weed out the weak. This is the most merciful way too. At present all the strong are being damaged, and their progress being hindered by the dead weight of the weak limbs and the missing limbs, the diseased limbs and the atrophied limbs. The Christians to the lions.[37]

This superficially seems Nietzschean, however Nietzsche is often interpreted as the antithesis of what he intended by a Darwinian-Nietzschean synthesis, that is not however part of the perennial tradition. One such aberrant synthesis for example would be Nazism. A literary example is that of Ragnar Redbeard's *Might Is Right*, which has become popular among rebellious sub-cultures.[38] The perennial tradition and Nietzsche are both at odds with Darwinism whether as a biological doctrine or as a social doctrine or a method of historical analysis Like Darwinian evolution in the biological sciences, modernist history is similarly Darwinian in its lineal progressive outlook, a 'world history' ascending from a 'primitive' to a 'modern' lineal progression. As Kaufmann clarifies, Nietzschean is not a philosophical or sociological application of Darwin; on the contrary Darwin's theory prompted Nietzsche to write in repudiation

---

[36]*Law is for All*, p.175-177.
[37]Ibid.
[38]Redbeard R., *Might is Right*, first published by Auditorium Press in 1890; it has had a continual publication history: 1896, 1903, 1910, 1927, 1962, 1969, 1972, 1984, 1986, 1999, 2003, 2005, 2008, and 2009 by Edition Esoterick.

of the naturalistic doctrine which sees man as animal as much at the mercy of natural selection as any other animal, rather than as the manifestation of a higher conscious will. Man's evolution to higher forms in the Nietzschean sense is a matter of conscious will rather than chance genetic mutation.[39]

Perennial tradition is at odds with Darwinism on all level, seeing man as devolving from a primordial higher state, as subject to laws of cyclic cultural decay from a Golden Age, rather than as progressing forward to higher biological, cultural and technical realms.[40]

Crowley's conception of a new aristocracy could have been motivated by his own bourgeois origins[41], and his desire for nobility, as indicated by referring to himself as "Sir Aleister Crowley."[42]

THELEMIC STATE

Crowley's rejection of democracy and anything of what might be termed a mass morality – or 'slave morality' as Nietzsche[43] put it - necessitates an alternative view of state organisation if one aims to be taken seriously as the founder of a new religious and ethical outlook to replace all others. Like others[44] of his time, not only traditionalists and occultists, but those concerned with the future of culture at the mercy of mercantilism and bolshevism, of the twin forces of materialism and the mass based on the machine as the new god, Crowley was concerned that an epoch of mass uniformity was emerging. Crowley

---

[39] According to Kaufmann, Nietzsche 'denounced vehemently' 'those who might interpret his conception of the over-man Darwinistically...' Kaufmann, W., *Nietzsche: Philosopher, Psychologist, Antichrist* (NY: Vintage Books, 1968), p.118.
[40] Evola, J., *Revolt Against the Modern World*, p.333.
[41] Wilson, op.cit. p.26.
[42] Designated as such in Crowley, A., *Ecclesiae Gnosticae Catholicae Canon Missae, The Saints*, 1984, op.cit.
[43] Nietzsche, F., *Beyond Good and Evil* (Middlesex: Penguin Books, 1984) , op.cit.
[44] Bolton, K., *Thinkers of the Right* (Luton: Luton Publications, 2003).

wrote of equality as being the harbinger of uniformity:

> There is no creature on earth the same. All the members, let them be different in their qualities, and let there be no creature equal with another. Here also is the voice of true science, crying aloud: 'Variety is the key of evolution.' Know then, o my son, that all laws, all systems, all customs, all ideals and standards which tend to produce uniformity, being in direct opposition to nature's will to change and develop through variety, are accursed. Do thou with all thou might of manhood strive against these forces, for they resist change which is life, and they are of death.[45]

Again it can be seen that Crowley renounced equality not in the name of the perennial tradition as did Evola or Guenon, but in the name conversely of a natural biological evolution. This biological rather than metaphysical approach was emphasised by reference to differences among humanity being caused by "race, climate and others such conditions. And this standard shall be based upon a large interpretation of Facts Biological."[46]

The democratic state as a manifestation of equality and of the forces of uniformity was to be replaced by what might be termed the 'organic state'. This state conception may be viewed both biologically as in the organism of the body with limbs functioning separately according to their own nature but for the good of the whole organism (hence the 'organic state') and metaphysically, and under different names has been advocated by secularists,[47] Catholics[48] and traditionalists[49] alike.

Referring to the passage in *Liber Legis* which states: "Ye are against the people, o my chosen!"[50] Crowley explained:

---

[45]Crowley, 1985, 228; citing *Liber Aleph*, ch. De lege motus.
[46]Ibid. p.229.
[47]The corporate State of Italian Fascism.
[48]Salazar's Portugal, Dolfuss' Austria.
[49]Evola, 2002, *Economy & Politics – Corporations – Unity of Work*, p.224-234.
[50]*Liber Legis* 2: 25 (Main: Samuel Weiser Inc., 1984).

The cant of democracy condemned. It is useless to pretend that men are equal: facts are against it. And we are not going to stay dull and contended as oxen, in the ruck of humanity.[51]

Crowley saw an era of turmoil preceding the Neo Aeon in which the masses and the elite, or the new aristocracy would be in conflict. Again it is shown that Crowley was referring to an ethos and élan that distinguishes this Thelemic aristocracy from the old aristocracy that can arguably be seen as having become decadent. Crowley wrote of this revolutionary precursor to the New Aeon: "And when the trouble begins, we aristocrats of freedom, form the castle to the cottage, the tower of the tenement, shall have the slave mob against us."[52]

There is a Nietzschean dichotomy of conflict between those representing the 'slave morality' and the 'master morality'. Of the masses who cannot overcome the slave morality and follow their 'true will', Crowley wrote in further explaining *Liber Legis* 2:25, of "the people" as "that canting, whining, servile breed of whipped dogs which refuses to admit its deity…"[53]

Under the Thelemic regime the undisciplined mob at the whim of its emotions, devoid of Will, is described as "the natural enemy of good government." The new aristocracy of governing elite will be those who have discovered and pursued their 'true will', who have mastered themselves through self-overcoming, to use Nietzschean terminology. This governing caste would pursue a *"consistent policy"* without being subjected to the democratic whims of the masses.[54]

What form this Thelemic government would take is described in *Liber Legis*: "Let it be the state of manyhood bound and loathing: thou has no right but to do what thou will."[55] Contrary to the anarchistic or

[51]Crowley, A., *The Law Is For All* (Arizona: Falcon Press, 1985), p.192.
[52]Ibid.
[53]Ibid.
[54]Ibid. p.193.
[55]Crowley, A., *Liber Legis* 1: 42 (Main: Samuel Weiser Inc.,1984).

nihilistic interpretation that might be put on Thelema's 'do what thou wilt', Crowley defined the Thelemic state as a free association for the common good. The individual will is accomplished through social co-operation. Individual will and social duty should be in accord, the individual "absolutely disciplined to serve his own, and the common purpose, without friction."[56]

Crowley emphasised his meaning so as not to be confused with anarchism or liberalism. While his *Liber Oz* (Rights of Man)[57] seems to be a formula for total individual sovereignty devoid of social restraint, Crowley stated: "This statement must not be regarded as individualism run wild."[58]

In what might appear to be his own effort at a 'papal encyclical' on good government, Crowley explains:

I have set limits to individual freedom. For each man in this state which I propose is fulfilling his own True Will by his eager Acquiescence in the Order necessary to the Welfare of all, and therefore of himself also.[59]

Once the obligations to the social order had been met, there should be *"a surplus of leisure and energy"* that can be spent in pursuit of individual satisfaction.[60] Sufficient amount of leisure time free from strictly material pursuits is seen as the basis of culture. Leisure and culture is a problem that has preoccupied numerous social theorists, from socialists to social creditors,[61] and cultural figures such as

---

[56]Crowley, A., *The Law Is For All* (Arizona: Falcon Press, 1985), p.101.

[57]Crowley, A., ibid, p.321.

[58]Ibid.

[59]Crowley, A., *De Fundamentis Civitatis*. (On the fundamentals of the state) clause 39 of *Liber Aleph Vel CXI, The Book of Wisdom or Folly (1991)*, www.hermetic.com/crowley/aleph/tbwf1.html

[60]Crowley, A., *The Law Is For All*, (Arizona: Falcon Press, 1985), p.230.

[61]Social credit theorist Eric Butler wrote of this: "Instead of the development of automation being regarded as a means of providing the individual with leisure and freedom for self-development, it is widely publicised as a "Problem" - to be "solved"

D'Annunzio and Ezra Pound harked back to the guild era when the economy allowed sufficient leisure time in which even the general populace could participate.

Crowley like the social creditors, although there is no evidence he had the slightest knowledge of their policy, stated that the economic system requires changing to reduce working hours. However, like the social creditors, he proposed that a change in the social and economic systems could only be effected by a change in the role of money. Crowley, one might argue rather perceptively, set out his economic and financial policy:

> What IS money? A means of exchange devised to facilitate the transaction of business. Oil in the engine. Very good then: if instead of letting it flow as smoothly and freely as possible, you baulk its very nature; you prevent it from doing its True Will. So every 'restriction' on the exchange of wealth is a direct violation of the Law of Thelema.[62]

Once the material welfare of the citizen is secured then the leisure that is found in sufficient material abundance can then be turned to the pursuit of culture. The other option is the pursuit of excess as a prelude to decadence and collapse, a matter that has concerned many cultural and social critics.[63] Under the Thelemic state the citizen would be directed by the ruling caste to pursue rather the higher aspects of life leading to the flowering of culture: "And because the people are oft-time unlearned, not understanding pleasure, let them be instructed on the Art of Life."[64] From thence would follow the flowering of a high culture in which each citizen would have the capacity to participate or at least appreciate: "These things being first secured, thou mayst

---

by finding other work for those displaced by automation. It does not matter how useless or destructive the work may be; the majority accept it passively because it distributes financial incomes." Butler, 1971.

[62]Crowley, A., *Magick Without Tears*, (Arizona: Falcon Press, 1983), p.346.
[63]Bolton, K., *Thinkers of the Right*, (Luton: Luton Publications, 2003).
[64]Crowley, A., *The Law Is For All*, (Arizona: Falcon Press, 1985), p.251.

afterward lead them to the Heavens of Poesy and Tale, of Music, Painting and Sculpture, and into the love of the mind itself, with its insatiable Joy of all Knowledge."[65]

It could be argued controversially and with the likely result of attracting odium and outrage, that Nazi Germany and Fascist Italy sought to achieve the socialisation of culture among the people via *Strength Through Joy* and the Afterwork Organisation *Dopolavoro* respectively. However one may view that, the Italian nationalist poet and war veteran D'Annunzio might have come closest to the Thelemite ideal with his short-lived City-State of Fiume, a regime governed by the arts that attracted numerous rebels, form anarchists and syndicalists to nationalists.[66] I am unable to find however any association between Crowley and D'Annunzio or mention of D'Annunzio in Crowley's works, although Crowley was in Italy in 1920 and D'Annunzio's enterprise did not finish until December of that year.[67]

As for the Italian Fascists, whose embarkation on trains from the north to converge on Rome and the assumption of power, Crowley wrote: "For some time I had interested myself in Fascismo which I regarded with entire sympathy even excluding its illegitimacy on the ground that constitutional authority had become to all intents and purposes a dead letter."[68]

Crowley saw the Fascisti in a characteristically poetic or romantic way, describing the blackshirts patrolling the railway as "delightful". "They had all the picturesqueness of opera brigands." [69] As for the coup or so-called 'march on Rome', Crowley stated that he thought

---

[65] Ibid.

[66] Rhodes, A., *The Poet As Superman – D'Annunzio* (London: Weidenfeld & Nicolson, 1959).

[67] Ibid., p.221.

[68] Crowley, A., *The Confessions of Aleister Crowley* (London: Routledge & Kegan Paul, 1986), p.911.

[69] Ibid.

the behaviour of the Fascisti "admirable".[70]

Crowley quickly became disillusioned however as he considered Mussolini had begun acting in the fashion of a typical politico, which presumably means that he was acting with a view to compromise for popular support; anathema to Thelemic governmental doctrine. Crowley observed development in Rome for three days, and was disappointed with the compromises that Mussolini was making with Catholicism, which Crowley regarded as Mussolini's *"most dangerous foe."*[71] He moved on to Cefalu where he would establish his "Abbey of Thelema" in a ramshackle house. The death of a follower Raoul Loveday resulted in Crowley's expulsion from Italy in 1923, by which time he had become an embarrassment to the Fascist regime.[72]

Under the Thelemic state every individual would be given the opportunity to fulfil their true will, however Crowley maintained that most true wills or 'stars' would be content with a satisfying material existence, and would be content to stay where they are in the hierarchy, having no ambition beyond 'ease and animal happiness.' Those whose true will was to pursue higher aims would be given opportunities to do so, to *"establish a class of morally and intellectually superior men and women."* In this state while the people *"lack for nothing"* their abilities according to their natures would be utilised by the ruling caste in the pursuance of a higher policy and a higher culture.[73]

Crowley's conception of an organic state is most clearly described in his *De Ordine Rerum*:

> In the body every cell is subordinated to the general physiological Control, and we who will that Control do not ask whether each individual Unit of that Structure be consciously happy. But we do

---

[70]Ibid.

[71]Ibid., p.912.

[72]Wilson, C., *Aleister Crowley: The Nature of the Beast* (*Northamptonshire*: The Aquarian Press, 1987), p.133.

[73]Crowley, *The Law Is For All*, p.227.

care that each shall fulfil its Function, with Contentment, respecting his own task as necessary and holy, not envious of another's. For only mayst thou build up a Free State, whose directing will shall be to the Welfare of all.[74]

Crowley's condemnation of democracy in Nietzschean terms and seeming contempt for the mass of people might be interpreted as a misanthropy that is not necessarily his intention. Again Crowley's description of the organic state in *Ordine Rerum* is reminiscent of Traditionalists such as Evola[75] and Catholic social doctrines expressed in the papal encyclicals, both harking back to the traditional social order of the medieval guild era.[76]

Machine & Craft

Crowley addressed the problem of industrialisation and the role of the machine in the process of dehumanisation, or what might also be termed by Traditionalists as desacralisation; a problem which continues to confront the post-industrial world with greater challenges than ever. Again Crowley, like Evola[77] sought a return to the Traditionalist order where craft, and the castes, from peasant to king, were earthly manifestations of the divine order. Crowley wrote:

Machines have already nearly completed the destruction of craftsmanship. A man is no longer a worker, but a machine-feeder. The product is standardised; the result, mediocrity... Instead of every man and every women being a star, we have an amorphous population of vermin.[78]

The tendency towards uniformity, towards the proletarianisation

---

[74]Ibid., p.251-252.
[75]Evola, 2002, p.224.
[76]Ibid.
[77]Ibid.
[78]Crowley, A., op.cit., p.281.

of what was once the craftsman and the peasant, created under capitalism and aggravated under communism, has not been resolved. Globalisation is the present cycle.

This sacralisation of work very much reflects the traditional social order of guilds, but this basic structure for a neo-traditional social order[79] does not seem to have been addressed by Crowley.

POLITICAL LEGACY?

If Crowley is not known as a traditionalist social and cultural critic like Evola or Guénon, but primarily as an eccentric occultist, it is because the political and social ideas implicit in Thelema were only rarely and sporadically addressed by Crowley among a large corpus of work. Although aiming to usher in a New Aeon, Crowley did not satisfactorily address himself to the details of this Aeon and how Thelema might be implemented on a practical level as an all-embracing doctrine that was to replace socialism and democracy, Christianity and Islam.

The result is that while some political activists and ideologues are drawn to Crowley, conversely few Crowleyites per se are drawn to political engagement. Evola recognised Crowley as an initiate of the perennial tradition, also referring to his predilection for notoriety, but did not seem to have commented on Crowley as a social or rather 'conservative' revolutionary.[80] Crowley for his part does not appear to have referred to Evola at all, perhaps jealous of his own claims to pre-eminence in the occult world.

One eminent individual who did begin his mystical journey as a

---

[79]Evola, op.cit.

[80]Evola devotes a chapter to Crowley in his Chapter IX, "*Il Satanismo*" ("Satanism", Maschera e volto dello spiritualismo contemporaneo, ("Mask and Face of Contemporary Spiritualism"), 1932. www.gornahoor.net/library/EvolaOnCrowley.pdf

Thelemite and found his way to British Fascism of the Mosley variety was J.F.C. Fuller who became the architect of modern tank warfare. Fuller had heard of Crowley in 1905, and was therefore one of Crowley's earliest devotees. He was like Crowley, a Nietzschean with occult interests, writing of socialism as 'the scum on the democratic cauldron', a levelling creed. His opposition to Christianity was likewise Nietzschean.[81] He met Crowley in London in 1906 and wrote the first biography, *The Star in the West*[82] as the winner and only entrant of a competition to promote Crowley's poetry. Although Fuller's interest in the occult and mysticism was lifelong he had broken with Crowley during 1911. In 1932 Fuller was still writing in Nietzschean terms of socialism and democracy as stemming from Christianity.[83]

Crowley himself never seems to have considered the practical application of his social and political critique other than apparently viewing Thelema's fulfilment in the New Aeon as an inevitable development through his own dialectical law of Aeons,[84] in similar manner to the outlook of Marxists in seeing the 'inevitability' of communism through a dialectical process. However Crowley, like the communists, called on Thelemites to become active agents in this dialectical process:

> We have to fight for freedom against oppressors, religious, social or industrial, and we are utterly opposed to compromise, every fight is to be a fight to the finish; each one of us for himself, to do his own will, and all of us for all, to establish the law of Liberty... Let every

---

[81]Trythall, A., *Boney Fuller: The Intellectual General* (London: Cassell, 1977).
[82]Ibid.
[83]Ibid.
[84]Crowley's perspective of history, of succeeding Aeons, seems more dialectical than cyclic. His system allows for the Aeons of Isis, Osiris and Horus, the latter of which he proclaimed himself the prophet. The dialectics can be discerned from the Aeon of Horus arising as synthesis from the interaction of the Aeons of Isis and Osiris: matriarchy and patriarchy respectively , followed by the "Crowned and Conquering Child" Horus, the synthesis heralding "Force and Fire." *Liber Legis* comprises the unfolding of three books as three epochs in human history, each representing the three dialectical concepts referred to.

man bear arms, swift to resent oppression... generous and ardent to draw sword in any cause, if justice or freedom summon him.[85]

These are fighting words in keeping with the war god Horus, the God of the New Aeon of Force and Fire, yet they are words that are hardly acted upon by Crowley's adherents, and when they are taken up in the name of opposing oppressors, religious, social or industrial, Thelemite occultists and mystics stand aggrieved at the perceived travesty of exploiting their prophet for political motives.

*****

K R Bolton is a Fellow of the Academy of Social and Political Research (Athens), publisher of the peer reviewed journal *Ab Aeterno*, 'contributing writer' for *Foreign Policy Journal*, and a regular contributor to *The Great Indian Dream* (Indian Institute of Planning & Management) and *New Dawn* (Australia). He has been widely published by the scholarly and broader media. Books include: *Revolution from Above* (London: Arktos Media Ltd., 2011), and *Artists of the Right* (San Francisco: Counter-Currents Publishing, 2012), with several others due out in 2012.

---

[85]Crowley, A., *The Law Is For All* (Arizona: Falcon Press, 1985), p.317.

The Traditionalist as a Liminal Model

William White

The nations of the West – meaning the nations founded by the peoples of Britain, as well as France, Germany, and much of Western and Northern Europe – are dominated by a social democratic political system. Even when "social democrats" per se do not hold power, the principles of social democracy, including an idea of "progress" and the moral perspectives that accompanies ideas of political and economic leveling, do. Because this perspective does not accord well with reality, social democracy is inherently violent and repressive in nature; only through force can irrational beliefs be maintained in the face of natural law. This violence, which has been increasing, particular in nations like the United States, which are only beginning to be converted to the social democratic system, poses a serious threat to those who adhere to the Traditionalist worldview. As such, those who maintain the idea of Tradition against the encroachment of the social democratic and internationalist worldview need to purge within themselves any notion of loyalty to the corruption inherent in democratic societies, and recognize that those who are not part of the social democratic system out of necessity must assume a liminal role.

Social Democracy and Internationalism Defined

Social Democracy is the latest term to be applied to a doctrine that has existed from the earliest moments of man's recorded history, and which has appeared in the past few years under names ranging from "liberalism" to "communism". Social Democracy distinguishes itself by the belief that internationalist "socialism" can be brought up through democratic reforms and electoral activism within bourgeois society.

Thus, the social democrat acts as an emissary of the "masses" against all true Traditional expressions, so he can wield the violence of the state against "counter-revolutionary" elements. Like the communist, gaining control of the mechanism of the state so as to be able to use state power to violently impose oneself on the general population is paramount, but the social democrat does not attempt to seize the state itself by violent means.

In the modern context, where social democracy already has a substantial presence in most western political systems, this philosophy better accords with political reality than the communist-revolutionary perspective. With the so-called "conservative" opposition to social democracy in most countries itself being just a watered down variant of the social democratic movement, there is no reason for social democrats to divorce themselves from the state; eventually, their aims will be achieved through state action.

The essence of social democracy, which unites it with its opposition, is the idea of internationalism – the notion that all of the nations of the world can and should be united into a single trans-national whole. In the post-monarchical period, which, for Western nations, begins as early as the 17th century in Britain[1] (which, admittedly, retains a nominal monarchy, even to this day), and as late as the 20th century in Russia,[2] the traditional divide within government has been between the mercantile caste – that segment of the population which views the accumulation of wealth as the greatest end – and the caste of the "workers" – the segment of the population which wishes it were in the position of the mercantile caste, but lacks the ability to create productive organizations, and thus is left demanding wealth

---

[1] As I discuss in my book *Centuries of Revolution,* the Golden Revolution in Britain was really the first eruption of modernism into a position of political power, where Masonic elements usurped the Traditional British monarchy.
[2] The Bolshevik Revolution in Russia, along with the other events that concluded the First World War, eliminated the last of Europe's Traditional monarchies, replacing it with a Jewish-Bolshevik system. This culminated the dismantling of Traditional European cultures by the forces of socialism and social democracy.

redistribution, whether in a literal form or in the form of higher pay, greater benefits, and better working and living conditions. This divide is not "natural", but is a result of the decapitation of society's proper governing castes,[3] and the effort of Western societies to survive without their natural leadership.

The interests of both castes are not, however, as antagonistic as writers such as Karl Marx have posited. In a proper Traditional world, the two interests would be reconciled in the greater interest of managing society for the benefit of all its people. In the chaotic and leaderless world of the modern west, the interests of the two groups are united in the demand for internationalism – in the opening of borders to exchanges of labor and capital. Though this is not in the actual interest of the social whole, it is in the perceived interest of both parties within the democratic state. The mercantile caste seeks new markets for their goods and less expensive labor in the short term, and wants borders opened so it can take advantage of the economic differences which the previously closed borders have created. The worker caste seeks open borders so it can migrate to new lands and take advantage of higher wages and lower cost goods that have been similarly created by the previously closed borders. In the end, the tendency of prices and wages across borders is to stabilize at a median rate; but the immediate effect of opening borders is what generally motivates policy and the short term political considerations of democratic states.

The tendency to destroy the cultural integrity of a nation causes Traditional societies to reject Western social democracy. For instance, the exportation of Western social democracy to the Islamic states has created a movement for so-called "moderate" Islam, a secular variant of the Islamic faith that is essentially the humanist doctrine of socialism with Islamic trappings. This is similar to the "liberal" Christianity or Catholicism preached within Western nations – it is nominally a religion, but substantially the secularist theory of the social democrats.

---

[3]Similar to the idea expressed in the *Mahanirvana Tantra*, which predicts the rise of five mixed castes in the Kali Yuga. This idea is derived from earlier Vedic texts.

These "moderates" have then turned against and waged war against the actual and legitimate proponents of their religion – individuals who do not wish to see their religious faith turned into a colorful variant of the internationalist faith.

Internationalism responds to challenges from those who question the wisdom of destroying national borders and homogenizing human society by homogenizing their opponents, utilizing terms like "fascist". Muslims who do not wish to see their nations homogenized into components of the internationalist Western socialist state are called "Islamo-fascists". Similarly, Europeans who recognize that placing barriers between European peoples and non-European peoples tends to create an improved standard of living for Europeans, based upon the greater capability of the Europeans within a given nation, are called "neo-fascists". Hindus who seek to maintain a uniquely Hindu culture within India are called "Hindu supremacists". Russians who wish to maintain their national independence from the globalist system are called "dictatorial" or are accused of practicing "modified democracy." Just as the internationalist movement attempts to homogenize itself, it seeks to homogenize its opponents. This leads to the amusing situation within the United States where libertarians and Constitutionalists are all labeled "fascists" – without any attempt to understand the differences between their organizations or political doctrines.

THE VIOLENT NATURE OF SOCIAL DEMOCRACY

Social Democracy, and its liberal and communist predecessors, supplanted the Traditional monarchies and nobilities of Europe through acts of extreme violence, often involving the genocide of entire families and lineages within the previous European ruling caste. In the modern world, social democracy has replaced the violence of the revolution with the violence of the state, and freely wages war not only against nations which refuse to be integrated into the globalist system, but against its own people, when those people refuse to accept the social democratic perspective on reality. Because the social democratic perspective is essentially flawed, the rise to power of social democratic elements within Western states has been accompanied with increasing violence, as social democrats have sought to obscure their flaws by suppressing any criticism of them. However, this refusal by the social democrats to accept the erroneous nature of their system has created fundamental economic and cultural divides which have destabilized the social democratic states, and led to increased dissidence among the governed peoples. A vicious cycle is now occurring which, as the social democrats consolidate their power, their failures become more glaring, more people are alienated, and the social democracy is compelled to use an increasing level of violence, war, and domestic repression to control the dissident elements. The end result of this cycle will be the collapse of a social democracy.

Cultural desemination and diaspora causes numerous problems in social democracies. The opening of borders on the internationalist model equalizes cultural groups within the new "international" nation, but does not eliminate inequalities between the principal actors. When the nations whose borders are opened have a substantially different ethnic composition, open borders tends to intensify, rather than diminish, disharmony between the groups, as open borders tends to unite previously divided cultural groupings and allow those peoples to focus on their marginalization.

For instance, the opening of the borders between the United States and Mexico allowed US companies to utilize Mexican labor, and allowed Mexicans to seek business opportunities within the United States. Prior to the opening of the border, Mexico had been governed by a small elite caste that controlled most of the nations' wealth, and which operated a socialist-style system in which its "publicly" controlled companies (companies operated by the governing elite) dominated many aspects of economic activity, and "private" business consisted primarily of the sale of personal labor in an unregulated manner. The opening of the border provided an opportunity for Mexican businesses – drug cartels in particular – to export their product to the United States. Because the Mexican economic system had been previously closed, thus collapse of economic control allowed new economic centers to form around the drug cartels, who used this economic force to create new political centers. These new political centers are based on ethnic and cultural groupings and tend to focus on the non-European Mexican underclass, which had been historically excluded from the Mexican governing class.

Similarly, mixed populations used the opening of the US-Mexican border to migrate to the United States, where they established themselves as a separate homogenous community, and where they enjoy a different standard of living than the other ethno-cultural communities within the United States. The inability of social democracy to close the cultural divide that continued after the migration of Mexican populations to the United States increased cultural animosity within the United States, as the immigrant population, unassimilated, demanded certain benefits and privileges, and as the European and, to a lesser degree, existing minority populations responded with movements to deny the new cultural group benefits which come at the existing groups expense. Further European workers were displaced by the new immigrants, causing a general fall in wages and leading directly to the current American position of economic weakness.

The response of the American social democratic system to the contradictions inherent in its internationalist doctrine has been violent. America has responded to the problems its policies have created in two ways, neither of which have involved modification of its policies. First, America has engaged in a policy of international aggression, part of the doctrinal demand that social democracy be expanded to include all of the nations of the Earth. Second, America has engaged in domestic repression to combat both dissent against its internal contradictions and the consequences of its aggression on an international scale.

Social Democracy and internationalism originate in the same religious and ethnic belief as Zionism. Both doctrines are tied inextricably to Zionism, and to the desire for world political and economic domination. For this reason, a key plank of internationalism and social democracy is the "defense" of the Zionist occupation of Palestine. This plank, combined with the doctrinal need to push the world into further "progress" through the destruction of all centers of Traditional culture have led the Western social democratic countries into launching a series of aggressive wars against ethnic and religiously oriented states in North Africa and Southern Asia – states which existed outside of the social democratic system and which were also perceived as threats to the continued occupation of Palestine.

The wars launched by the social democratic states against Traditional or independent states which are often much weaker, militarily, has led to a global "terrorist" conflict. In the mind of the social democratic states, they should be able to wage war and to murder others without any retaliation. To the social democrat and the internationalist, their own righteousness permits them to murder and torture without moral stain or liability. The fact that someone would respond to the murder, injury or torture of a friend or family member by taking up arms against the internationalist system or striking in a similar manner against social democratic states is considered completely irrational to the social democrat. The social democrat can only understand such motives as "hate" and such acts as "terrorism". Thus, the social democrat is completely unable to understand their own violent and anti-social acts in a universalist sense; they see no connection between themselves and the "enemies" they repress, and thus cannot understand that their own wrongdoing may lead to wrongdoing against them.

Those within their nations who understand that social democratic violence is not exempt from the universal laws that govern relations between men, and who warn social democratic states against acts of genocide, noting that such acts cause and justify retaliation, are similarly considered enemies by the social democratic state. Just as those who note the realities of cultural differences and the failure of social democracy to incorporate natural science into its cultural and economic policies are motivated by "hate", those who note that social democracy is not particularly righteous and not exempt from the laws of human and international relations are similarly "haters", "traitors" and sympathetic to it if not part of the "terrorist" problem.

The inability of social democracy to integrate fundamental criticisms of its goals and methods into its governing policies has caused social democratic states to resort to extremes of violence, as well as to create a system of public disinformation designed to conceal from the general public the true economic and political state of the social democratic nations. In the United States, the government, faced with an insufficient "terrorist" threat and a general inability to regulate such threat as does exist, has been forced into a policy of manufacturing "terrorist" plots in order to maintain the illusion that a sufficient threat exists to justify both social and cultural unity behind the social democratic state and to justify the massive expenditure of the resource of social democratic state on aggressive acts. This illusion of constant threat also distracts from the realities of the economic and cultural failures of internationalism and social democracy.

However, to maintain this illusion, the social democratic state has needed the weapon of the confession. Because these plots are essentially fabrications, perjured testimony and forged evidence is necessary to "convict" the alleged "terrorists" in the public mind. Thus, the social democratic states have had to implement a regimen of torture and violence to extract "confessions" from those they accuse. The mythology of social democracy further requires that all opponents of the state be essentially "violent" and "terroristic" in nature; otherwise, the violence of the state could not be justified. Thus, the arrest of political dissidents, often individuals who believe in the myth of citizenship and law, and the torture of political dissidents guilty of no crime greater than exposing the failures of internationalist and social democratic ideology, has become a necessary and routine function of the social democratic apparatus.

THE TRADITIONAL INDIVIDUAL WITHIN THE SOCIAL DEMOCRACY

Though the social democracies maintain a "cradle to grave" program of indoctrination, which begins with the consumption of mass media by children from an early age, which continues into early adulthood with a regimen of public schooling, and which is regulated by the mass media in adulthood through threats of "exposure" and social abuse of those who do not conform, the discrepancies between the doctrines of internationalism and the realities of the world are great enough that relatively large numbers of individuals cannot be controlled through these "soft" coercive processes. While Traditional doctrines are simply ignored by the mass media – or grossly misrepresented when they cannot be ignored – a smaller number of individuals have found philosophical centers outside of the social democratic system. As the kind of individual inclined to break from indoctrination tends to be more intelligent and capable than the general mass of the population, these individuals also tend to be potential leaders, and thus their existence poses a threat to the continuation of political systems that are based upon illusions and disinformation. To deal with this threat, social democracies use violence, generally after criminalizing the targeted individual through perjury, forgery and the slanders of the mass media.

The general belief in most Western nations is that the law is essentially "fair", and that the law is applied in accordance with the principles of law and justice. This belief is taught to youth at an early age, and there appears to be a genetic predisposition for Europeans to adhere to the demands of social institutions and the requirements of law. This predisposition has allowed Europeans to build intricate social organizations, but it becomes pathological when those social organizations have turned against the interests of the social-cultural whole.

The predisposition of Europeans to lawful and socially regulated behavior is manipulated by the forces of social democracy, who place a veneer of "law" over all of their actions. To do this, the internationalists have needed control of the organs of information, so as to produce and further the illusion that the actions they are taking are in accordance with the principles of truth and justice. Thus, the forces of social democracy may torture a man in order to obtain a confession, but they can be assured that, even if the mass media were to become aware that a man had been tortured, they would not report on it, and would instead report solely on the confession. Thus, those outside the small circle that has direct knowledge of the tactics used remain ignorant of the true situation – and continue the belief that the system "works" and that the law has been properly applied, even if they sympathize more with the views of the oppressed person rather than the social democratic state.

Individuals who reject the doctrines of social democracy often fail to realize the violent and repressive nature of internationalism. Social democracy furthers the myth of the "inclusive" society, in which the viewpoint of the individual is "freely" express. Thus, Traditionalists who dissent against the social democratic state often wrongfully believe that they are merely exercising their "rights", and that the ruling social democratic entity will "respect" their "freedom of expression."

In many European nations, there is no longer any such illusion. The government has simply criminalized political dissent, and has done so openly. In the United States, where there is the continuing myth of "freedom of speech", political dissidents continue to "assert their rights as citizens" by criticizing the social democratic state. Those who are effective in doing so, and who threaten to impact the electoral balance, or who otherwise challenge the governing system, are subjected to the same repression as their European comrades, but are generally more surprised by the violence that is wielded against them. Often, by the time they realize that the "justice" system is an illusion, and that the "crimes" prosecuted by American social democracy are frauds, they are already subject to such violence that they cannot meaningfully resist.

The Traditionalist within a social democratic society is by definition a

,liminal person. He is outside of social democratic society not because he has encroached upon the rights of his fellow man, but because the social democratic system is so weak – despite its instruments of violence and repression – that it cannot allow a single person who realizes its fundamentally flawed nature to exist within its social body. By "exercising rights", such as that to freedom of speech or assembly, the Traditionalist is simply notifying the system of his liminal nature. To call a public rally around a Traditionalist perspective is like a drug dealer calling the press and announcing he's selling crack at a given corner at a given time. The difference between the Traditionalist and the drug dealer is that the drug dealer is aware of the transgressive nature of his act and thus works to conceal it, whereas the Traditionalist, being deluded into believing he is not crossing socially constructed boundaries, openly acts in a manner that leads to his own destruction.

The implications of this frighten many who hold Traditional views. Once one gets past the delusion created by the mass media and recognizes that the arrests committed by the social democratic state are arbitrary, there is generally a chilling effect. Most Traditionalists are not naturally transgressive of natural social boundaries, and thus they are not used to existing within society in a liminal manner. Because of their inner cultural orientation, they wish to be law abiding. They are afraid to be outside of the law, even when they know that the "law" of the state is essentially lawless. The result is often paralyzation – an inability to act rationally. Further, there is always the residual belief that those who are actually breaking the law are somehow in greater danger from the state than those whom the state has chosen to target for political ends.

The reality of the social democratic state is that it is safer to actually break the law than it is to openly dissent against the internationalist system. Because the nature of the social democratic state is to invent crimes, one is less likely to be prosecuted for any real transgressions than one is for attempting to "lawfully" participate in the democratic system. Thus, it is safer to commit transgressive acts than it is to attempt political change through lawful means. One committing a transgressive act understands it needs to be concealed. Further, the system is not oriented to catch intelligent liminal actors who are attempting to conceal their activities. In contrast, those who believe their actions are within the law are not concealing their activities or taking precaution against prosecution, and are dealing with a system designed to manufacture crimes out of political speech.

THE TRADITIONALIST AS AN OUTSIDER

The laws of men are a compact between the individuals that comprise the state. They regulate interactions between individuals, as well as the relationship between the individual and "society," and the individual and the state apparatus. Once society and the state apparatus places one outside the law, the obligations one has towards all men who are part of that society and state apparatus are broken. When society or the state rejects any of its citizens, the citizen's duty to obey the social norms of that society and the citizens' obligations to any member of that society is abrogated, and may refuse to acknowledge the socially constructed boundaries of any person who adheres to the mores of the society that has rejected him.

This kind of liberation is similar to the liberation recognized by Tantric doctrine, when the individual, seeing the nature of destruction and the subjection of all things to the death principle, realizes that any action within the fabricated reality is permitted, because none of the things passing before the senses is particularly "real". It is similar to the transformation that occurs within the human cell when the cell turns cancerous. A cancer is a single cell reproducing itself without regard for the social whole (the society of cells) within which it exists. This often occurs when the cells around the cancerous cell have died, causing the cell to believe it is no longer part of a social whole, but an independent entity needing to reproduce in order to sustain itself. The difference in the Traditional individual who has been outlawed by social democratic society is that the social whole – the internationalist state and its adherents – is the cancer, and that the individual cell, abandoned by the social whole, is the healthy element, who needs to turn against the social whole of which it was once a part in order that it may reproduce and live. This recognition requires an inner transformation that is difficult for many to accept. Yet, by placing one's self outside of society and accepting one's independence from the society of which one was a part, one becomes part of a separate organism – the international network of Traditionalists who are persevering valiantly against the encroachment of social democratic internationalism. Though this social-cultural entity is still in a formative stage, its proper function is similar to that of the outsider concept of sociology. The Traditionalist remnant of society is a cultural organism that is – or should be – regulated by its own law and its obligations towards its own members, while maintaining an attitude of distance towards the social democratic world.

When one is truly outside of internationalist society, the laws of one's new association take higher priority than the laws of the state under which they happen to reside. Participants in the Traditionalist world recognize that they have an obligation towards the hierarchy and towards other members of their organism. They do not worry about the laws of the state when deciding how to interact with other members of their culture. Their first loyalty is towards the organism of which they have chosen to be a part.

Similarly, the Traditionalist, outlawed by social democracy, owes his first loyalty to other members of the Traditionalist organism. The Traditionalist must learn not to hesitate to abandon the social democratic organism in support of the struggle of their fellows in their endeavors against that organism. To break with social democracy and its institutions means to recognize a constant state of struggle against those institutions. However, to recognize a constant state of conflict as part of the nature of mankind is simply part of the acknowledgement of reality that led to one's being placed outside of society in the first place.

Too often Traditionalists try to straddle the line and exist both within social democratic society and as critics of social democratic society at the same time. This position is impossible. Internationalism is engaged in an occult – and often even overt – war against Tradition, and one cannot participate in both internationalist culture and Traditional culture at the same time. One either accepts the material comforts and soft lifestyle of the social democratic poison, or one commits to struggle against social democracy, steps outside of the social democratic society, and engages in a struggle that ends only with the victory of one side or the other.

Conclusion

Social democracy is doomed to ultimate failure because its principles do not accord well with reality. Despite powerful mechanisms for social control, the social democratic state is unable to universally impose its illusions on the people. Some of those who break free of that illusion find a new center in a Traditional worldview. These individuals are ruthlessly persecuted and outlawed by the social democratic state. In this persecution, the social democratic state understands no restraint of law, and makes no effort to adhere to "truth" or "justice". Arrests of political dissidents are often arbitrary and based upon perjured and manufactured evidence, with confession obtained by torture. Because social democracy eventually ostracizes and denies its protections to all who speak against it, all who speak against it should conceive of themselves as an outsider before being subjected to the violence of the social democratic state. This outsider status involves a complete dissolution of moral obligations not only to the social democratic state itself, but to all who choose to live within the context of the social democratic state. Such a status is not compatible with a lifestyle that seeks to enjoy material goods and comfort within social democracy while simultaneously struggling to alter it. Instead, the liminal individual becomes part of a another organism – of the international Traditional framework of the world – and one's moral obligations are transferred to those who participate in that organism, much as the loyalties of any individual in a esoteric order are to the order alone, and not any state apparatus.

THE CORNER AT THE CENTEROF THE WORLD:
TRADITIONAL METAPHYSICS IN A
LATE TALE OF HENRY JAMES

The human individual is, at one and the same time, much more and much less than is ordinarily supposed in the West; he is greater by reason of his possibilities of indefinite extension beyond the corporeal modality, ... but he is also much less since, far from constituting a complete and sufficient being in himself, he is only an exterior manifestation, a fleeting appearance clothing the true being, which in no way affects the essence of the latter in its immutability.
—René Guénon[1]

Time, space, and natural law hold for me suggestions of intolerable bondage, and I can form no picture of emotional satisfaction which does not involve their defeat—especially the defeat of time, so that one may merge oneself with the whole historic stream and be wholly emancipated from the transient and the ephemeral.
—H. P. Lovecraft[2]

"There's only one corner of the universe you can be sure of improving, and that's your own self ... [by] the sacrifice of self-will to make room for knowledge of God.
—Aldous Huxley[3]

JAMES J. O'MEARA

When last we looked in on James and Lovecraft, we found them occupying rather similar positions: wandering the streets of New York, "almost gasp[ing] with a sense of

---

[1]"Oriental Metaphysics".
[2]Letter to August Derleth (21 November 1930).
[3]*Time Must Have a Stop.*

isolation"[4] in a city transformed by immigration from a colony of the Nordic race to some loathsome futuristic Babylon.

Returning to their respective home bases, they were in quite different situations. Lovecraft returned to Providence and was taken in by his aunts, living in an increasingly shabby series of genteel houses, James, however, had not merely the funds of a reasonably successful writer[5] to provide for a comfortable residence; his share in the family real estate was making considerable gains under the surprisingly wise management of his nephew, Harry James (New York attorney and budding money manager, not the big band trumpeter).

After receiving some particularly good investment news ("Very interesting & valuable to me is your news of the new Syracuse arrangement. ... I feel as if it has placed my declining years a l'abri of destitution"[6]) James turned his hand to what would be his last great ghost story—"The Jolly Corner"[7]—that re-imagines his recent homecoming through the egotistical musings and nocturnal wanderings (in his luxurious family mansion on once-fashionable Irving Place, not in the street, like Lovecraft, whose "declining years" would also not escape destitution either) of a character who seems to combine Henry's imagination with Harry's grasping business sense— exactly what Lovecraft lacked in order to make his way in the new, capitalistic world.

[4]James, H., *The American Scene* (London: Chapman & Hall, 1907), p.86.

[5]And what greater irony than that the real nob, James, could make a living as a writer, while the impoverished Lovecraft sabotaged his career over and over again in order to keep up the pretense of being a "gentleman" amateur; one recalls more recently the über-WASP John Cheever, who at age eleven "promised his proud Yankee parents never to seek fame or wealth with his literary career;" see Blake Bailey, *Cheever: A life* (New York: Knopf, 2009), p.596.

[6]Quoted from Michael Anesko, *Monopolizing the Master: Henry James and the Politics of Modern Literary Scholarship* (Stanford: Stanford University Press, 2012), p.42.

[7]1908, with countless reprints. I am using the one on pp. 337-370 of *American Fantastic Tales: Terror and the Uncanny from Poe to the Pulps*, edited by Peter Straub (New York: Library of America, 2009).

Spencer Brydon returns to the city and house of his birth, after years of typically Jamesian vague epicurean wanderings in Europe, in order to look over his property—one building in the middle of the street, suitable for a lucrative remodeling, the other abutting the avenue, which he thinks of as the "Jolly Corner." Finding his fellow Americans boring, he spends his time exploring his properties, occasionally indulging in gossip and assurances of mutual admiration with his chaste confidante, Alice. She it is, however, who sets the weird plot in motion:

> Once Alice Silverton's conditional words—"if [you] had but stayed at home"—fix themselves in Brydon's consciousness, he responds to them by imagining that, somewhere within the recesses of the deserted birthplace on the jolly corner, his alter ego, the might have been self, lurks. With his newly discovered business acumen working as a catalyst for curiosity, Brydon yearns to track him down, confront him.[8]

What's going on in this uncanny story? Of course, there have been all the usual interpretations; Freudian (James confronting, or not, the childhood "wound" which kept him out of the army, and perhaps marriage as well), Jungian (an elderly man—56!—seeks wholeness by confronting his shadow), Marxist (James realizes the true face of American capitalism isn't his family's genteel wealth but the grasping robber barons[9]), and so on.

I think that here, once again, we can profit from looking at things from a Traditional point of view. To do so, let's lay out some of the puzzling, or at least noticeable, elements in this tale.

---

[8]Ibid, p.43.

[9]There is in fact a curious contemporary photo of J. P. Morgan which James may have seen while consulting over the illustrations in the recent New York Edition of his works, where Morgan seems to be about to gut the viewer with a hand, like that of the spectre in James' tale, that indeed is missing two fingers. See Adeline R. Tinter: *The twentieth-century world of Henry James: changes in his work after 1900* (Baton Rouge: Louisiana State University Press, 2000), p.44ff.

The first thing we need to notice—we can hardly avoid it, it dominates the text of the first part—is Brydon's extraordinary egotism. Right from the start, he tells us of how silly everyone is, asking for what he "thinks" about New York—"my thoughts [are] almost altogether about something that concerns only myself." Why is he here at all? "He had come—putting the thing pompously—to look at his "property," sounding a Stirnerite note. And he freely admits to coming home from "a selfish, frivolous, scandalous life. And you see what it has made of me." Indeed, 'me' is what it is all about: "He found all things come back to the question of what he personally might have been, how he might have led his life and "turned out," if he had not so, at the outset, given [a financial career] up."

And fortunately, for such a massive egotist, he has a confidante, Alice, who can assure him, if he had "turned out" differently, even as a "brute, a black stranger," a "monster," even: that he was "good enough," for, sounding like Seinfeld's mother, "How should I not have liked you?" Besides, she notes with approval, "You don't care for anything but yourself."[10]

Armed with such support, Brydon affirms his curious whim as if he were a Grail knight swearing to perform some Quest for his Lady: "But I do want to see him…And I can. And I shall."[11]

But at the last moment, he hits on different, rather more "cunning" plan,

---

[10]Again, Lovecraft, unlike the confirmed bachelor Brydon, actually had a wife, the Russian-born Brooklyn Jewess, Sonia Greene, who, unlike Harry James, was unsuccessful in business and left Lovecraft in New York, not with Brydon's choice of buildings, one to remodel (on Irving Place, not tenements for Syrian immigrants and the impecunious Lovecraft, surely, but for the declining remnants of Old New York), the other to indulge in nocturnal ghost hunts, but with a succession of tenements where Lovecraft would stint and starve while tormented by the "mad piping" not of Elder Gods but of Levantine flutes.

[11]If not a knight, then the Fisher King, who was punished for his pride in combat with an unmanning wound, like James' mysterious childhood injury, or the mutilated fingers of the spectre. See Julius Evola, *The Mystery of the Grail* (Rochester: VT, Inner Traditions, 1996), Chapter 16: "The Test of Pride."

as Blackadder's manservant Baldrick might say: rather than confront the spectre, he will one-up the spirit by exercising the supreme upper-class virtue: discretion. No coward ever retreated from the battlefield with more self-respect intact, even enhanced:

> ... though moved and privileged as, I believe, it has never been given to man, I retire, I renounce–never, on my honour, to try again. So rest for ever–and let *me!*

After all, he goal all along was to have "saved his dignity and kept his name, in such a case, out of the papers...."

Although the spectre won't, as it happens, let him leave without confrontation—resulting in another cowardly act, fainting—Alice arrives to rest his head in her comforting lap, and assure him that:

> "You came to yourself" she beautifully smiled.
> "Ah, I've come to myself now—thanks to you, dearest. But this brute, with his awful face—this brute's a black stranger. He's none of *me*, even as I *might* have been," Brydon sturdily declared . . .
> [W]ell, he must have been, you see, less dreadful to me. And it may have pleased him that I pitied him."..."He has a million a year," he lucidly added. "But he hasn't you."
> "And he isn't—no, he isn't—*you!*" she murmured, as he drew her to his breast.
>
> •

End on note of domestic bliss.

Lovecraft's narrators, by contrast, seem to err on the opposite side, foolhardiness. They may faint, but only after a determined facing of the truth, no matter how many warnings they may have gotten, and how much they latter hope for sweet forgetfulness or death.

Next, what is the house? The very first impression we are given of the house, as he begins to make his nocturnal rounds, evokes the traditional symbolism of Universal Manifestation as a graph of indefinite points along horizontal and vertical axes, or as a tapestry woven of warp and woof.

Traditional Metaphysics, as presented by René Guénon in a series of works that began appearing shortly after James' death,[12] envisions the Totality of Existence, or 'Universal Manifestation,' as, symbolically, a three dimensional grid, formed by the intersection of three planes, representing an indefinite series states of being. The individual being, the human being, for instance, is as it were a line drawn from the center to the periphery, along one possible state of being. But there are, of course, other and higher states, the acquisition of which is the goal of spiritual development. This can be thought of as a return from the periphery to the Center, so that the individual being has manifested all the possibilities of one level, and from which it can ascend to higher levels. In Sufi terms, the being who has actualized these possibilities is Primordial Man, in effect, the New Adam (the old Adam having left the Center, the Garden, and its central axis, or Tree) while the being that has further achieved all the higher states is Universal Man (the Adam Kadmon of the Qabbala).

As Brydon enters the house each night:

> He always caught the first effect of the steel point of his stick on the old marble of the hall pavement, *large black-and-white squares* that he remembered as the admiration of his childhood and that had then made in him, as he now saw, for the growth of an early conception of style.

There is an analogy between Universal Manifestation and personal

---

[12]See, for example, *Introduction to the Study of the Hindu Doctrines* (*Introduction générale à l'étude des doctrines hindoues*, 1921); *Man and His Becoming according to the Vedânta* (*L'homme et son devenir selon le Vêdânta*, 1925); *Symbolism of the Cross* (*Le symbolisme de la croix*, 1931); and *The Multiple States of the Being* (*Les états multiples de l'Être*, 1932), all of which exist in excellent English editions produced and kept in print by the estimable James Wetmore and his press, Sophia Perennis, in Ghent, New York.

development, though like all analogies it is inverted: physical manifestation entails diversity and a spreading out; personal development a return to simplicity. This is because by returning to the Primordial State, the Garden of Eden, one reaches the Center of the horizontal world, from which the vertical assent to higher possibilities and forms can be made.

This effect was the dim reverberating tinkle as of some far-off bell hung who should say where?—in the depths of the house, of the past, of *that mystical other world that might have flourished for him had he not, for weal or woe, abandoned it.* On this impression he did ever the same thing; he put his stick noiselessly away in a corner–feeling the place once more in the likeness of some great glass bowl, all precious concave crystal, set delicately humming by the play of a moist finger round its edge. The concave crystal held, as it were, this mystical other world, and the indescribably fine murmur of its rim was the sigh there, the scarce audible pathetic wail to his strained ear, of *all the old baffled forsworn possibilities.*

The image of a bowl of precious crystal, within which is manifested a pathetic little tone, by the tracing of a finger along its rim, is remarkable, and sounds like it ought to be a Traditional symbol of Universal Manifestation, but I can't really place it anywhere; here, Henry may have made a more original contribution to mysticism than either his father Henry or brother William!

The house itself clearly embodies the horizontal and vertical dimensions of universal manifestation, the three-dimensional unfolding of indefinite possibilities on each of an equally indefinite hierarchy of levels, forming an indefinite multiplicity of stages or stations. Such symbolism is often fairly explicitly manifested in the design of traditional buildings or dwellings, such as the Native American teepee (the hole in the apex of which allows smoke, or the soul, to escape) or the Muslim house built around an courtyard open to the sky.[13]

As Brydon "crapes" about his house (Irish servant dialect humor!) he finds himself confronting his obsession:

> that of his opening a door behind which he would have made sure of finding nothing, a door into *a room shuttered* and void, and yet so coming, with a great suppressed start, on *some quite erect confronting presence*, something *planted in the middle of the place and facing him* through *the dusk*.

The Center of the Primordial State is indeed associated in the world's traditions with erect presences of one sort or another, especially trees or castles, planted in the center of a Garden—as in Genesis—or an invisible or inaccessible Island—as in the Grail Legend. Dusk, of course, is the preeminent symbol of the liminal state where transformations can take place. And do we not have hear an echo of Lovecraft's "The Shuttered Room"?[14]

Reaching the top floor, where "the light he had set down on the mantel of the next room would have to figure his sword"—again, the ironic Grail note—he finds his goal:

> The door between the rooms was open, and from the second another door opened to a third. These rooms, as he remembered, gave all three upon a common corridor as well, but *there was a fourth, beyond them, without issue save through the preceding.*

Here one also recalls the three stages of reality or consciousness, analogous to the states of waking, dreaming and deep sleep, and the fourth, Turya, of primal bliss.[15]

---

[13]See, for example, Ananda Coomaraswamy, *The Door in the Sky* (Princeton, 1997).
[14]See Julius Evola, *The Hermetic Tradition,* Chapter 1, "The Tree, The Serpent and the Titans."
[15]See *Man and His Becoming according to the Vedânta,* Chapters XII - XV.

He had come into sight of the door in which the brief chain of communication ended and which he now surveyed from the nearer threshold, the one not directly facing it. Placed at some distance to the left of this point, it would have admitted him to the last room of the four, the room without other approach or egress, had it not, to his intimate conviction, been closed *since* his former visitation, the matter probably of a quarter of an hour before. He stared with all his eyes at the wonder of the fact, arrested again where he stood and again holding his breath while he sounded his sense. Surely it had been *subsequently closed*—that is it had been on his previous passage indubitably open!

As we have seen, his smug, self-regarding "discretion" allowed him to refuse to open that door, to pass, it would appear, a test set up for him since he had last seen the open door, and instead to retreat back to the lobby, only to faint when the spectre does appear, unwanted, and block his exit.

And as we also saw, after his failure and faint, he awakens in the lap of his motherly confidante:

on *the lowest degree* of the staircase, the rest of his long person remaining *stretched on his old black-and-white slabs.* They were cold, these marble squares of his youth; but *he* somehow was not, in this rich return of consciousness—the most wonderful hour, little by little, that he had ever known, leaving him, as it did, so gratefully, *so abysmally passive*, and yet as with a treasure of intelligence waiting all round him for quiet appropriation; dissolved, he might call it, in the air of the place and producing the golden glow of a late autumn afternoon. *He had come back*, yes—come back from further away than any man but himself had ever travelled; but it was strange how with this sense what he had come back *to* seemed really the great thing, and as if his prodigious journey had been all for the sake of it.

Back on the lowest degree of human development, yet congratulating himself like a Monty Python knight on his remarkable and triumphant journey, and rejoicing in the return of his egoic, and egotistical, daylight consciousness.

Finally, we must ask the main question: why is the ghost mutilated?

This is just classic misdirection, as in a magician's trick. Why are the ghost's fingers mutilated has absorbed the critics. But if the ghost is some representation of the narrator, then the ghost is like an image in a mirror. If the ghost's fingers are mutilated, rather than ask "Gee, why are the fingers in the mirror mutilated?" we should ask, "Why are the narrator's fingers mutilated?"

I would suggest that the spectre in the doorway (the "Thing on the Doorstep" or "Lurker on the Threshold") is NOT the thing behind the door. Brydon, having fled the chance of reaching the Center, is confronted rather by its inversion, the paltry ego which, however grand in worldly terms, is a sadly limited sight—a mutilation, in fact—in comparison to the fully developed Primordial Man who reigns at the Center. Brydon is far too proud of his single possibility, and perceives the fullness of the Primordial Man as a mutilation rather than the fulfillment of all possibilities.

Rather than standing erect in the primal darkness on the top floor (like the tree, or ithyphallic god, at the Center of the Garden; the 'darkness' of course is another traditional symbol-through-inversion, the overwhelming fullness of Universal Manifestation symbolized by darkness, like a strong light that blinds rather than illuminates) he awakens lying flat on the ground, in the morning sun, on the lap of his motherly confidante.

Brydon has in effect chosen to remain on the level he was born—the squares making up the floor of his childhood home—rather than move forward into the center (Primordial Man), nor, consequently, to rise from there to a higher level, eventually actualizing all possibilities of manifestation (Universal Man).[16] In the words of E. M. Forster (cited with approval by Camille Paglia): "Maimed creatures alone can breathe in Henry James' pages—maimed yet specialized."[17]

Or, as St. Mark asks, "What would it profit a man to gain the whole world [to say nothing of a real estate development, even one on Irving Place] and to lose his [chance of a fully developed] soul?"

Speaking of the New Testament, Brydon may be fruitfully contrasted with an earlier figure from classic American literature: Melville's Bartleby. While H. Bruce Franklin[18] has explored Bartleby's parallels to Christ and to Hindu asceticism—transmitted through Emerson's Transcendentalism—I think we can even more closely identify him with Guénon and Evola's realized being, who embodies;

> ... the style of an impersonal activity; *to prefer* what is essential and real in a higher sense, free from the trappings of sentimentalism and from pseudo-intellectual super-structures—and yet all this must be done by *remaining upright*, feeling the presence in life of that which leads beyond life, drawing from it precise norms of behaviour and action.[19]

[16]Brydon's egocentrism is to be entirely distinguished from the idea of the Absolute Ego which Evola had developed as a philosophical concept long before encountering Guénon. "In his full possession of power, man reaches absolute indifference, so that it makes no sense for him to act any more" [Evola, quoted by H. T. Hansen in his "Introduction" to *Men Among the Ruins* (Inner Traditions, 2002, p.30). The latter needs nothing, from a feeling of already having enough, of being, indeed, above both fullness and lack, indifferent to both, while Brydon continually needs the approval of the world—"I am good, aren't I." He is dedicated to "preserve his good name," while as Coomaraswamy observes, "Blessed is the man on whose tomb can be written *Hic jacet nemo*" [Here lies no one]. (Coomaraswamy, A. K., *Hinduism and Buddhism* (New York: Philosophical Library, n.d.), p.30).

[17]In *Sexual Personae: Art and Decadence from Nefertiti to Emily Dickinson* (New Haven: Yale University Press, 1990), p.616.

[18]The relevant chapter on Bartleby from his out of print monograph, *The Wake of the Gods: Melville's Mythology* can be found along with the story in *Melville's Short Novels* (New York: Norton, 2002).

[19]*Men Among the Ruins*, (Rochester: VT, Inner Traditions, 2002), p.220.

Bartleby has gone so far beyond Brydon that he no longer has a house or home at all, living surreptitiously in his employer's office (one can't really say "at his job") and, ultimately, lying in a prison yard and staring at the wall. While Bartleby is famous for his refusal to perform any of his employer's tasks with his "I would prefer not to," he also, at one point, insists that rather than do so he "would prefer to be stationary," making him functionally identical to the *Chakravartin*, the Realized Man who rules the universe from his unmoving position at the center.[20]

Bartleby's erstwhile employer, who narrates his tale, is clearly a member of what William James would later call the "healthy-minded" and, for all his sympathy and somewhat grudging efforts on Bartleby's behalf, unable to finally understand him.[21] He suggests that Bartleby's melancholy nature must have been amplified unduly by his tenure in the Dead Letter Office; yet it is precisely this daily confrontation with death, that is, the transience of what Salinger's Buddy Glass called "this goddamned phenomenal world" that enables one to rise above it. Unlike James' "discrete" Brydon, Bartleby has confronted death and used that extreme situation to leverage himself into the Center, erect and stationary, at rest as the world revolves around him.[22]

---

[20]See Guénon's *King of the World* (Ghent: N.Y., Sophia Perennis, 2005).

[21]As Evola notes, the philistine thinks that the realized man, the Magus, would be rich and exercise all kinds of magic powers, being incapable of understanding either that a disinterest in all such frivolity is a prerequisite for spiritual progress—"I would prefer not to"—as well as the "boomerang" effect of actions in the subtle realm having untoward results in this world; see his *Hermetic Tradition* (Rochester: VT, Inner Traditions, 1995), Chapter 51, "The Invisible Masters."

[22]Readers of William Burroughs will recall that Bartleby's prison was even then known colloquially as "The Tombs." It's true, that our last glimpse of Bartleby is lying in the prison yard, but again, the principle of inversion is at work here; the employer's limited perspective can only grasp Bartleby's position in a distorted way—Guénon, in *Man and His Becoming*, has some curious speculations about how the "delivered man" [the *mukta*] would seem to vanish from out three-dimensional vision—while also paralleling Brydon's opposite movement, from his failed trial to lying on the floor, snugly cradled in Alice's lap.

And his famous, sentimental conclusion—"Ah, Bartleby! Ah, humanity!"—would better be directed against such all too human specimens as Brydon. As for Bartleby, he has indeed "remain[ed] upright, feeling the presence in life of that which leads beyond life, drawing from it precise norms of behaviour and action."

THE TRINITY OF VOID

The Emptiness is the illusion, if it is not the Emptiness to Supremacy

- Azsacra Zarathustra

GWENDOLYN TAUNTON

E mptiness. Absence. Nothing. The concept of Nothing has been a topic that has inspired two responses in literary thought; either it has been one of immense fascination or a subject which has been entirely dismissed as not being worthy of serious speculation. For the purposes of this article, I shall be adopting a stand point in accordance with the former, in the regard that the concept of Nothing, of 'Absolute Zero' is one of the most profound and important aspects of philosophical thought which connects us with the deepest and most vital aspects of *Sanatana Dharma* or the Primordial Tradition.

Throughout this piece, it is our intention to examine how this understanding has influenced the work of Azsacra Zarathustra and is an integral part of the *Shunya Revolution*, which takes us on an implosive journey of self-annihilation until the point of 'Absolute Zero' is reached, leading us in a lightning flash across the Abyss towards the *Übernoumen*. The intention here is to weave together different strands of both Indian and European thought to provide a historical legacy which culminates in the *Shunya Revolution*. In order to commence then, we shall first examine the concept of *Shunya* itself.

> For this reason India should invent its own Pre-Indo-Aryan form of Absolute Revolution — SHUNYA REVOLUTION, which navigates in two directions — both inside the human Code, and in a concrete historical reality: Time has come to Blast the economic world at

Once — from within and outside!! … Only soaring Upwards in a Strong Vertical Fashion — through the all-destroying middle of Emptiness to Supremacy! — All the aggressive percussive centers of Will to Power ascend; up to the Supreme [Terrifying!] Zero Point — Nothing to Power! And even further — to Nothingness [Nothing-Will!] compressed in the Power of Over, thus breaching, at once, all infinite emptiness's and absences!![1]

Shuyna here, is of course not a mere mathematical expression which equates to 'zero'. The Hindu merchants of yore followed certain simple mathematical rules. If someone was in debt, the numbers should be negative, and if money was due to him, the numbers should be positive. If it was neither, the numbers would add up to zero. This introduced the concept of 'nothing' which is what Shunya is all about. Therefore, it does not equate to being a mere numerical expression, but is instead descriptive of a state of expression or existence. Early Sanskrit texts also refer to zero as *pujyam* not *Shunya*. Shuyna is therefore, Nothing. But how easy is it for us to understand Nothing – Absence in its purest expression as infinite Void? The answer is it is not, and *Shunya*, under a variety of names and in a dearth of different cultures, has always been regarded as one of the greatest metaphysical and philosophical mysteries. It is the core of the Primordial Tradition itself which inhales and exhales creation and destruction from its void of being, beyond time and space, form and function and the paradox of forms and ideals. *Shunya* is the mystery of mysteries and exists in a state which transgresses the boundary of existence itself. We can find expressions of this within the *Mahabharata*, the *Tao Te Ching*, the Buddhist writings of Nāgārjuna, and key European philosophers, who we shall cite later in this article to explain their connection to the concept of Azsacra Zarathustra's *Shunya*. Before examining the role of Shunya however, it is important to understand how the writings of an earlier philosopher, Friedrich Nietzsche, relate to the *Shunya Revolution*.

[1]Ganeshi, K., & Semenyaka, L., *The Absolute Revolution of Azsacra Zarathustra*, http://occupyessays.wordpress.com/2012/01/09/the-absolute-revolution-of-azsacra-zarathustra/.

I do not teach a primitive replacement of one human rule by another, which could be even more human, but the most severe capture of absolute superiority through Nothing to Power and the statement of total prevalence through Emptiness to Supremacy. That means: one having ears… finds them already cut off.

Azsacra Zarathustra, *Nothing to Power and Emptiness to Supremacy*

Azsacra Zarathustra's work with the ideas of Nietzsche is more correctly interpreted as an inevitable evolution of Nietzsche's thinking rather than as an academic dissertation or an implementation of an existing idea. In light of this, key elements of Nietzsche's thought, such as the Overman or *Übermensch* have been remodelled, as what I would term a natural progression of thought. The Übermensch is one who has successfully crossed that risky and dangerous tightrope that spans the yawning abyss betwixt God and Man, and is a creature blessed with both aspects. The *Übernoumen*, takes this concept even further and annihilates the 'Man' to replace it with a concept of mind which is far closer to mysticism and esoteric thought than that of Nietzsche's original concept, for to succeed in the total abnegation of the principle of 'Man' is to align thought with the principle of the cosmos itself. It is indeed a perspective where the whole anthropocentric view of 'Man' has been revealed in subordination to *amor fati* or 'love of fate'.

> The Overman indefatigably practices so that his Pure *Über*/"Over" could surpass the partial and small-biased "man", the tower of the vision of universal Non-existence. And this way is always one: from the Overman (*Übermensch*) — through his destruction — to Over Without "man" (*Überohnemensch*); and then and further away — to Overnoumen (*Übernoumen*).

It is not enough for one to merely cross the bridge…it must be incinerated so that return is impossible, and that once Man is surpassed, it is a part of his linear progression, that it is transcended, purged, and finally annihilated. It is in this final annihilation, that the concept of Shunya is introduced, as Man is sublimated by a nihilistic principle of Nothing. However, as we shall see, it is not a bleak, pessimistic and fearful Nothing, but rather a powerful transforming force that is entirely constructive and beneficial. In essence, it overcomes death, by becoming death, in a constant cycle of creative destruction.

Despite the claims of some, there is a hidden esoteric strand to Nietzsche's thought which applies itself naturally to the metaphysical – because of his staunch rebuttals towards the Christian Tradition, this is obscured somewhat until one examines his thoughts in conjunction with that of Indo-European Traditions such as Hinduism and the Hellenic Tradition, where it is revealed that Nietzsche is in fact highly influenced by both Vedic thought and the ideas of Ancient Greece. To Nietzsche, the West had become decadent, and he looked towards India and the ancient world for ideas to revitalise its flagging culture and decay.

One finds that in his discussions of these doctrines Nietzsche invariably makes references to Asian perspectives against which he compares or evaluates the particular Western 'truth' he is set on demolishing (indeed, the strategy of destruction/deconstruction which Heidegger and Derrida have recognized in Nietzsche's works). Perspectivism is defined as 'the "estranging" of what is one's own by questioning from behind (*hinterfragen*), from the perspective of the foreign.' Perspectivism also underscores a plurality of perspectives, without slippage into the 'childish' banality of relativism. This perspectivism is an important device by which Nietzsche places himself in the 'boots' of the cultural Other in the hope that the distance from his own entrenched situation might make visible the unconscious and concealed structures, prejudices, and weaknesses of his own culture. Nietzsche had no desire to 'go foreign' or adopt Asiatic ways, but sought instead to use Asian experiences as counter-images, and as deconstructive tropes, against which he could comfortably pass censor on many features of Judaism, Christianity, and in his eyes, an equally decadent Western secularism.[2]

Though it was not Nietzsche's desire for the West to adopt Hindu or Greek cultural practices, it is an inevitable consequence of his recourse to these texts that in essence Nietzsche's philosophy is more suited to Hindu and Hellenic cultures where the audience is already familiar with many of the ideas he deploys. In light of this, both Nietzsche and the developments made on his ideas by Azsacra Zarathustra should be regarded as being inherently possessed of Vedic and Hellenic intellectual heritage despite Nietzsche's biological European ancestry.

Returning to Nietzsche's Overman (Übermensch) and his progression through to become the Overnoumen (Übernoumen), in order to explain how this transformation takes place we first need to elucidate upon Nietzsche's definition of the will in relation to the Übermensch to understand how regulating the Will to Nothing by Azsacra Zarathustra consequently creates the Übernoumen.

It is in the character of the Übermensch that we see the unification of the Dionysian (instinct) and Apollonian (intellect) as the manifestation of the will to power, to which Nietzsche also attributes the following tautological value "The Will to Truth is the Will to Power". This statement can be interpreted as meaning that by attributing the will to instinct, truth exists as a naturally occurring phenomena – it exists independently of the intellect, which permits many different interpretations of the truth in its primordial state. [3]

The Apollonian/Dionysian impulse is another core aspect of Nietzsche's philosophy which relates directly to his concept of the will and the Übermensch, in which the two seemingly opposed characteristics dwell in balance. Dionysus, by contrast presides over music – his influence is unseen; it is only heard or felt. What he represents cannot be captured in form, for even in his role as the God of the Theatre,

---

[2]Bilimoria, P., Nietzsche as 'Europe's Buddha' and 'Asia's Superman', Springer Science & Business Media, 2008, p.364.
[3]Pfeffer. R, *Nietzsche: Disciple of Dionysus*, p.114.

he is always masked. The face of Dionysus is never seen. Usually the two gods are examined in their relation to the art world – but their opposition echoes back to another area; that of religion and the nature of ones relation to the divine. Apollo communicates to his brethren through the sedate art of dream. Dionysus whispers the words of madness to one's ear – the state of mind though which Dionysus communicates is via intoxication, whether this is in the form of theatre, music, madness or any other form of expression, what lies behind the Dionysian element is the expression of *pathos*, or emotion. As Nietzsche himself says, "In order to grasp these two tendencies, let us first conceive of them as the separate art-worlds of dreams and drunkenness. These physiological phenomena present a contrast analogous to that existing between the Apollonian and the Dionysian." The representations of Dionysus appear irrational or subconscious, those of Apollo rational. Furthermore, Apollo is a god of boundary drawing – both ethical and conceptual – he is the god of the *principium individuationis*. Apollo, therefore represents a sense of unity but also of restriction. Dionysus, by way of contrast, *expands his horizons by transcending boundaries* – hence for the Dionysian religious type 'intoxication' is a transcendence of everyday consciousness in which we overcome individuality. Of the two impulses, however Nietzsche repeatedly throughout his works refers to the Dionysian as being the superior mode of function, which we would therefore assume to be capable of being enhanced – this would therefore indicate that there is a more Dionysian state of being than that which is described in the Übermensch – the Absolute Dionysian or Übernoumen as it is called by Azsacra Zarathustra. The fact that Nietzsche himself prefers the Dionysian mode to that of a balanced synthesis betwixt Apollo and Dionysus is cited below.

Affirmation of life even it its strangest and sternest problems, the will to life rejoicing in its own inexhaustibility through the sacrifice of its highest types – that is what I call the Dionysian…Not so as to get rid of pity and terror, not so as to purify oneself of a dangerous emotion through its vehement discharge – it was thus Aristotle understood it - but, beyond pity and terror, to realize in oneself the eternal joy of becoming – that joy which also encompasses joy in destruction…And with that I again return to that place from which I set out – *The Birth of Tragedy* was my first revaluation of all values: with that I again plant myself in the soil out of which I draw all that I will and can – I, the last disciple of the philosopher Dionysus – I, the teacher of the eternal recurrence…(TI, *"What I Owe to the Ancients"*)[4]

This inevitably leads to the enquiry as to exactly what is the Dionysian will to life, because it is precisely this element which Nietzsche equates with the concept of the will in regards to the Übermensch. In the Hellenic Tradition, Dionysus represents the *Hidden* or *Black Sun* in contrast to that of his twin Apollo, the *Golden Sun* – and because of his power to survive in Winter, when Apollo symbolically 'dies' and retreats to the land of *Hyperborea*, Dionysus rules in his absence. Dionysus is thus associated with immortality and eternal life, which is expressed in the Greek concept of *zoë*

Plotinos called zoë the "time of the soul", during which the soul, in its course of rebirths, moves on from one *bios* to another […] the Greeks clung to a not-characterized "life" that underlies every bios and stands in a very different relationship to death than does a "life" that includes death among its characteristics […] This experience differs from the sum of experiences that constitute the bios, the content of each individual man's written or unwritten biography. The experience of life without characterization – of precisely that life which "resounded" for the Greeks in the word zoë – is, on the other hand, indescribable.[5]

Furthermore, there is a linguistic difference between zoë (pure, primordial life which is the domain of Dionysius, and that of bios, the biological life as is presided over by Apollo.) Zoë is not just life, it is the life which transcends death, the gift of Dionysus who is ritually

---

[4]Pfeffer, R., *Nietzsche: Disciple of Dionysus*, p.22.
[5]Kerényi, C., *Dionysos Archetypal Image of Indestructible Life*, (New Jersey: Princeton University Press, 1996), p.xxxxv.

dismembered to be reborn, just as his son Orpheus descends into the domain of the dead and returns to the upper world, where he also is dismembered but remains immortal. Zoë is life, but it is sacred life, which remains distinct from the mundane and worldly *bios*.

> Zoë is Life in its immortal and transcendent aspect, and is thus representative of the pure primordial state. Zoë is the presupposition of the death drive; death exists only in relation to zoë. It is a product of life in accordance with a dialectic that is a process not of thought, but of life itself, of the zoë in each individual bios.[6]

The zoë, the life of the Dionysian Übermensch, then is a life in a purely primordial state of mind which has sublimated life and death itself to enter into a pure world of formlessness…it has therefore surpassed the world of form and being itself. It is life in a subconscious mode of delivery. In order for the Übermensch to fully experience this, consciousness itself needs to be negated – hinting once again that Nietzsche's original presupposition for the origin of the will, was that it is subconscious in origin, as is indicated in *The Gay Science* where Nietzsche writes:

> For the longest time, thinking was considered as only conscious, only now do we discover the truth that the greatest part of our intellectual activity lies in the unconscious […] theories of Schopenhauer and his teaching of the primacy of the will over the intellect. The unconscious becomes a source of wisdom and knowledge that can reach into the fundamental aspects of human existence, while the intellect is held to be an abstracting and falsifying mechanism that is directed, not toward truth but toward "mastery and possession."[7]

Therefore, we have arrived at the conclusion that the Will to Power, in Nietzsche's definition is subconscious and purely primordial in its

---

[6]Ibid., p.204-205.
[7]Pfeffer, R., *Nietzsche: Disciple of Dionysus*, p.113.

raw Dionysian state – it therefore can be nothing else but the total negation of the conscious will, or as Azsacra Zarathustra says, it becomes Nothing.

Nothing it is delusion, if it is not the Nothing to Power! Emptiness — is insufficiently empty. It is only one more illusion, if it is not Emptiness to Supremacy! Thus speaks *Übernoumen* — the well-known in India the Russian thinker and creator of the *Shunya Revolution*. Even leading up our negation to the maximum (No), all of us inevitably slide down to the assertion (Yes). To be exact — it is the Will, which always is the Will to Rising. Nobody can deny in such a degree so that to eliminate all. Simple negation is not enough for this purpose. What is necessary for the aim to erect negation in the Absolute? Only going beyond of the maximum of the possibility — in Absolute Impossibility! Therefore, according to Azsacra Zarathustra's philosophy: Emptiness should become Emptiness to Supremacy and overturn the world of illusions — the illusory world.

But this is only part of the philosophy behind the *Shunya Revolution* – for Nietzsche is not the only philosopher to have placed emphasis on the will in regards to engendering a higher type of human – it is indeed a common mode of spiritual asceticism which is found in many Traditional practices. That consciousness is problematic for philosophers was also an idea which occupied the thoughts of the prominent Romanian philosopher Emil Cioran (also inspired by the works of Nietzsche), who cites in his famous aphorisms – "Consciousness is much more than the thorn, it is the dagger in the flesh" and "Fear creates consciousness—not natural fear but morbid fear. Otherwise animals would have achieved a level of consciousness higher than ours." Not only does Cioran also connect the will to the subconscious impulse, he actually takes this one step further to proclaim that the very consciousness of our desires and earthly motivations are precisely the source of man's discomfort. Thus, negation of the conscious will in Cioran's works would not only equate with the higher type exemplified by Nietzsche, it also becomes a source for mundane and worldly happiness. Taking this even further, Cioran (who although a religious disbeliever, deeply lamented his alienation from Godhead and yearned to be able to believe) found that the Will to Power was concentrated more in the religious/mystic experience than it was in any other aspect, noting in *Tears of the Saints* that it was these types whom were able to demonstrate their will by inflicting pain and suffering on themselves in an effort to align themselves with their spiritual beliefs via extreme asceticism.

Thus, we have the severe formulation of a new principle «Over-over, which is boundless in its possibilities and upwards reaching: Precisely Upwards!» as «crucial principle» of the Azsacra Zarathustra's Philosophy of Over is in itself a natural appendix to the Doctrine of Absolute Revolution, just as it is also a derivative of Über-Macht-Thought. This is expressed by its practical «corporally and Strong willed» embodiment: «Über-Macht-Thought is Not a «supra-normal» abstraction of thoughts, but rather a concrete Coronation of the Will of Over as FOREVER-POWER-TO-LIFE leading ultimately to [and solely for] the Risk of Luxury of ABSOLUTE REVOLUTION!!»[8]

In India we see this also in the will of the Yogi's who are capable of great acts of the will via ascetic practices, and we also see this demonstrated in some of Azsacra Zarathustra's ritual renditions. Thus, we see that the supreme act of the will is to be able to negate itself, to close its self-off and turn it's self towards a higher purpose – to become Nothing becomes the supreme sacrifice of the will – which we find in many religious beliefs around the world as well as in Cioran's writing.

Detachment from the world as an attachment to the ego... Who can realize the detachment in which you are as far away from yourself as you are from the world? To displace the center from nature to the individual and from the individual to God. This is the final end

---

[8]Ganeshi, K., & Semenyaka, L., *The Absolute Revolution of Azsacra Zarathustra*, http://occupyessays.wordpress.com/2012/01/09/the-absolute-revolution-of-azsacra-zarathustra/.

of grand detachment.[9]

But this is not the Emptiness nor the Nirvana which the Buddhist's seek – it is an active, virile emptiness which is altogether distinct from this in Zarathustra's work.

The Forever Impossible transition in Forever Impossible through the «Magic Zero Point» of *Shunya* (which was predicted by Ernst Jünger) is the only «possible condition» leading to Absolute Revolution. And it cannot be achieved through a «Buddhism of negativity» by means of *Shunyata* to Dissolution», but via the «Over-positive — the aggressive and creating atoms of Kshatriyas — through *Shunya* to Power». As a result of this percussive differentiation of two types of Emptiness [*Shunya* contra *Shunyata*], the shameful Buddhist Nirvana instantly «disappears, whereas the aggressively-Other-Emptiness — *Shunya!* — it is creating remains contrary to all. *Shunya* suddenly throws Itself into Total Absence as Emptiness to Supremacy. And then — [from this Supreme Absence of all!] the dead Hawk suddenly soars further and further ...» [10]

This is closer in essence to the great kshatriya epic the *Mahabharata* than the later teachings of the Buddha, for did Krishna not urge Arjuna to fight, but with detachment? Arjuna's secret of battle which Krishna relayed to him was to act, but without attachment to the *karma phalam* or fruits of action – in short to act, but to do so subconsciously, in accordance with the will of higher powers, and this involves the constant over coming of the will until it becomes a subconscious impulse or natural action – reducing the will to Nothing, the active Nothing of the kshatriya.

Renunciation of action and devotion through action are both means of final emancipation, but of these two devotion through

[9]Cioran, E. M., *Book of Delusions*, p.77.
[10]Ganeshi, K., & Semenyaka, L., *The Absolute Revolution of Azsacra Zarathustra*, http://occupyessays.wordpress.com/2012/01/09/the-absolute-revolution-of-azsacra-zarathustra/.

action is better than renunciation. He is considered to be an ascetic (1) who seeks nothing and nothing rejects, being free from the influence of the 'pairs of opposites,' (2) O thou of mighty arms; without trouble he is released from the bonds forged by action. Children only and not the wise speak of renunciation of action (3) and of right performance of action (4) as being different. He who perfectly practices the one receives the fruits of both, and the place (5) which is gained by the renouncer of action is also attained by him who is devoted in action. That man seeth with clear sight who seeth that the *Sankhya* and the Yoga doctrines are identical. But to attain to true renunciation of action without devotion through action is difficult, O thou of mighty arms; while the devotee who is engaged in the right practice of his duties approacheth the Supreme Spirit in no long time. The man of purified heart, having his body fully controlled, his senses restrained, and for whom the only self is the Self of all creatures, is not tainted although performing actions. The devotee who knows the divine truth thinketh 'I am doing nothing' in seeing, hearing, touching, smelling, eating, moving, sleeping, breathing; even when speaking, letting go or taking, opening or closing his eyes, he sayeth, 'the senses and organs move by natural impulse to their appropriate objects.' Whoever in acting dedicates his actions to the Supreme Spirit and puts aside all selfish interest in their result is untouched by sin, even as the leaf of the lotus is unaffected by the waters. The truly devoted, for the purification of the heart, perform actions with their bodies, their minds, their understanding, and their senses, putting away all self-interest. The man who is devoted and not attached to the fruit of his actions obtains tranquillity; whilst he who through desire has attachment for the fruit of action is bound down thereby. (6) The self-restrained sage having with his heart renounced all actions, dwells at rest in the 'nine gate city of his abode,' (7) neither acting nor causing to act. (8)

– *The Bhagavad Gita*

A similar sentiment is expressed within the R̥g Veda, where we see

"Sacrifice thyself for thine own exaltation".[11] The sacrifice is one's ego which binds them to the wheel of *samsara*. The path of inaction, of renunciation is not appropriate to the way of the kshatriya for it sits in opposition to their basic temperament – the kshatriya must act and must take part in the world, because it is their fundamental duty or dharma to do so. They must act, but without desire or attachment to the act itself – therefore the will of the kshatriya must be reduced to nothing, and the ego removed for the kshatriya to follow their appropriate dharma. By reducing their conscious will to the zero point, the dharma of the spiritual kshatriya naturally follows the course of *ṛta*, the golden law of the universe by which everything functions correctly.

The order and proper flow of the universe or cycle is regulated by ṛta, which is perhaps the most important component of Vedic thought, for it is by ṛta that all order and structure arises. This order, posed by ṛta, is extremely strict and inflexible. The best way in which to describe ṛta is perhaps to adopt Louis Renou's definition, "Ṛta, which for convenience sake be translated by order (cosmic order and moral order) or by law, is, more precisely, the result of correlations, the product of 'adaption', of the 'fitting together' between the microcosm and the macrocosm". In this way ṛta can be seen as a force of the expression of law in activity which we would call the law of becoming, or transformation, as is contained in the very root of the word itself √r which means to move, to go.[12]

This line of thought is not entirely restricted to the practices of the kshatriya, for it is also reflected in the etymology of yoga, which originally means to 'yoke' oneself to the mind of God. Meditative practice is the passive route to generate the tapas, but it can also be generated in an active sense, as we see in the spiritual battle of Arjuna. Tapas, the spiritual heat, is also the adhesive factor which joins together the strands of ṛta and dharma in the human practitioner.

---

[11]*Ṛg Veda*, X.81.5d.

[12]Taunton, G., *The Tantrik Tradition*, Numen Books, Forthcoming.

Tapas is held to be one of the key thoughts of the ṛṣi, the great seers who composed the *Vedas*. As Eliade explains, *tapas* is a concept that is documented in Vedic texts, and also holds a considerable place in Yogic-Tantric techniques. This heat is induced by holding the breath and especially by the "transmutation" of sexual energy, a Yogic-Tantric practice which, although quite obscure, is based on prāṇāyāma and various visualizations. Tapas is clearly documented in the *Ṛg Veda*, and its powers are creative on both the cosmic and spiritual planes; through tapas the ascetic becomes clairvoyant and even incarnates the gods. Comparing the magical increase of the temperature within the body, which Eliade goes on to describe as a universal feat amongst medicine men, shamans, and fakirs, he describes tapas as being one of the most typical yogico-tantric techniques for producing 'mystic heat' He then continues on to say that the continuity between the oldest known magical technique and Tantric Yoga, is in this particular instance, undeniable. The idea of mystic heat is not unknown outside of India, for as Georges Dumézil has shown, several terms in the Indo-European heroic vocabulary – *furor, ferg, wut, ménos* – express precisely this "extreme heat" and "rage" which, on other levels of sacrality, characterizes the incarnation of power. It is therefore clear that tapas can be raised by methods which are not purely contemplative practices, for these terms are linked to warrior traditions in Europe. In their own linguistic context, most of the words here have a connection with altered mind states that could also be linked to shamanism, which would identify the induction of a state of 'mystical heat' as a prerequisite for traditions which revolve around shamanism. In this context, tapas is the creative flame of contemplative exertion, the contracting to an innermost point of dissolution and the subsequent expansion to an finitude of creative possibilities. It is though the medium of tapas, that *sat* is witnessed and ṛta observed. Ṛta, however, is not just a cosmic function that regulates order in nature, for it also has applications at the social and moral level. Ṛta, at the level of philosophical abstraction, governs also the interplay of human relations, ensuring that moral and ethical codes are kept ordered. It is on this plane that ṛta finds expression as law and social order, representative of humanities intergradations and governance by the rule of cosmic law. On this level ṛta can be seen to be the expression of integration of humanity into the cosmic order, of which the social-ethical mode is but a reflection. In its totality, the concept of ṛta spans over three different spheres of reality - socio-ethical, religio-sacrifical, and natural law. Each of the three 'orders' – sacrificial, moral, and natural - are a manifestation of the same universal ṛta. As a principle of cosmic order, ṛta is similar to the concept of dharma. Though this word did not fall into common usage until later, its equivalent terms are readily traceable in the *Ṛg Veda*.[13] Once ṛta and dharma are understood and the tapas generated is sufficient, in all genuine Traditions this is the beginning of the process in which the microcosm homologises with the macrocosm to produce a higher cognitive state.

> What then is that which, dwelling within this little house, this lotus of the heart, is to be sought after, inquired about, and realized? As large as the universe outside, even so large is the universe within the lotus of the heart. Within it are heaven and earth, the sun, the moon, the lightening, and all the stars. What is in this macrocosm is in this microcosm. (*Chānd. Up.* 8.12.3)[14]

At this level of practice, the will is completely negated to the Absolute point of Zero, precisely because there is no longer any distinction between what is 'I' and what is 'Not I'. Once the adept has reached this stage, by whatever method of spiritual instruction, he or she is effectively "yoked' to the system of ṛta and will naturally follow the correct path of dharma without ever having to evoke the notion of 'will'. Therefore, by applying the will to certain spiritual methods, the will is constantly overcome until it becomes Nothing. In some Hindu Traditions we see this taken even further, such as in the iconography of Goddesses such as Kali, who bears a severed head in Her hand representing the removal of the 'ego' which is the ultimate impediment to the discovery of the Absolute Will.

---

[13]Miller, L., *The Vision of Cosmic Order in the Vedas*, (London: Routledge & Kegan Paul, 1985, p.3.
[14]Taunton, G., *The Tantrik Tradition*, Numen Books, Forthcoming.

All of these factors, and the link to a type of higher consciousness wherein the nothinginess of the will is attained via an amalgamation or 'yoking' of the microcosm of man to the 'macrocosm' of the universe, are found in texts devoted to the God Shiva. For example, the *Śāmbhavopāya*, 1.7 mentions that the 'fourth state of consciousness is experienced by piercing through the sates of waking consciousness, the dream state and the state of dreamless sleep, in blissful awareness of the true nature of reality.'[15] The fourth state of mind is furthermore defined within the *Śiva Sūtras* as being a state of mind which is not normally entered into. In the *Śiva Sūtras*, (*Āṇavopāya*, 3.9), it is even said that 'One who has realized his spiritual nature is like a dancer, dancing to the rhythm of the universe.'[16] Similarly, Wulff also states that there is a connection between Abhinavagupta's aesthetic theory and his practice of Kashmir Saivism; 'in aesthetic experience, as in yogic trance and in final release, subject and object disappear, and one transcends all desires and limited, ego-bound perceptions. Abhinavagupta terms the highest state of *vigalitavedyantara*, "one in which the object of knowledge has dissolved."'[17]

An earlier individual whom explored the importance of a kshatriya path to the divine, was the Italian writer Julius Evola, who not only comprehended the underlying principles in the *Bhagavad Gita* and Nietzsche, but also examined the role of this in Tantrism and early Theravada Buddhism. Early in his literary career Evola made the following statement:

> Tantrism may lead the way for a western elite which does not want to become the victim of these experiences whereby an entire civilization is on the verge of being submerged.
> – Julius Evola, "What Tantrism means to Modern Western Civilization"[18]

---

[15]Miller, L., *The Vision of Cosmic Order in the Vedas*, p.31.

[16]Worthington, R., *Finding the Hidden Self: a Study of the Siva Sutras* (Pennsylvania: The Himalayan Institute Press, 2002), p.15.

[17]Worthington, R., *Finding the Hidden Self: a Study of the Siva Sutras*, p.72.

[18]Wulff, D. M., <u>Religion in a New Mode: The Convergence of the Aesthetic and the</u>

Evola's opinion that the kshatriya path in Tantrism outranks that of the brahmanic or priestly path, is readily supported by the Tantric texts themselves, in which the *Vira* (The 'heroic' form of the Tantric Adept) or active mode of practice is exalted above that of the priestly mode in *Kaula* Tantrism. In this regard, the heroic or solar path of Tantrism represented to Evola, a system based not on theory, but on practice – an active path appropriate to be taught in the degenerate epoch of the Hindu *Kali Yuga* or Dark Age, in which purely intellectual or contemplative paths to divinity have suffered a great decrease in their effectiveness.[19] Thus much of Evola's philosophy should, contrary to his above statement, be regarded as an inherently Eastern influence which he hoped would provide intellectual stimulus to prevent the decline of the West. Many of these ideas where extrapolated and combined in a new premise in his work '*Ride the Tiger*'.

On the topic of Evola, Azsacra Zarathustra writes:

«Evola, actually, never tried to «Ride the Tiger», but only did all, that this Tiger of Will to Power instantly (in a trice!) could do to tear to pieces each of the «good equestrians» and «evil horsemen» simultaneously. Id est: on the «Tiger of Death it is impossible to Ride with the instrumentality of the «occult», it [only!] should be eaten by lions of Nothing to Power [it is necessary!], and then they (the lions) should be lacerated by the Dragon of Emptiness to Supremacy ...»

The Tiger is of course symbolic of the dark nature of the *Kali Yuga*, hence Azsacra Zarathustra's association of the tiger with Death. It is also worth noting here that the saying 'ride the tiger' is only part of the aphorism deployed by Evola; the full version of the saying implies that dismounting the tiger is impossible as it shall savage anyone who attempts to ride it. The only way to ride the tiger successfully is to become one with current of Kali Yuga – *forever*. The traditional view

Religious in Medieval India, in *The Journal of The American Academy of Religion* , 54 (4), p.677.
[19]Taunton, G. *The Tantrik Tradition*, Numen Books, Forthcoming.

of the Tantric path (the saying 'Ride the Tiger' is a Tantric one) is that the world itself is power, *Shakti* (the literal interpretation of Shakti is 'power') and that it is there to be used and absorbed by the adept (see Arthur Avalon's *World as Power*). Therein, the concept of power shifts from a personal one to a universal abstract conception wherein there is in truth no essence – the Tantric adept, the *Vira*, is power and nothing besides. Thus, the conception of the negation of the will, by focusing on the will, is an inherently Tantric worldview just as it is a classical Vedic one inherited from the *Mahabharata*. The proper approach to the divine for the kshatriya is not that of renunciation, but to act in accordance with power, the flow of Shakti that is both ṛta and dharma until the microcosm of man and the macrocosm of the universe become inseparable and will and power become one at the 'zero point'.

At first glance the unwary reader could also assume that there is a connection between Azsacra Zarathustra's concept of Shunya and that of the Buddhist *śūnyatā*, they are however, explicitly not the same interpretation of 'Nothing'. Though both essentially serve the same function, the Buddhist śūnyatā is essentially a passive path to renunciation, and an embrace of the emptiness. As we have shown from previous examples, the path of renunciation is inappropriate for those of kshatriya or warrior temperament. Their spiritual dharma is best suited to the active *Shunya* as described by Azsacra Zarathustra.

> *Shunya-revolution* as a blow from Nothing occurs within of a wheel of *Samsara*, where Shunya to Power rends a wheel of *Samsara* and breaks the spokes of all illusions. The Power of Shunya breaking loose from borders of a wheel of Life and Death and passing in/to Absolute Revolution already outside a Wheel of Good and Evil. Id est *Shunya Revolution* occurs only within the Samsara Chakra for possibility of Vertical Rising through all illusions of Wheel of Life and Death. *Shunya* to Power or True Pre-Buddha — Antibuddha! — destroys even Nirvana and Death beyond Death and without Death.

The theme of emptiness (śūnyatā) emerged from the Buddhist doctrines of the nonexistence of the self (Pāli: *anatta*, Sanskrit: *anātman*) and teaches that existence is empty, a conclusion which is derived as part of the Buddha's Enlightenment resulting from the process known as *pratītyasamutpāda* or the theory of *Dependent Origination* wherein all actions are connected together, until eventually one regresses back to a primal cause, thus depriving the object and events of an individual existence. The primal cause is therefore assumed to be a form of primordial emptiness. Nāgārjuna also equates emptiness with Dependent Origination in the *Mūlamadhyamakakārikā*. According to Nāgārjuna any enduring essential nature (*svabhāva*) would prevent the process of dependent origination, and would prevent any kind of origination at all, for things would simply always have been and will always continue to be, i.e. as existents (*bhāva*). Nāgārjuna equates *svabhāva* (essence) with bhāva.

The Sanskrit word *Śūnya* means empty. *Śūnyatā* means emptiness. However, there is a subtle difference in the connotations of the two, as deemed by the two sects of religion. According to the Buddhist Mahayana Tradition, nothing in this world exists inherently independent of itself. Either it is the cause(s), or their part(s), or the imputation(s) of a sentient being's mind that any phenomena manifests itself out from. Hence, all things existing in the universe are totally empty of any defining essence. It is always in a state of flux and hence, impermanent and ever-changing. Since, it is always in a transformative stage as gathered by the mind of a sentient being, hence is always subjective and the existence of an objective reality is and can never be a possibility in the Mahayana Buddhist Tradition. The only reality is the Śūnyatā or the emptiness.[20]

Though Nāgārjuna and the Buddha both espouse a form of renunciation and detachment derived from emptiness, it is again a passive emptiness it is not the active emptiness advocated it the

---

[20]Evola, J., *Men Among the Ruins: Post-War Reflections of a Radical Traditionalist*, (Vermont: Inner Traditions, 2003), p.89.

Shunya Revoltuion. Zarathusta places the Shunya of the kshatriya in opposition to the Śūnyatā of Buddha.

Perhaps closer to the Hindu concept of dharma and the world as Shakti, is the Taoist concept of *Wu Wei* which involves natural action in which everything knows how to act appropriately, without the necessity for contemplation of the act. The literal meaning of Wu Wei is 'without action', 'without effort', or 'without control', and is often included in the paradox *wei wu wei*: 'action without action' or 'effortless doing'. This again utilises the theory of merging or negating conscious activity to the point where it becomes one with the way or *Tao*, which is essentially the same as the Hindu conception of ṛta. Wu wei is also applied in certain martial arts techniques such as *T'ai chi ch'uan, Baguazhang* and *Xing Yi.*

Shunya is a Trinity of Void – Absence, Emptiness and Nothing. But it is not the same, and is in fact contrary to Śūnyatā. This inevitably leads to a complex epistemological quandary; how can Nothing (being essentiality with form and quality) have two different forms of being existing in opposition? This statement that there are diametrically opposed modes of Nothing which essentially form a dyad is not as paradoxical as it sounds. Dualism is a common element to many Traditions. Both Hinduism and Daoism share this element in the forms of *Shiva/Shakti* and *Yin/Yang*. There are in fact two different approaches to the divine, one of which is active/kshatriya and other which is passive/brahmanic – together these elements form the monad, the bindu or absolute point which represents unity. The Śūnyatā of the Buddhists is the contemplative/meditative aspect which is more suited to those of a passive temperament, whilst the Shunya of Azsacra Zarathustra is the active element, an aggressive model of Emptiness which is in a constant state of overcoming and destroying itself in the service of a higher purpose. Neither the Shunya or the Śūnyatā is in truth superior or inferior; they are both the essence of an eternal primordial Nothing that is the Absolute Point of Zero in which both paths culminate. The Shunya is suited for those of the kshatriya temperament, the Śūnyatā for those of a brahmanic temperament.

As explained above, Shunya is explicitly a concept related to the kshatriya. The fact that the kshatriya are not the traditional priestly model of the India citizen (the brahmin) does not render them spiritually less capable of advancement. There are countless illustrations of highly educated and spiritual kshatriya throughout the religious history of India, most notably Arjuna the hero of the great epic the *Mahabharata*, of which his spiritual struggle in the *Bhagadvad Gita* is one of the most popular tales in the modern world. To a certain extent, the *Upanishads* also represent a breaking point with the Traditional model of brahmanic religious authority as some of these texts are attributed to kshatriya authors. Likewise, the *Tantras* reject traditional notions of *varna* and establish an interior system based on temperament instead of birth, in which a vira and *divya* adept are described – both of which approach the *Tantras* themselves in a different manner. As noted before, the *vira* mode is the Tantric equivalent of the kshatriya path. It is also worth noting that the Buddha himself was born in the kshatriya varna. It is therefore apparent that the kshatriya caste is capable of wielding equal spiritual merit to that of the brahmin. The point is that difference approaches are suitable, based on individual temperament, and Shunya corresponds to a kshatriya teaching.

In regards to the Übernoumen, there is also an element of death at play too, for it involves the psyche being in a constant state of flux, where things are constantly overcome and destroyed in order to create a state of mind which reflects the nature of Nothing, Absence, and Emptiness. Death, is of course symbolic to such a state of mind which is in a pronounced stage of worldly detachment. This technique is not unknown within certain Traditions, who looked not upon death as an object of fear, but one of reverence and as a powerful tool for self-transformation. As I hinted earlier in this article, Dionysus, who is the deity behind Nietzsche's philosophy, is also associated with death and the underworld through his connection with the zoë (eternal life). The transformative power of death is also found in other Traditions besides the Hellenic one, and is present in early Tibetan Buddhism (*Varayana*). The *Heruka* and *Hevajra Tantras* place emphasis on mortuary practice (meditation and ascetic practices in cremation grounds and other places of death). Also within the Tantric Tradition in India it is commonly noted that the proper attitude of a true practitioner of Tantra is to be 'one who is dead to the world'. Sects such as the *Aghora* also adopt an existence in which the currents of life and death are merged, negating the polarity of mortal life and death. In this stage the human psyche is broken down and the will strengthened to a point in which it eventually transgresses Death, in precisely the manner of continuous over coming through embracing emptiness as the Übernoumen. One Guru within the *Kapalika* Tantric Tradition even teaches that such an attitude is a requirement to practice the path, for which he endorses his students to embrace death rather than avoid it and advocates a theorem known as *'Yama's Gate'*. Thus the constant death and destruction which is the state of the Übernoumen, should not be viewed as one that is negative; rather it is an extremely potent psychological process for self-transformation which exists in other parts of the world of Traditional metaphysical lore. Death is the ultimate psychological hurdle and the ultimate horror of human existence – which the true adept or philosopher should directly confront. To know the Absolute Void and the Essence of Emptiness, one must know Death as they know Life.

Shunya clearly is a kshatriya discipline and is comparable to the instruction of Arjuna by Krishna in the *Bhagavad Gita*, in which action not renunciation is clearly expounded as the path appropriate to the kshatriya. That Arjuna is told to act, but to avoid the fruits of action relays the impression that appropriate action is controlled by dharma and ṛta and not by the conscious will – it is fact, comparable to Shunya in the regard that it is a subconscious and constant overcoming, in which consciousness is reduced to Nothing in the service of a higher purpose and individual dharma. Thus, success on the battlefield is caused by the sublimation of the self. It is also the equivalent of wu wei, in which one acts in accordance with the Tao. Therefore the supreme act of the will is to negate itself and become one with the flow of ṛta/dharma – this is the instruction that Krishna provides to Arjuna and the highest teaching of the kshatriya. It is also the amor fati of Nietzsche.

> It is a Dionysian Yea-Saying to the world as it is, without deduction, exception and selection…it is the highest attitude that a philosopher can reach; to stand Dionysiacally toward existence: my formula for this is *amor fati*.[21]

As explained earlier, Nietzsche's rejection of religion stems from what he perceived to be the negative influence of Christianity as a principle cause of cultural decadence in the West. It does not extend to either Hellenic or Vedic models of thought, as both of these are repeatedly extolled in his texts. Indeed, on the cultural level there is a high degree of compatibility betwixt Hellenic and Vedic thought which stems from early Proto-Indo-European influences in language and religion. The Hellenic dichotomy Nietzsche deploys in his theory on Apollo/Dionysus also has correlations to relationships between the Hindu Gods Vishnu and Shiva. Therefore, the concept of the Übermensch of Nietzsche and the Übernoumen of Azscara Zarathustra who sits at the vanguard of the Shunya Revolution, are entirely suited to the Indian mind-set, especially if we regard the Übernoumen as an incarnation of Nataraja Himself, engaged in the *tandava* dance and evolved in the prefect Trinity of Void – Emptiness, Absence, Nothing - and the creative power of destruction embodied in the constant overcoming of the self, which is the Will to Nothing. It is destruction in a state of flux with creation, ever changing and dying in the supreme transformative state.

> Thus: «Will of Over Without man [Gott-Tod!] as Nothing to Power and Emptiness to Supremacy is burning all «reasonable safety devices» before entering into Will to Power as such. And thusly, Not-shown Over is ensconced in the Hidden and Invisible from which it doesn't disappear, but is Totally Governed by Absence Eternally!!». And it is real: «Without the Nothing to Power and Emptiness to Supremacy the life of God is only the «inability» to

---

[21]Pfeffer, R., *Nietzsche: Disciple of Dionysus*, p.261.

Think — «shortage of the will»! — conditioned by its Own Death [22]

---

[22] Ganeshi, K., & Semenyaka, L., *The Absolute Revolution of Azsacra Zarathustra*, http://occupyessays.wordpress.com/2012/01/09/the-absolute-revolution-of-azsacra-zarathustra/.

Traditionalism vs. Traditonalism

Roy Orlogstru

About 10 years ago I got acquainted with Traditionalism, mostly the author René Guénon (1886-1951). I started reading English translations of his books (which are easily accessible) and later on read other authors from the so-called 'Traditionalist school'. Guénon remained my most-read and most-appreciated author. After a while I had the idea that I kept reading the same all the time, but in different words and I started to read less Traditionalistic literature.

Either or not because of my teenage involvement with the - in Traditionalistic circles - dreaded "Theosophism"; the ideas of the Traditionalistic school felt like homecoming. I also thought that there was a single Source for all religions. Other ideas that I found within the literature felt familiar too, but of course, a lot was new. Yet, the overall 'structure' of his way of thinking comes to me as completely logical, but at some points this 'system' is limiting to say the least. I am afraid that this is a price I have to pay. I will come to this later. At the time I had a Traditionalistic teacher, who did not teach me and my fellow students Traditionalism, but he taught from a Traditionalistic background. He and I were usually in surprising accordance, but the big difference was that he is a 'realised' initiate, a stage that I will probably never reach myself, *because* of my limiting Traditionalistic ideas...

After several years without the teacher I did continue studying Traditionalism along with my many other interests, but after a while it seemed as if nobody, not even the former fellow students, had any interest in the subject. I started to look around for other Traditionalists, not books, but people to exchange ideas with and ask questions to. Fortunately with the world wide web it is easy to communicate with people from all over the world, find out about smaller or larger initiatives and order them from anywhere in the world. I found out that there are many shades of Traditionalists and that is what I want to say a few things about in this short text.

Music Scene Traditionalism

Mark Sedgewick (1960-) is a British/Irish scholar with an interest in Traditionalism. His book *Against The Modern World* (2004) gives a history of Traditionalism that is not received with applause in the entire Traditionalistic community. Sedgewick also has a website (www. traditionalists.org) with a blog. On 20 May 2007 Sedgewick mentioned on this blog that he discovered a new kind of Traditionalism: 'Music Scene Traditionalism'.[1] Now since the music scene that Sedgewick describes is the one where I mostly find my own material to listen to, I am quite familiar with what Sedgewick describes, only, I hardly agree with the man. It is true that some sort of Traditionalism receives a rising attention every decade or so, but to me, this is at best a very thin form of Traditionalism. What we see in music (sub) genres that we can refer to as 'neofolk' and some parts of the 'metal' scene can hardly be described as Traditionalism. Instead of Guénon, the inspiration is usually Julius Evola (1898-1974) which as you probably know was an Italian author who was in contact with Guénon and who agreed with Guénon on some points, but the two disagreed on many others. From what I find in the writings of Evola, I do not regard him as a Traditionalist per se, but this is not what I want to talk about here. What Sedgewick sees as Traditionalism in the music scene, to me seems more anti-modernity and some politics claiming to be based on authors such as Evola and Oswald Spengler (1880-1936). That the West is in decline is clear. That our community desacralises with the day is clear too. Some bands like to sing about that and combine these notions with more or less politically inspired elements. Some call for a return to native spirituality. However though some themes and

---

[1] http://traditionalistblog.blogspot.nl/2007/05/music-scene-traditionalism.html accessed 6/10/2012.

inspiration certainly resemble those of Traditionalism, I would hardly call this Traditionalism.

Radical Traditionalism

Perhaps not entirely unexpected, but within and 'around' this music scene, some more serious things happen. There are a growing number of publications and websites that sometimes combine music with philosophy or even focus mostly on the latter. The best example is the American *Tyr Journal*. In 2002 the first volume of this well-printed journal appeared. However in a way a magazine, it had the size of a book. Topics included went from anti-modernism, European heathenry to more controversial topics and references to the Second World War. Controversial as it is, the publication was ground breaking, interesting and thought-provoking. The authors called themselves "Radical Traditionalists". To quote the back cover:

> ['Radical Traditionalism'] means to reject the modern, materialist reign of 'quantity over quality,' the absence of any meaningful spiritual values, environmental devastation, the mechanization and over-specialization of urban life, and the imperialism of corporate mono-culture, with its vulgar 'values' of progress and efficiency. It means to yearn for the small, homogeneous tribal societies that flourished before Christianity — societies in which every aspect of life was integrated into a holistic system.

Like I said, hardly Traditionalistic, but certainly an initiative to applaud. *Tyr* was supposed to be an annual publication, but with only three volumes (2002, 2004, 2006) so far, this was perhaps a bit over-ambitious.

Tyr Journal is available through 'regular' channels such as Amazon, but also through many of the mail orders from the music scene that Sedgewick referred to (especially because volume two came with a CD). There are other more or less similar publications which are either available or recommended within that music scene. *The Initiate*, a journal that now has two issues available (2008, 2010) is quite a Traditionalistic publication, but leans much on the political side. It is nowadays made available by Arktos, a publisher of both books and music. There are other magazines and journals, but *if* there is a Traditionalistic touch, it is certainly much softer than the two titles I just mentioned.

'Real' Traditionalists

For a few years I had been looking for 'real' Traditionalists, since in my eyes all the above is 'Traditionalism light' or at least lighter than how I look at things myself. I was, of course, aware of Traditionalistic publishers with obvious names such as Sophia Perennis (the publisher of Guénon in English) or World Wisdom (home of many living Traditionalists), but do these authors and their readers meet? Where can I found out about authors that I do *not* know and if some book is any good? Is there not something of a Traditionalistic discussion board, some virtual group, a Facebook group, a mailing list, or anything? When I found nothing of my liking, I started my own group.[2] Soon after I ran into the Traditional Studies forum[3]. Now there we have living and breathing Traditionalists! It seems mostly a relatively small group of intellectuals with an interpretation of the same books that I read myself.

Hardliners

To an outsider like myself, this group seems to consist of scholars and their followers. Publications that I heard of, but never read come from this angle. *The Sophia Journal*[4], *Sacred Web*[5], the relatively new

---

[2]Traditionalism Discussion Group, to be found at www.monas.nl.
[3]www.traditionalstudies.freeforums.org/.
[4]www.sophiajournal.com.
[5]www.sacredweb.com.

Luvah online journal[6], they are often written by the Traditionalists of our own day. Seyyed Hossein Nasr (1933-), Charles Upton (1948-), Huston Smith (1919-) and many others that I never heard of. Each of them practises a world religion and tries to find a balance between credibility in their professional community and in the Traditionalistic or religious community. Needless to say that as a religious scholar in a desacralised world, this is an almost impossible task.

What I soon noticed when I started reading and conversing with these new Traditionalists was that we have a rather fundamentally different view on some key subjects within the field, in spite of mostly reading the same literature. I have jokingly called them 'hardliners' and 'theologians' and this is where I will proceed to some more substantive discussions instead of just telling you stories. I hope you are familiar with some of the basics of the Traditionalistic worldview, but even if you are not, you will get a little wiser from what follows. Quite certainly, the below will give you a few things to think about.

THE BASICS OF TRADITIONALISM

In basis the ideas behind Traditionalism are as simple as they are far-reaching. There is one Source for everything. This Source has many names, God, Allah, Brahma, make your pick. This Source is not a creator, God is not an entity separate from creation, but everything is *emanated* from It. This of course does not only concern the material, which is hardly interesting, but more importantly religion. There are many religions and philosophies which all can be sees as paths on a mountain going upwards to the same peak. That peak is (depending on how you describe it) not necessarily the Source, but the 'first emanation of wisdom' that in Traditionalistic literature is also described with different terms. A popular term is philosophia perennis or in English perennial philosophy (perennialism is another term sometimes used

---

for Traditionalism). I prefer *sophia perennis* over the first term since it does not refer to the *love for* wisdom, but to eternal wisdom itself. Some authors use *religio perennis* or its Muslim counterpart *al-din al-hanif*. René Guénon simply used the term Tradition.

The benefit of Guénon's term, in my eyes, is that the term does not only refer to a starting point, but also to its connection to the present and this is where we come to another crucial point of Traditionalism. However many religions, philosophies, etc. there may be, there are not all that many *valid* ones. This is where the term orthodoxy emerges and this very term will prove to be the very reason that there seems to be differences between Traditionalists.

Let me first continue with the basics. According to Guénon there is a 'something' coming from the sophia perennis, something which he describes as a spiritual influence.[7] In Muslim terms this often is spoken of as Grace.[8] It is this influence that is transferred and which thus guarantees an unbroken link, or filiation with the Source. The way that this filiation is created is another point of discussion. The basic idea is, a religion is only valid when it has an unbroken link to the Perennial Wisdom and an individual is only connected to that Source when (s)he received the spiritual influence. Consequently, only a filiated individual can continue the chain.

Orthodoxy

In what follows some more Traditionalistic ideas may appear, but here you have the basis in the simplest explanation. Now let us have a look what Traditionalists call "orthodox".

For a religion to be considered intrinsically orthodox [...] it must be founded on a doctrine of the Absolute which, taken as a whole, is

---

[7]For example in "Perspectives On Initiation" p.23 and 27.
[8]Schuon, F., "*The Essential Frithjof Schuon*" p.158.

adequate; this religion must then advocate and achieve a spirituality that is proportioned to this doctrine, which is to say that it must comprise sanctity both in notion and in fact. Therefore, the religion must be of divine and not of philosophical origin, and consequently it must be the vessel for a sacramental or theurgic presence made manifest notably in miracles and also—though this may be surprising to some—in sacred art. Specific formal elements, such as apostolic personages and sacred events, are subordinated inasmuch as they are forms to the principal elements just mentioned; their meaning or value can therefore change from one religion to another—human diversity making such fluctuations inevitable—without this constituting any contradiction with regard to the essential criteriology that concerns both metaphysical truth and salvific efficacy, and secondarily—and on that basis—human stability.[9]

Or another quote:

> It may be said that religion essentially entails the conjunction of three elements belonging to different orders, a dogma, a moral law and a cult or form of worship; wherever one or other of these elements happens to be wanting, there can no longer be any question of religion in the proper sense of the word. We will add forthwith that the first element forms the intellectual part of religion, the second its social portion, while the third, which is the ritual element, participates in both these functions.[10]

You can see that the whole idea of orthodoxy goes quite far. A religion has to be based on revelation *and* has an unbroken tradition to the present in order to be valid. For how many religions of today will this be true? Christianity? There are many forms of Christianity. Which of them can be really traced back to Christ himself? Are the forms of Christianity as we know them today orthodox with all the forms of Protestantism that emerged only a few hundred years ago? I, with

---

[9]Schuon, F., *"Form and Substance in the Religions"* p.13.
[10]Guénon, R., *Introduction to the Study of Hindu Doctrines*, p.65.

other Traditionalists, think that some can, but I still differ in opinion on some details.

What about other religions? Is Buddhism an orthodox religion? Hinduism? I do not plan to go into details, but let me take a very clear example of an orthodox and living religion: Islam. As you know, Islam is the last of the revealed religions and it emerged in the seventh century. I do not suppose you will think that since that time Islam has died and relived again, hence, Islam is the ultimate example of an orthodox religion? All forms? Just as with Christianity this is a question, but not a question for the current essay. A fact is, that a great many of the Traditionalists were and are Muslim. René Guénon died as Abdel Wahid Yahia in Cairo. Frithjof Schuon (1907-1998) was a Muslim by birth. The most famous contemporary Traditionalist, the earlier mentioned Nasr is a Muslim, as is for example the late Martin Lings (1909-2005). They all wanted to be part of an orthodox religion. In spite of this and despite of the fact that Islam itself has a strong notion of the *Sophia Perennis*, including respect for other orthodox religions (which is a natural result when you realise that all religions are paths up the same mountain), there is not all that much attention for Islam in Traditionalistic literature. *Was* I should actually say, because in the more serious Traditionalistic circles of today, Islam seems to start to surface big time.

When you visit the Traditional Studies forum, you might first think that you stranded on a Muslim discussion board. The design on top, the "avatars" of many users *and* the subjects under discussion often bear a Muslim stamp. Also when you read journals such as *Sacred Web, Sophia or Luvah* you can see this 'trend'. A very nice article of Zachary Markwith[11] in *Sophia* tells us why. Islam (among its other faces that we usually see on the news) appears to be the keeper of the sophia perennis.

---

[11]Markwith, Z., *Muslim Intellectuals and the Perennial Philosophy* in *Sophia* volume 13, issue 2, winter 2007/2008 (this lengthy essay is both a nice introduction to Traditionalism as of the subject under discussion).

I want to quote Markwith from that article to make a jump to the next subject.

How to Connect

> For one cannot realize the One who transcends forms, except by adhering to a form that the One has revealed.[12]

This is an often-heard and logical conclusion for a Traditionalist. A bit further Markwith even states that: "[...] realized knowledge, [...] requires a living tradition, as well as the guidance of a spiritual master."[13]

There we go, being a Traditionalist you have to either be lucky enough to have been raised in an orthodox religion (and with more luck you even have 'access' to a realised master), or you have to connect yourself to one. That may not be what many people within occultic, heathen or new-age circles want to hear. It is a logical conclusion of the Traditionalistic way of thinking though.

And how does that work then exactly? I do not know for sure, since I have led myself in a blind alley. I am a baptised Roman Catholic, but stopped attending church in my teen-years. As such I am a perfect example of a Western man. As I understand some people look at it, during mass in an orthodox congregation, the priest 'radiates' what I earlier called the "spiritual influence" and those receptive and ready could thus be initiated. On the other hand, we saw Markwith saying that "[...] realized knowledge, [...] requires a living tradition, as well as the guidance of a spiritual master." This seems to imply that is it the spiritual master who makes you part of the chain, perhaps even in a one-on-one situation. That sounds like "initiation" does it not?

[12] Ibid. p.89.
[13] Ibid. p.104.

Esotericism

René Guénon spent an entire book about this subject. *Perspectives On Initiation* was the first book that I read of the man and I can tell you, it is not an easy work. By now I think that you can guess that Guénon states that an initiation is only valid when the initiator possesses the spiritual influence. In this book Guénon does not write about religions, but about mystery schools and perhaps this is why in my head there is somewhat of a split between esotericism and exotericism. When we take a step back to Islam, you see that it has an esoteric branch in the form of Sufism. In the West the schism is even clearer (this is not strange, because the West is of course the most degraded of all) where you have Freemasonry.[14] This is an organisation that you can join regardless if you are Christian, from another religion or have no religion at all. You only have to believe in 'something higher'. You can take your oath on the Bible, but also on another holy book. Comparably I have heard of Sufi organisations inviting non-Muslims to join. Does that mean that 'filiation is possible' for people outside an orthodox religion?

Similar questions bug me with my Traditionalistic outlook that I, in spite of all, combine with an unorthodox religion, at least, in the eyes of some. Let me shake the tree a bit more.

Revelation

What is revelation? Markwith writes in his earlier quoted article:

The greatest masterpieces of traditional art and architecture are

---

[14]According to Guénon (*Perspectives On Initiation*, p.96) there are two valid forms of esotericism left in the West, but both in decline, Freemasonry and the Compagnonnage. Later in his life he even denied the filiation to both according to Harry Oldmeadow (1947-) quoted in the biography of Guénon on the website of World Wisdom (http://www.worldwisdom.com/public/authors/Rene-Guenon.aspx accessed 8/10/12).

clear signs of a living intellectual tradition, even if religious or philosophical manuscripts are absent. In addition, many esoteric traditions continue to be transmitted orally.[15]

Certainly I would not say that revelation requires *a* prophet and *a* book. Actually I would argue that the primordial tradition should *not* be put to paper, since it is a universal truth, but appearing in a specific time and place. How people described the primordial tradition 1500 years ago is not necessarily the way an initiate would talk about it nowadays. Scripture would be a degradation of the primordial tradition since it became static. I do not mean to say that there is no value in religions of the book, just that it is not the book that is the transmitter of Tradition. It is the master who transmits It to his student.

Does revelation only happen once every few centuries with the start of a new religion, or does revelation occur more often? Are there 'levels' in revelation? Did the avatars Christ, Buddha or Mohammed get a bigger portion of the truth than a Jacob Böhme[16]? Would the latter have 'received enough' to start a new tradition? Most interestingly, does revelation still happen today?

TRADITION

The quotes of Nasr and Guénon that I gave earlier, and an argument of some contemporary Traditionalists, is that an orthodox tradition requires *tradition*. Some forms of Christianity and Islam are orthodox because they have a liturgy that has not changed since the revelation. An orthodox religion requires a complete package, in the words of Guénon a dogma, a moral law and a cult or form of worship; wherever one or other of these elements happens to be wanting, there can no longer be any question of religion in the proper sense of the word.

---

[15]*Sophia* 13/2 p.90.
[16]Jacob Böhme (1575-1624), was a German mystic and has been regarded an authority on esotericism since he lived.

This is why scorn often befalls Traditionalists outside of the the main world religions, sending them off as 'reconstructionists' or 'neo-somethings'. I wonder, though, does the continuation of the burning flame really require the 'whole pack' or can that flame become small but remain alive in just a few people, in habits and believes of the 'common folk' and relive after a period of slumbering? Also, cannot, as with real fire, the flame be (re)lit from another fire? Or to stay more in Traditionalistic lines of thinking, is there actually not *one flame* and as long as we do not let it die all over the world, there is still hope for people who live in the dark?

Then there is this other point. *Can* the transmission only be performed within an orthodox religion? Despite of what some Traditionalists think and say about Freemasonry, I am personally convinced that there are fractions within it that can still 'do the trick' whether everybody realises this or not. I do not intend to discuss 'regularity' versus 'irregularity' within Freemasonry, nor the state of either regular or irregular Freemasonry. Also I am no mason myself, I am just quite convinced that this is the situation.

The point is just that the way I see it, only religion is not enough. What we need is a religion that is somehow connected to the primordial tradition along with an 'esoteric connection' with that same Source. Now I personally have no doubt about this in my own situation[17] (woe on me), but I do have serious concerns about the second. I do not think that we have genuine Western esotericism left in my country and I have not decided if it is an option to look for valid non-Western esotericism. It would be a bit weird, a Sufi Asatruar, would it not?

No Conclusion

An open question remains if a person without 'filiation' can rightly

---

[17]See my article Traditionalistic Asatru: Esoteric Heathenry in *Mimir: Journal of North European Traditions*, (ed, Taunton, G., Numen Books, 2012.)

be a Traditionalist. Perhaps not, but does it matter? The only thing I want to show you with the above is that Traditionalism is more than just a critical view on modernity, atheism and that the Traditionalistic worldview can lead to some unwelcome conclusions that I personally chose not to deny. Also there are different shades in Traditionalism. I do not wish to start a right/wrong discussion, just to present yet another shade.

The End

[Kalki returns to the cave atop the highest mountain at the centre of the world, and enters to converse with the Great Prophet Zarathustra.]

Kalki: O Zarathustra, Wise One, was I not reborn in the heart of sacred Shambala, where all Time and Space ceases? I am Kalki, I am the First and Last Avatar of the Eternal Return. Have I have not been the most faithful and most studious of your disciples? From Beginning to End we are understood Zarathustra. It is the duty of every faithful student to leave his teacher, and I have come to bid thee farewell. But first, O Zarathustra, there is something of which I must speak.

Zarathustra: Kalki, always thou hast been the most treasured of my students. Long have I yearned to hear you speak these words! Too long have I spent conversing with dead men, in you Kalki, I sense one of the Living – a bright flame that will lure many of the Herd's brightest and best away. To those with eyes you burn in darkness like a thousand suns; but those who dance too close to the flames will perish in your burning intensity. But I am Zarathustra the Godless – I fear nothing and none - why should I fear even your words Kalki?

Kalki: O Zarathustra: Thou art wrong. I was born when Time froze, in the lineage of the Moon and the Sun aligned; Time and Space both I split asunder. I would take your animals; even now the eagle alights above my head, the serpent writhes beneath my feet. Both I shall wield as sovereign; both Eagle and Serpent I craft into my emblem; the Great Dragon as Master of both Heaven and Earth. I am the Golden Sun - the Black Sun - the Principle of Expansion and of Contraction – both Time and the Absence of Time. I freeze the tongue of poets, curse the blood of kings and rip the conscious of my enemies from their bodies with but a whisper spread upon the winds. And I tell you that you are wrong O Zarathustra - thou knows nothing of women nor of war, and God still lives.

321

Zarathustra: You tell me that I am wrong. That I know nothing of women and war; but through your words Kalki, I shall come to know both. You are the Eternal Return itself but it was I who taught you to lift the veil of Truth. I would expect nothing less of you but to steal my words, and my animals. Man fears the celestial bird of prey; man fears the venom of the serpent deep in the earth. But even more does he fear their power united as One. Take them with my blessings... but, I am not wrong. I know of War. I know you Kalki, and you are the Great War. Your secret is known to your creator, to Zarathustra. You are the Great War, and as I created you, I therefore know War.

Kalki: I am Doubled Crowned as Sovereign of Heaven and Earth; and I tell you again O Zarathustra. Thou art wrong. Man is a bridge, a rope that spans the Abyss between the Beast and the Divine; but without the Transcendental element, he cannot cross. Without the Lightening spark from heaven and the rapture of the inner flame, the perilous journey across the chasm is doomed. And thus O Zarathustra, many of your disciples fall.

God is not dead. Man cannot slay God, only the illusion of God. The immortal, the infinite cannot be killed, only its rendition. What thou has slain, O Zarathustra is not God, not the Absolute itself, but only an illusion of God. Thou has slain only the image of Abraham.

Zarathustra: It is true: I took aim at the Holy Lie and all that made man weak. But again I am not wrong Kalki. This I made clear in my parables. Man must be strong enough to embody the divine not in another world, but in this. You can pass Kalki, for you are God made Man. You were destined to cross the Abyss long before either you or I were even born.

Kalki: We will all pass thy Abyss Zarathustra - I shall take all my kindred safely across thy chasm to all that is Divine in Man. The Ugliest Man speakest to me in riddles; I know his secret shame and his fear of the Last Man. I feel the animosity; the tremendous Doctrine of Burning grows stronger within me everyday – the call to War and the words that must be written.

Time ceases when I am born; all measurement of the Ages is a Human Abstraction – Space is likewise an illusion. I am the Eye of the Heart and the Mirror of the Soul, only that which is Pure shall I let pass thy Abyss Zarathustra. This is why you are wrong O wisest of Prophets. Those who dare not behold their soul refracted in my Obsidian Mirror shall never pass over this Abyss, for here the abominations are brought to Light. That which is bestial cannot pass, it is part of the Last Men, the remanants of the Old Age. Therefore O Zarathustra, I tell you now – God still lives – and that which is Divine in man cannot be allowed to die.

Zarathustra: Thou art Time and thou art the Eternal Return. Thou art Kalki, and you are my favourite student, but I, Zarathustra, am never wrong.

Kalki: Both the Priests and Warriors will follow; one to guide the other to protect – from there all else proceeds. That which is not of our kind shall not and cannot transcend the Abyss. And so Zarathustra, I tell thee this as Kalki, the brightest and most devoted of your students. Thou art wrong. God is not Dead. God yet lives, and breathes. And it is by the hand of God alone that we shall pass. And I know you will listen to me Zarathustra, for you know me well; my name is known as the leader of the Noble Ones, both Preserver and Destroyer. And I ask you again O Zarathustra, to look within your Heart and ask – is God truly Dead? Or is it merely another man's God you have slain? Dionysus lives in your verse, he dances and takes his disciples across the Abyss. At your feet I see only the corpse of Abraham.

I am Sun, I am Wind, and I am War. I can teach the secret that will take all your disciples across to the far shore. I will lift the Veil that blinds the Initiate; I will guide the Adepts. But I shall bare no blade against the weak, the injured nor the innocent – mine shall be a War in which no blood is shed; the Great War alone is what shall take those over the Abyss. Those who do not possess the Inner Flame are not of my kin, nor are those who would harm the Last Men. They will follow those who possess the true Doctrine of Burning and the Empty Secret - and thus the Twice Born shall take the elect over thy Abyss O Zarathustra. This was always thy secret intent. Even before you wrote your words O prophet, my presence was in your Heart, and the name of Kalki lay unspoken on your tongue.

Throughout the Aeons reborn have I been from Age to Age in wind and fire; summoned by desire and need. I spit upon the False; defile the Untrue. That which is not of the Cosmic Law is to be burned and destroyed O Zarathustra, in this we agree. The old law codes and values must be smashed – what is, was and will be of value must be re-assessed. Thou has broken many tablets already Zarathustra, but without new ones? All is lost. The Death of Abraham did not bring the Creators you hoped for O Prophet, only a nation of destroyers and murderers whose hands are stained with the blood of thy crime O Zarathustra.

Zarathustra: My error is the Death of Abraham? It is you who are wrong Kalki. I have already told you, you are my favourite student. The Death of Abraham was necessary for your Return. Without this, you could never have been Kalki, Priest of the Warriors. Take my law codes and inscribe them on new Tablets O Kalki, and let it be known that thou art the new voice for Zarathustra. And understand that without my error, you could never have been born again. Zarathustra and Kalki share the same spirit, as Master to Disciple.

Kalki: O Zarathustra, we upon the far shores who have fought the Great War, and spanned the Abyss shall inscribe these new tablets! I who can see into the Hearts of men from across the waters shall compose the new text. O Great Prophet, we who are both born of the Eternal Return shall together transcribe the Law Code for the coming age. Thus it shall be known that Kalki was the once the most humble student of the greatest and wisest of sages, the prophet Zarathustra.

CPSIA information can be obtained at www.ICGtesting.com
Printed in the USA
BVOW02s0917110216

436361BV00001B/20/P